Women and Modernity in Weimar Germany

For Mor, Dida og Gudmor

Women and Modernity in Weimar Germany

Reality and its Representation in Popular Fiction

Vibeke Rützou Petersen

Berghahn Books
NEW YORK • OXFORD

First published in 2001 by

Berghahn Books
www.berghahnbooks.com

Library of Congress Cataloging-in-Publication Data

Petersen, Vibeke Rützou, 1943-
Women and modernity in Weimar Germany : reality and its representation in popular fiction / by Vibeke Rützou Petersen.
p. cm.
Includes bibliographical references.
ISBN 1-57181-154-0 (alk. paper)
1. German fiction--20th century--History and criticism. 2. Women in literature. 3. Popular culture--Germany. 4. Women--Germany--Weimar (Thuringia)--History--20th century. 5. Weimar (Thuringia, Germany)--History--20th century. I. Title.

PT772 .P438 2000
833'.91209352042--dc21 00-062103

British Library Cataloguing in Publication Data

A catalogue record for this book is available from the British Library.

Printed in the United States on acid-free paper.

Part of chapter 5 of the present work appeared in a slightly different version, entitled "The Best of Both Worlds? Jewish Representations of Assimilation, Self, and Other in Weimar Popular Fiction," in *The German Quarterly*, 68, no. 2 (spring 1995): 160-73. © by *The German Quarterly*.

Contents

List of Illustrations

Preface

This project grew out of an National Endowment for the Humanities summer seminar at the University of California, Berkeley in 1991 where a group of scholars under the guidance of Anton Kaes met to discuss Weimar and Modernity. While others concentrated on film, dance, body culture, history, and the major philosophers and writers of the period, my first impulse was to examine the highly politicized culture through the range of politically affiliated publishing houses. But even scholarly projects are at the mercy of their material conditions and a trip to the stacks revealed that out of all their fabulous holdings, the library shelved only some Vicki Baum novels for immediate access.

Remembering that a musical named *Grand Hotel* had recently had a long and very successful run on Broadway, I set to reading Baum's 1929 novel of the same name and knew right away that fate had dealt me a trump card. The work had been an immediate bestseller, both in Germany and the United States, but, more significantly for my purposes, its many parallel plots took place in an urban metropolis and in many ways constituted a representation of modernity, this Benjaminian explosion of linearity into a million little pieces, albeit in a much reduced manner. The impact of modernity on the lives of characters from various walks of life as represented in *Grand Hotel* echoed the conundrum in the material reality of the first German Repulic. At the same time, novels such as Baum's were important elements of the cultural landscape and were thus part of the cultural discursive practices dealing with modernity at that time.

I soon realized that popular fiction in the Weimar years reached far beyond this particular author. I expanded my reading to include authors of popular fiction who, on the one hand, had not been admitted to the hallowed halls of belles lettres like Bertolt Brecht, Anna Seghers, and Thomas Mann, but most of whom, on the other hand, were not writing dime novels either. These "middle brow" authors vary enormously in style, intention, and closeness to the respectability of canonicity. Many may shudder at finding Irmgard Keun, Vicki Baum, Gustav Frenssen, Erich Maria Remarque, and Erich Kästner, or even Joseph Roth in the same category, and they may be right on several points. Nevertheless, I am not interested in making qualitative judgments about their works but rather in pointing out that the texts included in this examination have certain commonalities. The aesthetics, vocabulary, and the overt philosophies of these works are accessible to an average reader. Moreover, and more importantly, the stories by and large focus on coming to terms, each in its own manner, with a world of frightening modernity, so totally different from their authors' childhood worlds. Each work is an accumulation of comments on everyday Weimar life and because, in these fictions as in reality, the obstacles to happiness vary—according to class, gender, and sexuality, among other things—the works constitute an important element in the self-fashioning, so to speak, of the Weimar population in general; the following examination focuses on Weimar women in particular.

It is now that I have the chance to thank the many people and institutions who have helped me in the process of writing this book. Of all institutions involved in some manner in my project, I owe the most to the National Endowment for the Humanities, for without the existence of the 1991 Summer Seminar, the impetus and initial direction of my research would not have taken shape. The University of Tulsa gave me a summer fellowship to continue my research and I am most recently indebted to Drake University for summer research leaves and a Faculty Development Grant. Its generosity made archival research in Princeton and Berlin possible.

I am grateful to the Berkeley University Library and its staff for helping me in the initial stages. The librarians in Princeton's Rare Books and Special Collections deserve a special mention for their untiring assistance in my quest; of particular mention is Dr. Jochen Twele and Dr. Don Skemer, as well as Alice Clark who pointed out the existence of the Herbert Blau Collection among the holdings of the Firestone Library. The Ullstein Press Archives in Berlin and Dr. Laabs generously provided me with many more volumes of *Die Dame* than I could consume in my time in Berlin. The Cowles Library staff at Drake university, particularly the interlibrary loan librarian, Barbara Corson, must be thanked for her heroic efforts to acquire exotic titles for my edification. I also wish to thank the library staff at the University of Iowa and its photographic services for their assistance in gathering the illustrations for the book. Denise Wicker in Educational Media Services at Drake University deserves a separate mention for her advice and preparation of the same.

There are many more individuals who have helped this project throughout its creation. I thank Tony Kaes for his guidance and encouragement in its early stages. Bruce Campbell, Vic Udwin, Reggie Hyatt, Holly Laird, Barbara Hodgdon, Margot Lovett, and David Veeder saw some chapters in their early form and discussions with Louise Noun and Marc Keith helped give the work some direction. When I was in doubt, Britt Keith and Bitten Bridge gave me constant encouragement and proof that women are indeed capable of doing it all. I thank William Stoppel for reading and commenting on the finished manuscript, Anne Wallestad for her sharp bibliographical eye, and I am eternally grateful to Susan Hanson for her untiring attempts to clarify my arguments and language. Thank you, Susan Chase and Joseph Kestner, for insisting that I could and should write this book; your encouragement never ceased, even after reading some early parts; my heartfelt thanks also go out to Robert Cohen whose quiet but strong moral support was always with me.

A very special acknowledgment goes to Tanya Beer, a student and colleague in Women's Studies at Drake, who collaborated with me and co-wrote a section of Chapter Five, "Lesbian Excess," as a paper. I will always treasure the intellectual and emotional friendship she extended to me. My thanks also go to my colleague and friend, Rick McCormick, whose feed back not only erased some otherwise embarrassing mistakes but also informed many of my readings. My dear friend, Stephen Brockmann, read more versions of the manuscript than he thought was possible and his invaluable suggestions and enthusiasm for the project always came when I was most in need. But words cannot express the gratitude I feel for my partner in life, Karl Schaefer, who offered me his intellectual insights, organizational ideas, library science, and editing skills at my smallest sigh, and, without whose love and support this book simply would not have been written.

Brandy advertisement showing a *femme fatale*
plying a tiny, formally-dressed (male) bird with alcohol.
Leipziger Illustrirte Zeitung, 162, no. 4119 (February 7, 1924): 93.

Note the sinofied letters of the titles which enhances the exotic Erotic.

Leipziger Illustrirte Zeitung, 162, no. 4136 (June 19, 1924): 747.

Motorcycle advertisement depicting male and female figure in similar riding outfits, emphasizing the intersection of technological advances and shifting female roles.

Leipziger Illustrirte Zeitung, 161, no. 4109 (September 20, 1923): 209.

Cover of a 1926 issue of the *Leipziger Illustrirte Zeitung* shows a striking representation of a feminized male or a "new" masculinity.

Leipziger Illustrirte Zeitung, 166, no. 4238 (June 3, 1926): Title page.

Cover of a 1928 issue of the *Leipziger Illustrirte Zeitung* depicts couples dancing to music heard through headphones. Here urban dwellers are embracing technology in one if its more bizarre manifestations.

Leipziger Illustrirte Zeitung, 170, no. 4332 (March 22, 1928): Title page.

A toothpaste advertisement which uses blatantly racial caricatures to emphasize its whitening ability.

Leipziger Illustrirte Zeitung, 170, no. 4335 (April 12, 1928): 571.

Chapter One

Mass Culture and Weimar Modernity

> [M]ass production of fiction is the culture of what might be called the 'novellistic,' the constant narration of the social relations of individuals, the ordering of meanings for the individual in society.
>
> — Stephen Heath

Among the many works written in this country about Weimar culture, the overwhelming majority that examined popular culture did so from the vantage point of film. It is only recently that these examinations have included gender issues in the reception of films.[1] Moreover, early examinations of popular culture generally ignored the consuming public and in those few instances when the public was considered, it was perceived as a passive, unified entity. The 1960s and 1970s, however, ushered in a material criticism which, by introducing class as a category and critical approach, began to dismantle the monolithic concept of an audience or a reading public. Further, in the 1980s, the burgeoning fields of feminist and cultural criticisms foregrounded notions of race and gender as crucial issues in the culture industry.

One of the most important works on Weimar popular culture and women in recent years is Patrice Petro's 1989 study, *Joyless Streets: Women and Melodramatic Representation in Weimar*. This study examines the ways in which Weimar films and magazines addressed a female audience. In so doing, it opened new avenues of investigation into women as agents in cultural production, their consumption of popular culture, and reciprocally, popular culture's role in women's self-fashioning. Still, very few full-length studies have focused on

Notes for this section begin on page 12.

the role of popular fiction in the lives of Weimar women.[2] My study aims to fill part of that gap.

When a study draws conclusions about a society based on readings of texts rather than the life experience of the writers, questions arise about the cross-over from "fact" to "fiction." To wit: how can that bridge be crossed? What assumptions can be made from fictional characters about a material world? Can anything about "real" life be inferred from symbolic processes? If we believe, as I do, that fictions are also repositories of social observations translated into narratives and that literary figures are constructs of the writers' creative will, then it is reasonable to conclude, as Jochen Schulte-Sasse has pointed out, that textual culture plays an integral part in how modern individuals constitute their subjectivities.[3] Based on criteria of constructedness that include, among others, material as well as subconscious circumstances, I cannot insist on a sharp delineation between literary figures and "real" ones; both can be seen to constitute a nexus of certain shaping discourses. This is particularly noticeable when the literary figure, frozen in time and inscribed onto the page, is contemplated by a reader from another time and place.

The manner in which readers connect literary texts with their socio-economic, historical, or political backgrounds reflects on their—the readers'—own ideological negotiations of various cultural texts. One thing seems certain to this critic: we live in a world of contingencies, and literature constitutes a forum for an exchange of meanings that passes out of the abstract into the corporeal and back; it is part of a cultural system of meaning that constitutes our "real" lives. In this light, what follows represents my readings, subjective but informed, of a highly volatile period in German modernity; most specifically of the women of that period, of the representations of them, and the related issues that arise alongside such representation in contemporary popular literature.

Previously, critics were divided with regard to popular culture. This division is similar to that of earlier film critics. The overwhelming majority, guided by artistic and socially conscious criteria, condemned popular culture as affirmative, stereotypical, and aesthetically unadventurous; but there were also those who proclaimed it meaningless, harmless, and satisfying a popular demand. Since the rise of cultural studies in this country, this binary opposition has dissolved into several disparate groups, whose views of popular culture divulge much more complex notions of that which "is the very element we all breathe."[4] This first chapter will discuss the facets of (popular) culture as they pertain to Germany, with a special view to the gender specificity of the issues.

Raymond Williams writes that, in the parlance of social Darwinism, struggle is a necessary activity of the strong, and "women are identified as special examples of the weak who hold back the strong." (51) Writing about modernism, Ann Ardis states that "reading the gynocentric writing of the end of the nineteenth century in conjunction with masterworks of high modernism makes modernism's reactionary cultural politics stand out in high relief—makes it possible to see how the female subject, not mass culture, functions as modernism's Other."[5] If we link these statements, there emerges a clear notion of women as obstacles to the progress of civilization and high art, as defined by patriarchal discourse. Although Ardis makes a point of separating women from mass culture, other critics have pointed out how the divisions of high and low as cultural categories are gendered: "high" culture is masculine, while "low" is feminine.

Joseph von Sternberg's 1929 film, *The Blue Angel,* carries the inscription of the *Kulturdebatte* in its narrative. The film that marked the real beginning of Marlene Dietrich's illustrious career is the perfect paradigm for the cultural *Angst* of the Weimar bourgeoisie, although it is set in the Wilhelminian period. Dietrich's character, the singer Lola-Lola, assumes the vulgar, seductive, deceitful, and ultimately destructive characteristics that are attributed to mass culture. The professor can be seen as the exemplar of *das gebildete Bürgertum* (the educated bourgeoisie), complete with its powerlessness, concomitant sadism, and canonical culture. The narrative plays on several levels comprising female sexuality and Wilhelminian petit-bourgeois morality, but among the many discourses embedded in the film, one is crystal clear: feminine mass culture is devouring and destroying not only the category of "the masculine," but masculine canonical high culture.

Co-existent with the notion of the maleness of modernism's high culture is the notion of woman as the embodiment of the darker sides of modernity, the irrational, threatening, and decadent aspects. Undoubtedly, particular sets of social conditions in Weimar were instrumental in both creating and supporting those notions: the influx of women into the labor market during the early part of the twentieth century, the increase in organized labor movements, the growth of membership in the SPD (Social Democratic Party), the KPD (Communist Party), and the NSDAP (Nazi Party) all intensified middle-class fears of losing privilege and of engulfment by the (similarly feminized) masses. The gender-specific modifiers of low (female)/ high (male) culture combined with the notion that women were not only the embodiment of negative modernity but were also playing a major part in shaping this same modernity, heightened the anxiety linked with women's cultural roles at the time.

When we look at female characters in Weimar literary texts, it becomes clear that these fictional women are indeed creatures of modernity. They operate in a tangle of fictionality and commodification. Figments of the writer's imagination, they are the reification of authorial notions of modern womanhood created with an eye to the commercial success of a work of fiction. The production and consumption of these characters constitute a certain bridge between the blurred arena of fiction and reality: in a very real way, these characters and the texts wherein they appear constitute a nexus in the cultural production of the commodification of femininity, female self-fashioning through fashion, and consumerism within an urban environment.

How important *is* popular culture in the process of subjectivity formation? The question is an irksome one since we can only speculate upon its answer. But a look at the debate in early twentieth-century Germany, which deplored the "bad" content of popular culture, seems to indicate an overwhelming concern with the direction that culture was taking as well as with its effect on its consumers. At one end of the popular spectrum are the *Schmutz und Schund* ("trashy novels") whose publication began in the late nineteenth century. They included many perceived evils: installment novels sold door to door (colportage novels), dime novels, series of paper-bound romance, detective, Western, and adventure stories as well as true-life stories (often of sexual exploits, for example, those of Marquis de Sade and Don Juan) in various shades of purple prose. I examine only a few texts that would belong to the above categories, but the dismissive condemnation of such literature appears to have metastasized into a moral stance that lumped together most forms of popular culture and implicated them in the deterioration of the moral fiber of the German nation.

In 1909, Ernst Schultze categorized *Schmutz und Schund* texts into two categories: 1) literarily bad but morally inoffensive and 2) literarily bad and morally dangerous. Wilhelminian defenders of morality claimed that such reading material had "an unhealthy influence on telling good from evil" and that it "glorified crime."[6] Such was the concern for the moral fiber of the nation that in 1926 an amendment was made to the Weimar Constitution (which prohibited censorship) to permit measures to protect the nation's youth from trashy literature.

This lament strikes a familiar cord in the United States of the 1990s. The title of an 1890 conference, "Do dime novels represent a moral danger to the German people?" easily makes a one-hundred-year Benjaminian "tiger's leap" to resonate with worries from both the left and the right about Hollywood's purportedly detrimental effect on the American people.[7]

Of course, this worry over the adverse effect of popular culture underscores the belief that we are somehow shaped by culture. Adorno and Horkheimer claimed that the true products of the culture industry were the consumers of cultural commodities. Post-structural arguments confirm this assumption when they aver that subjectivities are shaped in discourse and representation rather than existing as stable, integral categories. It therefore follows that culture, "high" or "low," is prime terrain for investigations into gender discourses and, in turn, women's participation in and experiences of their national culture.

One of my primary concerns in writing this book is to establish that popular culture is a forum where debates about subjectivity, gender, sexuality, social conditions, and nationhood were, in the early twentieth century, discussed with as much fervor as they were in what was traditionally known as high culture. Moreover, it is important to understand that these discourses are not reflections of a purely material reality. Rather, discursive formations are themselves crucial constitutive elements of the very cultural debate they represent. In fact, the traditional (elite) cultural production in Weimar Germany, owned and produced largely by educated middle-class men, was increasingly interrupted and threatened by a culture industry whose appeal was to the population at large.[8] By studying "mass" media, we learn, in Leo Löewenthal's terms, about the "typical forms of behavior, attitudes, commonly held beliefs, prejudices, and aspirations of large numbers of people" (xii).

The subject matter I will be examining here is a popular culture that is clearly infused by modernity and its technologies. One focus of my study is the extent to which popular fiction encouraged—or at least made visible—nontraditional or new forms of life praxis. In Chapter Two, "Female Domestication or Marriage, Reproduction, and Family," I argue that popular texts not only represent norms and prescriptions of the day but also that the bound energies of these texts frequently reveal very real alternatives to customary praxes. Moreover, popular fictional works featuring abortion issues provided another forum for discussion of issues crucial to women's lives, thus constituting, in fact, a female public sphere.

As I was reading, at times indiscriminately, through popular Weimar stories and novels, I was intrigued by the sheer number of issues that jumped out of the texts, issues that spoke to what was going on during this time in the Weimar Republic. Many of them touched particularly on women's work; thus the third chapter of this study examines the interplay between work (in the context of industrialized processes) and *Körperkultur* (body culture), as it plays out in the culture of the time. Caught in the rational choreography of Taylor's efficiency industrialism, Ford's assembly line, American jazz, the Charleston, the increasing availability of cars, and outdoor activities such as organized sport, many German bodies participated in some form of *Körperkultur*. Others tried to free themselves not only from the constraints imposed by such discourses but also from an increasingly constricting urban existence.

During the interwar years in Germany, a rigid social system was seriously undermined. Due to the inflation and severe economic circumstances that plagued most of the Weimar years, middle-class families were forced to accept their daughters' entry into the work force, thus eroding one of the more decisive differences between them and the working classes. Rural and small-town women migrated to the cities, where they swelled the ranks of factory workers and sales and office clerks. In turn, this movement across social barriers also blurred the lines of morality and respectability. In her article "Something Old, Something New: Women between the Two World Wars," Renate Bridenthal writes that "the working girl and the sexually loose woman became conflated into the same figure. Her sheer existence threatened the stability of bourgeois values and lifestyles and her non-reproductive sexuality … supported the need for a more controlling population policy to some."[9] With those issues in mind, Chapter Four, entitled "Classed Genders and Sexualities," analyzes the nexus of sexuality, gender, and class in Weimar culture. The juncture of these elements moves according to its historical whereabouts; in Weimar, what we find in the struggle are the left-over moralizing discourses of the Wilhelminian era and the laissez-faire attitudes of the 1920s.

There is a virtually unanimous agreement among traditional German scholars that the most important force shaping early twentieth-century German citizens was World War One. Recent scholarship has examined the possible existence of a German "cult of violence" that, from the turn of the century, gradually permeated all or most aspects of life. Supposedly, it was eventually harnessed by the extreme right in the late 1920s and went on to culminate in the

Final Solution.[10] This is a tempting reading of the period, but it is erroneous to view German culture only through the spectacles of violence and brutality. Such a view urges us to accept a monolithic teleology, an unavoidability in the cultural trends of Weimar that end in fascism and the Holocaust.

Notwithstanding the brutality and unspeakable horror of the twelve Nazi years that followed the Weimar Republic and the "war to end all wars" that preceded it, a focus on a cult of violence is predicated on a male subjectivity; such a focus represents a gendered, masculinist reading of the cultural terrain and its signifiers. Indubitably, masculine subjectivities were shaped largely by the violence of the war and the revolutions that followed in its wake. Yet it is debatable whether the war registered in women with the same, acute brutality as it did in men. In fact, Maria Tatar argues that sexual murders in Weimar may very well have been committed by men revenging themselves on women precisely because the latter had escaped the war, thus indicating that women were in some sense perceived as accomplices in sending men to the trenches (12). Be that as it may, women's subjectivities then, as today, were fashioned by and, in turn, helped to shape discursive practices that often differed from those that formed men. One such shaping discourse was the stories they read.

Popular culture features as a basic element of our subjectivities, those moving targets that flit through a culturescape, absorbing, discarding and, as importantly, producing and changing culture while on the move. And since popular culture also enunciates, as it informs, a national identity, it is of particular interest here insofar as an intense celebration of the German national subject had been part of popular cultural discursive practices since the middle of the nineteenth century. *Blut und Boden* (blood and soil) is not only the best known of such paradigms, it is also the one whose continuous grip on the national imagination was the strongest. If phobias of all kinds circulated in Weimar, they did so in the company of cultural experimentations that often cut across classes; both thus make visible groups and behavior patterns previously shut out of polite society. It will become progressively clear to the reader that there existed in Weimar popular culture a diversity of elements that prevents us from making a monolithic and totalizing pronouncement about the prehistory of fascist culture. In Chapter Five, "Beyond the Pale: Others, Selves, and Nationhood" I nonetheless examine stereotyped images of various Others in Weimar and their exoticization or demonization, indicating that various definitions of un/German-ness—and thus inversely of nationhood—circulated freely in Weimar popular fiction.

To return to the relations of gender on which this study focuses, it can be said that the decadence of the city in particular, and modernity in general, is fictionalized as an unchecked female sexuality that is, as such, an active constituent in Weimar cultural production. Such a sexuality is, no doubt, a product of the very modernity it is perceived to undermine.[11] The construction of a class-less (read middle-class), heterosexual femininity is a project very much in evidence throughout Weimar culture on the whole; popular fiction was one of the major components in the process if for no other reason than its large audience. Thus Chapter Six, "The Shape of Things," takes on an issue which has been underlying the entire study: the body and sexuality of the "new" woman. In the chapter, the dissolution of traditional categories of gender and sexuality is read as one manifestation of the crisis that was Weimar. Looking into the similarity in corporal representations of the Weimar "new" woman and "new" man, and their cultural and political contexts, I claim that women are portrayed as emblems of chaos and men as carriers of the desire for stability. Keeping in mind the historical reality of the Nazi years (1933-1945) that followed the Weimar Republic, my findings support the contention that popular texts were also a space wherein desires for traditional gender roles and social stability, both sorely missing in the Weimar Republic, were articulated.

While scholarship on modernity has cast women as the primary consumers in urban communities, few serious investigations have explored the question of why women consumed—in the broadest sense—what they did. The study of popular fiction plays an important role in this inquiry since in the 1920s Germany, popular literature constituted a new, consumer-oriented public sphere. Available to both genders, this modern *Öffenlichkeit* (public sphere) was of crucial importance to women in their attempts to grapple with the twentieth century. Many subgenres of popular fiction center on aspects of the world that are familiar to women: work, consumption, films, abortion, love, marriage, and the family, among others, figure prominently in the narratives of popular fiction's various genres.

The struggle to connect the private and public spheres in a meaningful way is the object of many texts of modernity. As middle-class women entered the labor market in increasing numbers, popular literature became an arena where this struggle was probed and negotiated, but not exclusively from a middle-class point of view. Reading about it, as well as writing about it in a successful manner, as many women of the Weimar Republic did, were in themselves ways of bringing order to a new world.

Given all this, the notion of popular fiction as a female public sphere, as well as the anxious debate in Weimar about the decline of culture through the onslaught of mass culture bear closer examination. Andreas Huyssen describes the dominant attitude regarding the increasing volume of popular cultural production in Weimar as a "commodification and colonization of cultural space." (57) Such a position conveys the vision of a single indigenous (high) culture which is subsequently overrun and subsumed by a horde of low-culture, barbarian textual practices. Once more we note the tendency to universalize consumers and to posit a single pre-existent culture whose consumers have access to and identify with cultural paradigms in an unambiguous and similar fashion.

Once we examine the phenomenon of the universal cultural consumer, the notion of an integral cultural space turns out to be a fallacy. The moment we assign to the cultural subject/consumer a number of specific characteristics such as gender, race, class, and sexual orientation, it becomes clear that the mythical space posited as "integral" was in fact a turf already occupied and patrolled by the powerful, here the white, bourgeois, heterosexual male.

Therefore, if we gender the cultural consumer and make her female, the metaphor of invasion may change to one of mobility. Popular culture, especially fiction, has, more than any form of "high" culture, created texts where life is mediated through a woman's story. This one aspect of a fictional work has often been so controversial that it alone can disqualify it from being granted a place in "high" culture. Yet, by insisting on the notion of the ubiquitous female consumer (and producer) of culture and its artifacts, we change the set of moves that can be made. Rather than reading mass culture as being equal to a "commodification and colonization of cultural space," one can understand mass culture as reading also of the trivialities or travails of every-day life. Our language now evokes a rather different notion of the concepts, namely, that mass culture is capable of facilitating women's stories in cultural paradigms, as well as giving female access to the same. It all depends from whose vantage point we describe these events.

The act of reading itself had great cultural significance during the Weimar years.[12] Discussions about the literary market-place were often vehicles for voicing utopian sentiments about literature as an arena for public discussion; this suggests that literature played an important part in democratization of the public sphere. Some sections of the intelligentsia held that writers should be revolutionaries regardless of whether they were canonical writers, members of the avant-garde, or members of the writing proletariat. And yet, popular fiction is rarely mentioned, if at all, in these discussions.

There is little doubt that popular fiction is less aesthetically sophisticated than most canonical literature. One finds little experimentation with form or language in works of popular fiction. Rather, mass consumption of such texts relies on adherence to well-tried formulae concerning vocabulary, length of chapters, and the overall work. In modern popular fiction this often has less to do with the authors' individual abilities than with the policies of publishing houses—the mass production of Harlequin novels in the US is a case in point. To give an example from Germany, serial novel pamphlets from the 1880s and 1890s all were of sixty-four pages, priced from ten to twenty-five pfennig, depending on the publisher.[13] During the Weimar years, the Mignon Verlag in Dresden published a series of *Sittenromane* (moral tales), each one exactly seventy-nine pages long.

The plots and character configurations in most popular works also lean toward clichés and stereotypes.[14] The formulaic actions of thriller, spy novels, and the rags-to-riches paradigm of love stories are all too well known to require special treatment here. Nevertheless, it is precisely their adherence to an aesthetic as well as to a particular contents that makes such works appealing to a large readership. The common and the usual –everyday life, in other words–are often the metatopoi of popular texts and it is presumably the non-alienating, non-displaced representation of the quotidian that distinguishes these texts from other literary texts traditionally considered to be of higher artistic value.

All the above characteristics of popular fiction points toward a complicity with the status quo, a charge that is difficult to dismiss. This notion of the affirmative culture industry, proposed by Adorno and the New Left, represents a deeply pessimistic view of popular culture under the sway of monopoly capitalism. Such a view is doubtlessly justified on many levels. However, cultural affirmations, decried by critical theorists, are not impervious to resisting ideologies. If this resistance were not possible, then readers would actually be victims of the irreducible givenness of a text; and by the same token, we would no longer be able to talk about an active cultural production but only of a passive cultural reception and consumption.[15]

It is the thesis of this study, therefore, that texts are not hermetically sealed realms closed to non-hegemonic thoughts; thus, in our view, alternatives to the status quo may well be present in a text, albeit covertly. Furthermore, if we accept that readers may be quite active and unique and that they interact with a fictional text according to learned cultural codes and interpretive processes (Radway 1984, 52), we thereby empower them to appropriate (parts of) texts for their own uses, according to their own anxieties and desires.[16] And since these are no longer considered universal properties, but rather social constructs, their historical, class, gender, and sexual specificity must be admitted.

The claim that the consciousness of readers stays as it was before reading a popular text is presumably made on the general assumption that all readers are the same and in agreement with the material status quo. But the sheer porosity of any narrative allows enough slippage to occur for readers to find a diversity of subversive coping strategies. In other words, rather than leaving her consciousness intact, popular texts may in fact make visible to their female reader pleasures and alternatives not previously thought of. Although alternative or subversive possibilities may be contained later in the text, they will have surfaced and perhaps created, for however brief a moment, an "unconscious ambivalence" about the status quo.[17] If we acknowledge this, it makes little sense to state categorically that popular fiction is exclusively affirmative of a given state of affairs, serving only to reproduce and reinforce the prevailing ideology. Hence it is probable that readers with diverse cultural and social locations will produce diverse readings of a popular text, even readings that are contradictory to presumably uniform and obvious messages in both text and culture.[18]

Optimistically speaking, where the reader finds confirmation and ratification of her choices and her world in works of popular fiction, her reading is an empowering enterprise. Of course, the power derived from this process is not considered progress unless it is transformed into political action.[19] While her readings may inform her that her world is the way to true happiness there is no guarantee that she finds everything in it agreeable. Acquiring a certain measure of self-confidence therefore could in fact facilitate coping mechanisms for a difficult reality and could furthermore foster a desire to inquire into and perhaps change perceived wrongs. Our difficulty lies in proving links between reading and behavior. As Radway pointed out, greater assertiveness on the part of women may come from changes in the culture at large rather than reading (although it is our claim that popular fiction is a crucial constituent of that very culture). Conversely, acceptance of traditional roles may be caused by an economic climate, among others, rather than a conservative impact of reading popular novels.[20] We can only speculate and interpret.

The present work is not intended as a eulogy of popular fiction. Rather, it is an effort to bring into view a literary field–the popular fiction of the Weimar Republic–that has been largely ignored in scholarship. As an attempt to construct a theory regarding what role such works may have played in the lives of their female readers, my examination contends that whether or not of high literary quality, popular works constituted an arena wherein women experienced and participated in varying enunciations about gender, race, nationhood, class, and marriage, to name but a few important sites of subject formation. It is also here that women readers may have found affirmation of traditions or glimpses of alternative forms of life praxis. It is in part through this textual culture that female subjectivity has been formed. It is my hope that the following will shed some light on the workings of popular fiction as an important part of the social production of female subjectivity in the Weimar Republic.

Notes

1. There are too many to mention and the following is but a small selection: *Kino-Debatte: Texte zum Verhältnis von Literatur und Film 1909-1929*, ed. Anton Kaes (Tubingen, 1978); Miriam Hansen, "Early Silent Cinema: Whose Public Sphere?" *New German Critique* 29 (Spring/Summer 1983): 147-84; Patrice Petro, *Joyless Streets: Women and Melodramatic Representation in Weimar Germany* (Princeton, 1989); Richard McCormick, "From *Caligari* to Dietrich: Sexual, Social, and Cinematic Discourses in Weimar Film," *Signs* 18, no. 3 (Spring 1993): 640-68; also *New German Critique* 40 (Winter 1987) & 51 (Fall 1990), special issues on Weimar Film Theory and Weimar Mass Culture.
2. Notable exceptions are Lynda J. King, *Best-sellers by Design: Vicki Baum and the House of Ullstein* (Detroit, 1988) and *Women in the Metropolis: Gender and Modernity in Weimar Culture*, ed. Katharina von Ankum (Berkeley and Los Angeles, 1997).
3. Jochen Schulte-Sasse, "High/Low and Other Dichotomies," *High and Low Cultures: German Attempts at Mediation*, eds. Reinhold Grimm and Jost Hermand (Madison, 1994),
4. Michael Denning, "The End of Mass Culture," *Modernity and Mass Culture*, eds. James Naremore and Patrick Brantlinger (Bloomington, 1991), 267.

5. Ann L. Ardis, *New Women, New Novels: Feminism and Early Modernism*. (New Brunswick, 1990), 174, as quoted in the review by Anne Hermann in *Signs* 18, no. 3 (Spring 1993): 728.
6. Ernst Schultze, *Die Schundliteratur. Ihr Vordringen. Ihre Folgen. Ihre Bekämpfung* (Halle A S., 1909), 7, as quoted in Georg Jäger, "Der Kampf gegen Schmutz und Schund: Die Reaktion der Gebildeten auf die Unterhaltungsindustrie," *Archiv für Geschichte des Buchwesens* 31 (1988): 173.
7. *Fach-Zeitung für Sortiments- und Colportage-Buchhandel*, VII. 1-3 (Jan/Feb. 1891): 2-23 as quoted in Georg Jäger "Der Kampf," 165.
8. Ibid., 176-78.
9. Renate Bridenthal, "Something Old, Something New: Women Between the Two World Wars," *Becoming Visible: Women in European History*, eds. Renate Bridenthal, Claudia Koonz, and Susan Stuard (Boston, 1987), 493.
10. Cf. Michael Geyer, "The Stigma of Violence, Nationalism, and War in Twentieth Century Germany," *German Studies Review*, Special Issue: German Identity (Winter 1992): 75-110.
11. Cf. Rita Felski, *The Gender of Modernity* (Cambridge, Mass., 1995).
12. *Die Dame* (December 1932) states that 26,961 books were printed in Germany compared to 9,176 in France and 15,393 in England.
13. Georg Jäger, "Der Kampf," 164.
14. See also Peter Nusser, *Trivialliteratur*, vol 262, Sammlung Metzler (Stuttgart, 1991).
15. See also Hans Magnus Enzensberger, *Einzelheiten I. Bewußtseins-Industrie* (Frankfurt am Main, 1964).
16. Janice Radway, "Interpretive Communities and Variable Literacies: The Functions of Romance Reading," *Daedalus* 113, no, 3 (1984): 52.
17. Janice Radway, "The Utopian Impulse in Popular Literature: Gothic Romances and "Feminist" Protest," *American Quarterly* 33, no. 2 (1981): 157-58.
18. James Naremore and Patrick Brantlinger, "Introduction," *Modernity and Mass Culture*, 4-5.
19. Lynda J. King, "Vicki Baum and the "Making" of Popular Success: "Mass" Culture or "Popular" Culture?" *Women in German Yearbook*, 11 (1995): 162.
20. Radway, "The Utopian Impulse," 69.

Chapter Two

Female Domestication or Marriage, Reproduction, and Family

Die Ehe ist nicht die richtige Ausdrucksform für mich. Dafür interessieren mich die Männer zu sehr.

— Erich Kästner, *Fabian*

Most young men are so stupid that they take more trouble over the purchase of a cow than over the choice of a wife—and then they pay for it afterwards.

— Gustav Frenssen *The Pastor of Poggsee*

It became increasingly clear to us that the institution of marriage 'protects' women in the same way that the institution of slavery was said to 'protect' blacks—that is, that the word 'protection' in this case is simply a euphemism for oppression.

— Sheila Cronan, "Marriage"

Narratives that speak about women's traditional spheres—marriage, reproduction, and the family—constitute a domain for their readers to engage in discussions about the domestic realm. Stories about marriage also constitute an arena where conflicting notions about women's paid labor, working conditions, starvation wages, desires for independence and for marriage may well intersect. In modern periods of social and cultural shifts, explorations of marriage, divorce, and (single) motherhood have been constitutive elements as well as barometers of such shifts. Just as issues regarding marriage, reproduction, and family have reemerged in the arena of public debate in the United States over the last couple of decades, so did these same topics come under scrutiny during the Weimar

Notes for this section begin on page 40.

years. What follows is an attempt to map this debate, so crucial for women, as it appeared in popular texts of the time. Having said that, it should also be pointed out that this chapter will investigate these domains from a heteronormative point of view: popular fiction then (as now) was an almost exclusively heterosexual discourse, embedded in the dominant straight culture as well as being a constitutive element of the same.

Many novels gave the reader an opportunity to reflect upon her own life and identity insofar as they created ways for her to participate in modernity. The arguments for and against in the debates over these issues were diverse. While much official energy was expended on making the traditional domestic package palatable to young women of the 1920s, the more independence women gained, the less it seemed that a traditional marriage and its gender-specific division of labor was attractive to them. Even so, tradition had a strong pull, as did the safe (and, the woman hoped, romantic) harbor that marriage was perceived to offer. In Rudolf Braune's novel from 1930, entitled *Das Mädchen an der Orga Privat*, a young female typist articulates the dilemma in the following manner: "Men earn the money and they won't let us have any. But we all want to be happy, get married and have kids."[1] Class consciousness is woven into the novel like a red thread advocating, among other things, an honest day's pay for an honest day's work. And yet, marriage is introduced as a happy goal. The words reveal the conflicting desires of young working women and a tension between work and marriage. Taken together, these elements lead the reader to speculate that perhaps women would not get married so readily if their wages could sustain a better standard of living.

A well-paying job was but a dream for most working women. Ute Frevert points out that women as a rule earned between twenty to forty percent less than men for the same job.[2] This tenacious reality is translated into the terse but sincere advice a young typist receives from an older, sick, and unmarried woman colleague in Christa Anita Brück's 1930 novel, *Schicksale hinter Schreibmaschinen*: "Get married, Miss Brückner, get married, get married."[3] The older woman's exhortation peels all romantic notions from marriage and exposes it as an institution whose merit lies in the economic security which has eluded the older woman. Poverty and illness kill her within the next few pages of the novel.

But even for traditionalists, marriage in the 1920s was not what it had been. After the First World War, such profound changes occurred in Germany, in particular in urban society, that it was difficult to maintain the turn-of-the-century notion of the bourgeois institution of marriage. The advent of women's suffrage sent shudders through traditional patriarchy as did the thought of what suffrage might indeed mean to marriage and motherhood. Until this time, marriage had been a sphere of male empowerment where husbands might act as educators in all areas of life, including especially, sexual matters.[4] Hence, women's emancipation was also perceived as a threat to the male monopoly on sexual knowledge, dealing one more strike against an already fragile state of male potency. The profound uncertainty and unease that surrounded modern gender and sexual relations constituted a fundamental philosophical problem. On the one hand, the "new" woman was progressive and represented freedom from the oppression of patriarchal marriage; on the other, that freedom brought with it its own targets, pressures, and problems. In Heinz Bernd's 1921 novel, *Wrong Morals*, Burghaufen, the male protagonist, discusses unhappy marriages and assures his female audience that he has made an effort to look upon the phenomenon objectively. When marriages go wrong, he maintains, "and here you have to believe me ... nine times out of ten the woman has been at fault."[5] It appears that along with female agency came the lion's share of relational responsibility.

Loud voices in the Weimar Republic proclaimed the decline of marriage, the family, the decay of social mores, and, implicitly therefore, the dissolution of Western culture.[6] Statistics may have exacerbated such fears and Germany's birth rate had indeed been in decline since the last decades of the nineteenth century: the number of live births per 1,000 inhabitants dropped from thirty-nine in the 1870s to thirty-six in the 1890s, thirty-three in the 1900s and to twenty-eight in the first decade of the 1900s. Simultaneously, the death rate had been falling in parallel, thus keeping the population constant. It was the twin factors of the death of young and middle-aged men in the First World War and the ensuing drop of the birth rate that gave great cause for alarm.[7] National worries about marriage and the family appeared to increase in inverse proportion to the birth rate and as a result, public discussion regarding marriage in the Weimar Republic included concern both for social morality and for the growth and health of the population.[8] It is interesting to note that although no female occupation was publicly as highly praised as that of housewife, there is no official statistical mention of it in the censuses from 1882, 1907, 1925, and 1933 where women's occupations were included.[9]

Inextricably bound up with the issue of marriage were those of female sexuality and "frigidity," birth control, and abortion. The political arena in Weimar Germany was a jousting field where opposing groups concerned with family policy issues' struggled for power. Political instability led to constantly changing legislatures that nevertheless made some attempts to adapt social policy to the change in women's roles that modernity required. However, the social maneuvering that went on during this time was not perforce synonymous with emancipatory struggles. In the midst of radical change in both discourse and reality, there were also stasis and conservatism, especially in the rural and southern, Catholic areas of Germany. *Die Frauenfrage*—the question of women's rights—resonated in cultural utterances of all kinds; and if this discourse was not always present in the sphere of political administration, it reigned supreme in the cultural consciousness of men and women in the German Republic, as we shall see below.

In Weimar reality, as in its fiction, then, the domestic realm constituted a site of struggle. In both realms, all aspects of marriage, whether traditional, modern, or even experimental, challenged each other, enacting, it would seem, the first feminist principle: "the personal is the political." The private sphere, purported to be that of the woman, was in fact thoroughly infused with and shaped by rules decided upon in the public, "masculine," sphere. But the reciprocity of influence between the public and private spheres was evident in the extent to which management and control of women determined political and cultural discourses in the Weimar Republic.

Bachelor Girls

Women and their independence—whether real or imagined, present or still to come—was without question one of the most charged themes in the German Republic. Magazines and weeklies constantly featured articles and vignettes dealing with this topic. The same topic also finds its place as the central issue in most of the period's popular novels, each with a differing set of desires that circumscribes the end or goal of their protagonists. In Vicki Baum's novel from 1928, *stud. chem. Helene Willfüer*, the title character is a young woman from an academic background who discovers, while pursuing graduate studies in chemistry, that she is pregnant.[10] Since she cannot pay for a safe but illegal abortion, she and her lover, Fritz, plan a double suicide. Despite her desperate straits, Helene abandons the plan in the eleventh hour. Fritz kills himself, and Helene is arrested for his murder, but she is found not guilty and released from prison. In due time,

Helene gives birth to a baby boy and finishes her dissertation, whereupon her former professor, Ambrosius, finds her a position as a research chemist on a private project. As the narrative unfolds, Dr. Helene Willfüer rises through the ranks; it is only much later, while vacationing with her child in Italy, that she happens upon Professor Ambrosius, and they finally realize they love each other.

Among other things, *Helene* establishes two conflicting sets of opposites: the private versus the public and the individual versus society.[11] But what makes the novel relevant to this discussion is that its woman protagonist attempts to negotiate a world that clearly is not set up to facilitate her passage through it. The novel does in fact offer the possibility of an emancipated life for women, (that is, independent of a father's or a spouse's household) if—and that is a substantial if—they have at their disposal staunch determination and purpose, intelligence, education, and, not to be forgotten, male connections.

Helene's rite of passage from a lone female graduate student to successful scientist and business woman may indeed sound like a stock phenomenon: You suffer, but if you try hard enough, you will succeed. This is one of the prevalent readings produced by the consumption of popular novels. Had Helene had a brother, he might have lived out that dictum with much greater ease; for Helene and her sisters things looked different. However, with the twentieth century came the first opportunity ever for young middle-class women to get an education outside the traditional female fields of nursing and teaching. As George Mosse points out, the establishment of workmen's colleges in the 1880s and 1890s helped to erode education as a privilege of the (male) bourgeoisie.[12] The last bulwark against universal education, gender, began to crumble soon afterwards. In the late 1890s women still had to obtain ministerial permission to attend university lectures, but in 1901, the University of Heidelberg admitted female students to all faculties for the first time. In 1913, at the beginning of the fall term, 3,649 women were enrolled in universities all over Germany and accounted for 6.3 per cent of the total university student population.[13] Thus, the issues for a woman like Helene had not been tried or tested by previous generations of women. There were few, if any, role models for women among scientists or business executives in Weimar Germany, and as economic conditions deteriorated, the workplace as a whole grew increasingly hostile to the female workforce.

Women with terminal academic degrees did not abound in Weimar, either in fiction or reality. Besides Baum's *Helene*, Erich Kästner's *Fabian: Die Geschichte eines Moralisten* (1931) is one of the few exceptions to the rule in that it features a woman lawyer.[14] However, in keeping with the novel's dystopian bent, she decides to leave the legal field; she instead uses her degree to get her foot in the door of a film company and then becomes a film star by granting sexual favors to the producer. Whether or not it was a frequent occurrence in Weimar reality, spurning education in favor of glamor in popular fiction is interesting on various, if at times conflicting, counts. While portrayals of women who throw away the hard-won right to a higher education and the acquisition of the same confirm traditional assumptions about women's disinterest in the intellect, they are also indicative of the anxiety-induced hostility men assumingly harbored toward educated women. Linked to this issue is a second point, taken from Kästner's scenario: the fascination with film. Irmgard Keun's 1932 novel, *Das kunstseidene Mädchen* , also discusses this pull and both novels articulate, each in their own way, the Hollywood star craze and philo-Americanism so prevalent in Weimar Germany.[15] The subtext that here resonates best with conventional views of women is the one that insists that female sexuality, i.e. women's perceived traditional power, will always win out over the benefits of education (and thus even over the power and authority it may grant). Indeed, such a view disassembles modernity's *Frauenfrage*, and argues for a return to a desirable, stable gender hierarchy.

The great number of books that appeared throughout the 1920s addressing marriage indicate the degree of trouble that the institution of marriage was in and consequently also how traditional, ordered life was out of kilter. Indeed, population figures from the time indicate some of the trends that gave cause for alarm: in 1925, there were two and a quarter million more women than men over twenty years of age; of this group, more than half (one and a quarter million) was between the ages of twenty-five and forty; further, there were nearly three million widows and consequently, women were heads of three quarters of all the single-head households in the nation.[16] In addition to the sheer demographic facts, men's prolonged absence away at war very probably boosted women's independence and emancipation.[17]

One answer to the perceived need for explanation and guidance in issues surrounding marriage appeared in *The Book of Marriage: A New Interpretation by Twenty-four Leaders of Contemporary Thought* (1926), edited by Count Hermann Keyserling.[18] If we are to believe this anthology, it is not so much the institution itself but women's emancipation that is to blame for the dissolution of marriage as we know it. As one of the women contributors to the volume explains, a country that had granted citizenship, i.e. suffrage, to women thereby also removed one of the foundations of traditional marriage, since it was through her husband that a woman received social standing and sanction for her existence.[19] It sounds therefore as though, with women's newly found freedom to ride a bicycle, earn a living, and vote, there had to be newer and more persuasive reasons for young women to marry. Thomas Mann observed: "We see, then, marriage and the "household" menaced and rendered problematic by the husband through licentiousness, the right to happiness and the right to change if his felicity does not appear to him to be perfect; by the wife, by the children, and by the servants through emancipation, attained self-assurance, liberty, and personality."[20] Matrimony was indeed threatened by all the above claims. It is therefore not unexpected that the subject of marriage would also occupy a prominent place in many works of popular fiction, although the novels do not universally approve of the experiments that were taking place throughout the Twenties.

"Certainly the structure of marriage remained the same ... but women ... could earn their living as well as any man. The consequences were an ominous decline of marriages and births, issues that had already caused extensive debate in the Reichstag."[21] This sentiment appears in Wolfgang von Lengerke's novel *Die Amazone Gloria* (1928). According to its foreword the novel was conceived of as a satire against the American women's movement which is deemed "completely out of hand." (7) The anxiety underlying both the foreword by Felix Holländer, a cultural guru of the Weimar period, and the novel's subject matter—the founding and foundering of a Women's Independent State—is apparent. Women's economic independence, which in fact remained more mythical than real, was perceived to be one of the major causes of the destruction of civilized society. Nonetheless, Von Lengerke's lament is curiously at odds with the novel's female characters few of whom are working women and all but one are "women who, due to their husbands' millions, were able to be idle ...." (32) This incongruity sets up a reading wherein the perception of marriage is not so much that of an institution that is crumbling due to economic viability of female work, but rather that it may be a socio-economic arrangement often based on the women's economic needs.

Given the growing middle-class concern about marriage, one would expect to find statistics that would point toward its decline. And yet, the figures concerning marriage do not divulge any great need for panic. Until World War One, the number of marriages per 1,000 population per year had been 7.7. In spite of the large number of male war casualties, the figures actually rose from 1927-1931 to between eight and nine. By 1932 the number of marriages had declined slightly to 7.9 but, as the figures show, the marriage rate showed no drastic downward trend. It could even be said that since the adult male population after 1918 was smaller by nearly three million, more men were getting married in the interwar years than before the war.[22] The number of adult females had also declined by almost a million in 1919. If the same number of people per thousand were marrying, even though there were fewer adults, we must therefore infer that there were, in fact, proportionally more marriages after the war than before, given that the size of the marriageable portion of the population had shrunk.

If the "problem" with marriage is not one of quantity we are forced to look elsewhere for the cause of the reigning consternation. Could it be that the quality of marriage was the reason for the nervousness so pervasive in good society? One look at the divorce rate is enough to indicate that a major cause for anxiety lay here. The following figures for divorces per 100,000 inhabitants tell a clear story: 1913–26.6; 1920–59.1; 1923–61.6; 1932–65.0.[23] It appears that the incidence of divorce more than doubled in the seven years between 1913 and 1920 and that it continued to rise for another decade. One explanation for this may lie in the dissolution of war marriages. Many of these had been entered into in the heat of battle, but with peace time came also low morale, lack of employment, and political unrest. Once the breadline replaced the frontline, emotional and sexual energies were diverted from war to a different kind of survival that did not sustain flash romantic encounters.

It was the divorce figures rather than the statistics on marriage that indicated that one of the major patriarchal institutions, marriage, and the concomitant male control over female sexuality might be weakening. Seen from the perspective that the passage of time offers us, it becomes clear to what degree the "daily and hourly self-sacrifice, renunciation, and the shouldering of responsibility and blame" evidently required for marriage fell disproportionately on women's shoulders.[24] At the time, such a perspective was perhaps present but not articulated very often; after all, women's consciousness-raising groups were still a good forty years away. By and large, there was no wholesale rejection of marriage as an institution, as the numbers indicate. Nevertheless, members of the generation that had come of age during the war harbored a general dissatisfaction with traditional marriages as they had witnessed it in their parental homes. It was the subordinate role of the wife in a traditional marriage that held no attraction for young, would-be independent women. In practice, this meant that a modern woman wanted a responsible, modern husband, a small family, the right to work, and to a private income; most importantly, she aspired to self-realization.[25] Those kinds of tensions—that is, between discontent with marriage as well as a lingering acquiescence to it and a desire to reform or, even more radically, to abolish the institution—are what set the parameters of the issue when the question of marriage appears in the popular fiction of the time.

Still, when all is said and done, so few of the examined novels touch on divorce that it is virtually invisible in Weimar popular fiction. Why? The very few characters who are divorced or separated are minor characters with the exception of Gloria Garrick from von Lengerke's *Gloria the Amazon* (1928) and Ulrike Sebald from Oskar Gluth's 1933 tongue-in-cheek novel *Bayerische Himmelfahrt*. Whereas Gloria's divorce is pardonable—her husband whipped her—Frau Sebald's character is given a less charitable testimony from a parishioner: "Didn't the pastor know that this woman was involved with theater and divorced from her husband? (10)" The humorous tone of Gluth's novel highlights its critique of narrow-minded perceptions of both artists and divorcées, while through their representation, also verifying not only those very perceptions but also the existence of divorce. In reality, divorce was both difficult and expensive to obtain and as the novels show, marriage was too often the only road to economic viability for women. The mode of production of novels almost always predetermined a positive outcome of the plot and its characters, and therefore female role models or successful women in popular fiction were not divorcées. They were woman who were happily married or took their vows about "for better or for worse" seriously and stuck with their marriages. Less frequently, they were unmarried women who due to education and well-paying careers, like Helene, chose to live on their own. Reading through popular literature that was written in the socio-historical context of wide-spread anxieties concerning population growth and morality, the sheer un-presence of textual divorce elicits a sense of the magnitude of its taboo. It brings to mind lesbianism and its representational conundrum: if you deny its representation you likewise deny its existence but you also miss the opportunity to vilify it.

Marriages were nevertheless not always portrayed as an earthly paradise. A short story, "Der Weg," published in 1925 by Vicki

Baum, serves to exemplify the dystopian aspects of marriage. It is the story of the last few days in the life of a housewife, Frau Elisabeth Zienkann, before she chooses to die from a cold. Her life is defined exclusively by family and her attention to general household affairs. When, in the very beginning of the story, Baum describes the housewife's daily work, the excruciatingly thorough description not only produces for the reader the atmosphere in which Frau Zienkann can no longer live, but also evokes in the reader a certain measure of sympathy for her decision to let go of life:

> She wakes the children ... shakes awake the sluggish little servant girl and has in the meantime put water on the gas burner to boil for breakfast ... She prepares and packs lunch bags and quickly sews on a button. She wakes up the little sleepy servant girl again and sets the table for breakfast. Her hands always shake a little anxiously in the morning until she has seen to her husband and the children and got them out of the house on time. Then ... she balances the household accounts and plans the day. She cleans the canary's cage; waters the flowers. She tidies up the bedroom and her hands grow blue with the cold. She dusts the living room and scolds the little servant girl, who never does things by more than half. She stands at the coal-elevator, helps pull the coal bucket up and supervises the heating process. She dons an old rain hat, grabs a shopping net and trots to the market for affordable fish. She sails home with the heavy, filled shopping net, argues with the servant girl, and polishes the floor herself ... She cooks. She irons a blouse for Marianne ... She cooks again .... (3)

The list goes on, and when the woman finally sits down at night it is not with idle hands, of course, but with some crochet work. The narrator is careful to point out that there is nothing special about this Frau Elizabeth Zienkann (4). Women readers recognized her as one of the tens of thousands of women whose lives are lived out in similar fashion and the passage cited above provides ample proof of the fragmentation and decentralization which characterized women's work in the home. It is therefore not surprising, that Frau Zienkann envisions in death the only means of resting, finally, in peace.

This little story is radical. The mother of two adolescents and wife of a "good" man (Mr. Zienkann is employed), chooses death over life for no reason at all, at least not for reasons apparent to her family. But to Frau Zienkann, her reality is deadening. Her invalidated work, which she considers a duty, leaves her no room for a sense of self-fulfillment; further, her attempts at playing the piano lead her to melancholic reveries accompanied by uncomprehending, patronizing smiles from spouse and children, clearly indicating a lack of recognition of her subjectivity. As is so often the case, in fiction as in reality, marriage has replaced love and desire with duties and a family. It is not a search for emancipation that kills Frau Zienkann. Rather, it is the lack of alternatives, caught as she is in the claustrophobic structure of the household duties she carries out without recognition.[26] When her search for a household item brings on a cold and then death, it is clearly the pursuit of these duties that kills her.

Another unenthusiastically married woman protagonist, this one from Baum's 1931 novel, *Zwischenfall in Lohwinckel* (*And Life Goes On*), is Elizabeth Persenthein who has married a somewhat eccentric village doctor, Nick Persenthein.[27] Elizabeth's views on marriage do not amount to a glowing recommendation, and in the beginning of the novel they are formulated thus in her tired thoughts: "But what does marriage consist of except these questions: Are your tired? When do you want dinner? Why can't you sleep?" (29). Elizabeth, like her namesake from "Der Weg," is yearning for something else, something better than this.

An alternative to Elizabeth's disenchantment with marriage is proffered elsewhere in the novel with the open-ended relationship between two of its characters, Peter and Leore, the latter a beautiful filmstar and Peter's current companion. Their relationship is one in which "the love that united them was the love of this modern age: without any foundation in the past and without any regard for the future. Without any obligation ...." (201-2) Options such as this one can be found in many of Weimar popular works. Even though (mostly heterosexual) love triumphs in the end, marriage is not the only alternative proffered in popular texts. It may be the goal that at least most fictional women steer toward and the looser relationships–ones between servant women and their masters, for example–frequently turn out to be unsustainable.[28] Still, extra-marital relationships are portrayed, and their existence is verified, sometimes as the age-old male prerogative, but also as a modern phenomenon, desired and maintained by the woman. In *And Life Goes On*, the fact that Nick and Elizabeth's relationship is continuous makes it the primary focus in the novel. All the other intimacies portrayed, emotional, sexual, or simply flirtatious ones, are of much shorter duration, and Elizabeth's ability to return to "home base" to regroup her thoughts and consider her actions contrasts sharply with the rootlessness of the other characters. All the same, unlike "Der Weg," which condemns marriage like no other text examined here, *And Life Goes On* does not invalidate other forms of relationships as much as it reinstates the possibility of marriage as a good working option. The time of this work's conception is important: it first appeared in 1930, at a time when 1920s optimism and the search for liberated life styles was being supplanted by the pessimism of the third and most serious economic crisis in the short history of the Weimar Republic. Hopes of a new, brighter future and the desire for experimentation were giving way to a desperate return to "safe" traditional ways of life.

Tensions, conflicts, and contradictions about love, marriage, and experimental relationships similar to those that preoccupied the German Republic reside both in and between the individual works. Such were the Weimar years that it was almost impossible not to be enmeshed in contending notions of contemporary conduct. That shifting cultural values had found their way even into rural areas is evidenced by the many popular texts that denounce urban degeneracy and turn to traditional outlooks. Insofar as works of popular fiction affirmed traditional views on marriage, women readers could indeed find their own doubts or desires resonating in these texts, which ensured that their engagement with circulating narratives and ideologies were multivalent. The texts are pervaded with an almost hegemonic heteronormativity that suppresses alternate sexualities and desires in all but a few novels, and when linked to the textual absence of divorce, they are a complex contradiction to a lived (urban) reality with its obvious and prolific presences of divorcées and lesbians. These conflicting discourses and realities not only shaped the contemporary culture in which women took part, but also shaped their experience as participants in its formation which in turn constituted part of the process of the readers' own subject formation.

Reproductive T/Issues

As a response to a polite enquiry about life in the village, Vicki Baum writes the following in her 1926 novel, *Feme. Bußfahrt einer verirrten Jugend* (*Secret Sentence*, London, 1932): "The men are fond of drinking too much, and the girls have babies that they shouldn't, just like it happens all over the world."[29] This remark seems odd at first but upon a closer look, we can read it as a comment on a highly charged and topical issue— reproduction. While traditional behavioral codes seemed to join the moral casualty list of Western culture, a rise of pregnancies among unmarried women followed closely in the wake of the "discovery" and recognition of female sexuality: a vast number of popular Weimar novels featured at least one young, unmarried, pregnant woman. Whether they are passengers in trains as in Baum's *Helene*, Gilgi herself in Keun's novel of the same name, a secondary character in Braune's *Orga Privat*, one of the many sales clerks in Georgy's *Der Konfektionsbaron*, or a trendy young woman in Kästner's *Fabian*, unmarried pregnancy is ubiquitous. Another example is Hans Fallada's 1933 novel *Kleiner Mann, was nun?*, one of the most widely read novels about the depression era. It starts in the following manner.

> Five minutes past four. A neatly dressed, fair-haired young man stands in front of No. 24 Rothenbaumstrasse.
>
> At a quarter to four Bunny was to have been here to meet him. Pinneberg put his watch back in his pocket, and surveyed a brass plate affixed to the Wall.
>
> Dr. Sesam
> *Gynecologist*
> Consulting Hours: 9–12 and 4–6
>
> "Good afternoon," said a voice. In the doorway stood Dr. Sesam, the famous Dr. Sesam of whom it was whispered over half the city and a quarter of the province that he had a large heart, and many people also said, a good heart. Anyhow he had written a popular pamphlet on sexual problems, which was why Pinneberg had summoned up courage to write to him and seek an appointment for himself and Bunny.[30]

The very opening of Fallada's novel forefronts reproductive issues in a demonstrative manner, thus reflecting how commonplace out-of-wedlock pregnancies and abortions were in the 1920s. Granted, pregnant women or women seeking an abortion were not often major fictional characters, but rather figures in the human landscape, their condition mentioned as an aside. The importance of such figures lies in the fact that they appear so frequently and in such large numbers throughout the popular culture of the Twenties. The sexual climate in Weimar Germany was such that sexual relationships between unmarried men and women were frequent; consequently, so were incidents of single motherhood.[31]

Records show that the German pharmaceutical industry produced between eighty and ninety million condoms annually.[32] Other birth control measures—diaphragms, dutch caps, and various foam contraceptives—were known, largely due to the many medical and lay people working in the movement for sexual reform. One of the many results of this movement came when independent feminist

Helene Stöcker founded *Bund für Mutterschütz und Sexualreform* (League for the Protection of Motherhood and Sexual Reform) in 1905 in order to fight for women's right to a free sexuality and unmarried motherhood. Unfortunately, not only was birth control generally too costly for the lower income classes, it was in reality only available if prescribed by a doctor or if you were a member of one of the many leagues or clubs that were founded to educate the general population about sex.[33] As an example, by 1931, Prussia had established 200 clinics according to the Ministry of Social Welfare's guidelines but in none of them were the staff supposed to discuss birth control. Grossmann reports that by the end of the Weimar Republic, however, there were at least forty installations in Berlin that offered some form of birth control as well as marriage and sex counseling.[34] Obviously, a woman's class and geographical location determined whether she had access to clinics that dispensed birth control. The farther removed from large urban centers she lived, the more obstacles there were between her and contraceptives. Therefore, pregnancy was more prevalent among low income and rural women than among urban middle- and upper-class women.

In fiction as in reality, some unmarried women decided to bring their pregnancies to full term in spite of the social and economic hardships of single parenthood. Conditions for a single mother had improved measurably since the Wilhelminian era. The rate of children born out of wedlock had also risen consistently, from 8.5 percent in 1905 to twelve percent in 1925 (with an all time high of thirteen percent for the year 1918). A woman gynecologist in Baum's *Helene* assures Helene Willfüer that times have changed: "When the time comes ... (you will be admitted to a) lying-in hospital. There'll be no charge ....Thank God we've managed these last years to see that the unmarried mother gets her social rights ... you're even allowed to call yourself 'Mrs.'...." (142)

A child born out of wedlock was not the ruination of a working-class woman's moral reputation. Unwed mothers were accepted more readily among the working classes, who did not necessarily share the bourgeois assumption that respectability was almost entirely predicated on chastity.[35] Working-class morality permitted premarital sexuality as long as the couple had agreed to get married at some future point. Nonetheless, discriminatory and class-specific attitudes prevailed in the institutional treatment of women from lower income groups. Working-class mothers presumably had the same social rights as those of the middle classes, but if the woman were poor, she was obliged to subject herself to science to a humiliating degree, thus paying by other means for her lower social status. Baum's novel, *Helene*, whose concerns relate both to fiction and to reality, contains passages describing the mortification to which poor unwed mothers had to subject themselves. They could enter the hospital six weeks before the birth of the child and stay there with it for six weeks after, but during that time they might have to serve "as material for study." A medical student tells Helene: "Not long ago we examined a pregnant woman—a girl—who was expecting an illegitimate child—a house case as they're called here. We were twenty-four guys and one after another we examined the girl. She lay on the table and kept her eyes tightly shut." (230, 82)

Among contemporary observers, Wilhelm Reich summarizes the situation that provides the basis for the above incident with his comment that "[t]he ... idealization of motherhood is grossly at variance with the brutality with which mothers among the working population are actually treated."[36] "Mamschka," a novella by Hans Franck, lends support to Reich's observation. In this short story, Marylla Urbinelakowsky, a rural day laborer, gives birth to a child out of wedlock at the same time as the mistress of the house has a son. Marylla is "promoted" to wet nurse but is forced to leave her own child in foster care where it subsequently dies. The rationale the masters give the servant for asking her to abandon her child is: "[H]owever abundantly her milk may flow, she certainly could not feed two infants."[37] In reality, the perception given expression here is that the poor are not as attached to their children as are people from other classes.

The intersection of historical narratives, contemporary statements, and fictional stories underscores the chasm between the social rhetoric of "sacred motherhood" and the harsh reality of reproductive issues for many women. In Franck's novella there is the added element of ethnocentrism—Marylla is Polish—giving it an extra and pernicious eugenic twist: in the late 1920s, the desire to improve the birth rate was tempered by the desire to control the purity of progeny. A Weimar reader would, of course, be attuned to this concern. Speaking, as I do, from a post-Holocaust vantage point, it is difficult not to imagine a reader's reaction to Marylla's predicament: sadness, anger, or perhaps even outrage at the ruthless treatment of the servant woman. Nevertheless, as the story progresses, Marylla's love for the master's child soon erases the loss of the little Polish boy in the reader's mind especially since the master's son reciprocates Marylla's love. Women readers could hardly avoid reacting to such a story, although individual readings are dependent upon the confluence of too many conditions to be entirely predictable. But whatever their actual effect on any single reader, stories like Franck's point to popular fiction as a public sphere where decisions on crucial, real, public issues were being made every day, as readers interacted with them on a fictional level.

As long as the Weimar economy was booming (1924–1927), the Republic was able to sustain state- or employer-supported pre- and post-natal care, infant care, school lunches, and other social programs that helped relieve the single-income family.[38] Still, that did not remove the difficulties for a single mother. There were no effective measures in place to ensure paternal child support, nor did an unmarried mother have any legal right over her child.[39] As the economic situation deteriorated from 1929 onward, the above-mentioned public health measures were increasingly privatized or simply eliminated. As unemployment rose and real wages fell, the need consequently grew even greater for those same public health services.[40] Under such economic conditions, abortion became a very real option for low-income women. Lack of income and of available institutional support invariably influenced women's decisions about whether they would let a pregnancy come to term or choose abortion. In 1931, at the depth of the depression, there were officially six million unemployed, and the number of abortions is said to have reached the one million mark.[41]

In fictional form, Baum's best-selling novel, *Helene*, mediates the dilemmas that many real women faced. At first, Helene chooses to have an abortion. As the narrator soothingly tells her and the reader: "It's true that you're answerable only to yourself, that you enjoy every possible freedom, that you know nothing of the narrow conceptions of a former day, that you haven't the faintest fault to find with the unmarried mother on moral grounds. But one does not have a child when one is studying ...." (133)

This paragraph condenses the increasingly intense debate over abortion and birth control, individual versus societal obligations, motherhood, and work in Weimar. The narrator assumes a rather conciliatory, even apologetic, note when addressing Helene's crisis, and this befits the personality parameter that the author and the publishing house, Ullstein Press, had established for her young protagonist. The motherliness and nurturing concern for people that pervade the narrative lead the reader to understand that the decision to have an abortion is made with the head, not with the heart. Popular texts often operate within the dualistic pattern of intellect versus heart or instinct—an approach that to this day is presumed viable when explaining women—and it is at this juncture that Helene's decision to have an abortion is situated. Her intellect guides her up to that point; but when all attempts at terminating the pregnancy fail, her true instinct, the "naturally female" nurturing instinct, takes the upper hand. In this manner, Helene actually switches to wonder and love for the life within her. Her material circumstances have not changed, nor have the moral framework of society around her. Nevertheless, by means of what may be interpreted as inner fortitude and her newly found feminine nature, she emerges from her personal struggles with a boy child.

This conciliatory solution to an unwanted pregnancy stands in sharp contrast to other popular novels mentioned here, among them Keun's *Gilgi—eine von uns* (1931).[42] In this novel, the title character, Gilgi, consults a male gynecologist who confirms her pregnancy and congratulates her. Gilgi's wish not to have the baby falls on deaf ears. She insists: "Listen, Doctor. It is the height of immorality and absurdity to make a woman give birth to a child that she cannot feed. But it is even more immoral and absurd to force a woman give birth to a child that she does not want." (117)

The differences between Helene's and Gilgi's approaches are obvious, and the reasons for them are manifold. One powerful motivation behind Helene's conciliatory approach is undoubtedly Baum's position as an employee in the House of Ullstein. Although Baum was Ullstein's rising star, the mighty publishing house still designed its products very carefully; indeed, Ullstein publications intended to give their readers entertainment, not problem novels. The suggestion of having a "hard-working girl" [*sic*] as the protagonist came from Hermann Ullstein, and the values Helene portrays—optimism, individualism, hard work, and a belief in humanistic values—match those of the publishing house.[43] But even more crucial for commercial ventures such as novels, the values expounded in them would be expected to match those of the targeted middle-class readership. Keun, a self-employed writer, on the other hand, had neither the favor nor the design-constraints of a publishing house. Consequently, she presumably had less assurance of economic success but more artistic leeway.

If Helene's early inclination toward abortion is unconvinced and half-hearted, Gilgi does not mince words. She is much more aware of the larger moral and social issues involved in reproduction and abortion than is Helene. This awareness is clearly not one that is born of an advanced education, but rather out of a political interpretation of the reality that faces the protagonist. The material reality for young, white-collar women like Gilgi was akin to that of the established working classes, that is to say, grim.

It is therefore a startling moment when the reader comes across the cavalier manner in which one of Kästner's female middle-class characters from *Fabian* mentions having had a "surgical procedure" performed (87). Working-class women—among whom illegal abortions were a mass phenomenon in the 1920s—had less psychic detachment and clinical cleanliness at their disposal than their higher-paid sisters. In Baum's *Helene*, a medical student describes a working woman "who has tried by illicit means to intercept [*sic*] her sixth pregnancy, and who lies there now, exhausted and drained of blood—she would prefer death." (27) The plot of Rudolph Braune's *Das Mädchen an der Orga Privat* features an illegal and fatal abortion performed on a female clerk, Trude Leußner. Her treatment at the hands of a lecherous boss precipitates a sympathy strike among her women colleagues, which does not prevent her subsequent death from the complications of the illegal abortion. The strikers return to work, defeated by their horror, grief, and need for work while they are also empowered by their first experience of solidarity with other women.

These fictional examples as well as many others not mentioned here echo some disturbing statistics. In *The Working Class in Weimar*, Erich Fromm writes that "over 10,000 women died annually from the after-effects of abortions ... even more [than from] contracted chronic diseases."[44] While the sheer number of pregnant working-class women who appear in popular texts may be an indicator of the general perception of working-class women—eternally pregnant and mothers of numerous children—it simultaneously illustrates the fact that working-class women could less afford to take measures to avoid pregnancy than could middle-class women. Leonhard Frank's short novel from 1927 about a working-class couple, *Carl and Anna*, indicates living conditions in tenements with large families in the following passage: "The crying of babies rose here and there like the croaking of frogs in a marshy pool; often they combined in a chorus for minutes on end." (38) Family-planning clinics were not widely available although, in 1931, forty-three cities (not including Berlin) were reported to have some kind of marriage counseling program. Women who had access to one were often more likely to be given instruction in the proper care of infants, what to do in case they contracted venereal disease, and how to detect incest in their families than they were to receive contraceptives.[45]

Abortion was a hotly debated issue then as it is now. In France, in 1920, mere advocacy of abortion was punishable by prison and a fine.[46] In 1929, the German Reichstag Criminal Justice Committee took steps toward developing a new criminal code. The Weimar Republic's Paragraph 218, a focal point of women's issues, stated that anyone performing abortions for commercial gain faced an indefinite prison sentence. This is misleading, however, for the law could be—and often was—interpreted very broadly. And in fact, it was not only those who received payment for their services who were punished: in 1930, a miner's wife who had performed 140 abortions without payment—and more importantly, without causing injury—was sentenced to three years in the penitentiary.[47]

The huge number of illegal abortions was indicative of a critical contradiction between theory and practice or, said differently, between the law and the material conditions. On the one hand, improved hygiene and better pre- and post-natal care had lowered the infant mortality rate. In 1905, infant deaths amounted to twenty percent of all live births; in 1913, the figure had fallen to fifteen percent; by 1930, it was only 8.5 percent.[48] Although the percentage of infant deaths was higher among infants born to unwed mothers, a drop of 11.5 percent in less than two decades is significant. It appears that advances in modern medicine, public housing, and hygiene outweighed the spending cuts in some areas of public health. However, even though more children now lived to adulthood, there was no central or official effort to make contraception legal. Indeed, Paragraph 184.3 prohibited any advertisement or display of contraceptive means and methods, because, it was thought, they would be used for indecent purposes.[49] To counter the few birth control clinics that existed, the Evangelical and Catholic Churches set up their own counseling centers where they instructed clients in the Pauline notion of marriage and offered neither sexual nor medical advice.[50]

The issue was, and is, class-specific. The fact that middle-class families generally were smaller than working-class families points to a differential in the availability of and knowledge about birth control as a result of differences in money and education. And yet, within the working class itself, a distinction was being made between those families whose way of life was modern and, considering married women's work and housing shortage, limited the size of their family and those who did not.[51] But when all is said and done, legal abortions were available under circumstances that were by and large safe from both legal and health complications to those who could afford them. This becomes clear if one compares the sanitized mention of the abortion issue in Kästner's middle-class text *Fabian* ("a surgical procedure") with the brutal outcome of Braune's working-class novel, *Orga Privat*. It is also interesting to note that most of the bourgeois feminist associations in the Weimar Republic distanced themselves from the urgency of the discussion. They, in unison with the churches, supported "family values." *Helene* articulates this conflict through the title character's dilemma and decision to keep her child.

The abortion struggle was bitter, and everyone was touched by it, even those who tried to distance themselves from it. It came to a head in 1931, but no constitutional change ensued. A Berlin newspaper was flooded with nearly half a million replies to a poll on abortion; only 150 respondents were in favor of the extant law.[52] Had she been real, Keun's title character, Gilgi, would have been among the former respondents: her character resonated so strongly with the SPD's views on the right to abortion that its party organ *Vorwärts* invited its female readership to discuss the novel and suggest modifications of its plot and female character. Similarly, the film, *Gilgi—eine von uns,* was received very favorably by *Vorwärts* in 1932.[53]

In the case of Baum's novel, Helene's difficulty as she envisions an abortion lies partly in its illegality. She knows she has to seek "slimy and forbidden detours." A female gynecologist, Dr. Gropius, heightens Helene's dilemma: "I can't help—I daren't help. I've got to send these poor women away—women with five and six and seven children, who don't know which way to turn for misery. I—if it were up to me! There'd have been a welfare institution established long ago for official birth control. But that's a long way off yet. And we have our prohibitory laws." (134, 144) As a matter of fact, while Baum was writing *Helene,* opponents of Paragraph 218 were hard at work. In 1928, the first Doctors' Course in Birth Control and Abortion Techniques was conducted in Berlin by Helene Stöcker's Committee for Birth Control, by doctors who were members of the Communist Party, and the Association of Berlin Public Health Services.[54]

What was left when all else failed? Atina Grossmann points out that the pages of left-wing women's magazines were filled with reports of suicides and both completed and attempted infanticides. "Indeed, suicide, often taking children along ... was as much of a cultural motif in the presentation of the proletarian as was abortion, and the two were frequently connected."[55] When one looks into the popular culture of the late Weimar period, this solution does indeed manifest itself rather often as the following examples indicate: Phil Jutzi's 1929 film, *Mutter Krausens Fahrt ins Glück,* features Mother Krause and her children's struggle for economic survival; when their financial straits finally seem hopeless, she turns on the gas and takes her youngest child with her into death. Similarly, *Gilgi*, written in the depths of the Depression, draws a spare but shocking picture of a family who has seen better days: the man has become a door-to-door salesman, but at a time when nobody spends any money, he cannot but sink into desperate poverty. The arrival of yet another baby is too much for them to bear, and the whole family is found one morning, dead in their little room, with the gas taps turned on. Baum's *Helene* involves the same issue. In this case, the lovers consider double suicide by lethal injection. He wants to die as his burning desire to become a musician has been thwarted due to his father's cancer. He is required to become a doctor, like his dying father, in order to care for his mother and siblings. Helene also considers suicide, presumably because of the unwanted child. If her death wish is passed over lightly in the novel, it is no doubt due, once more, to readership considerations. A "hardworking girl" with morbid tendencies is not a good selling point for "light" entertainment.

Sex and the Single Girl

Female sexuality is seen as intimately connected with issues of marriage and reproduction at the same time as it is considered a crucial signifier of the "new" woman. This was a volatile property that few popular texts were without although there was deep divergence as to how to represent it. In *Helene*, the heroine's eroticism and sexual desires are side-tracked by her nurturing "instincts" (and later on, career focus) and she exhibits only maternal feelings toward her lover, Fritz Rainer: "Sometimes she felt like a big wise old mother beside this slender boyish, immature creature." Even in their most intimate moments she harbors no overt passion: "I'd like to hold you ... in my arms, nothing more. I'm a girl, maybe that's why. Or the great ecstacy isn't meant for me ...."(78, 97) Similarly, an unwavering nurturing spirit characterizes her relationship with her mentor, Professor Ambrosius. She desires only to hold him in her arms and to protect him. As a new phenomenon, Helene, the woman scientist with a brilliant career, has been constructed as asexual, even frigid, an occurrence that in the context of the novel has the appearance of a trade-off between education and desire.

As mentioned earlier in this chapter, the fear of female eros mixed with brain power has a long history. By the 1920s, a shift had occurred from the nineteenth-century notion that cerebral development could only occur at the cost of the woman's reproductive powers. Instead, it was now assumed that intellectual activity could cause a decreased capacity for passion and desire. The word was out: since deploying brain power took the edge off the erotic appetite, educated women were less able to enjoy sex.

Modernity's struggle with this and other aspects of women's emancipation is palpable in Helene's character where a compromise, almost a barter arrangement, has taken place. Since her education threatens the previously exclusive male preserve of science, she must counteract this by encompassing traditional characteristics; thus she is furnished with the vindicating quality of mothering infants as well as adults (all of which are males in the novel). While she has broken society's taboos regarding premarital sex, higher education for women, and their gainful employment, Helene as a nurturing matrix at the same time accommodates bourgeois notions of the de-eroticized—and thus non-threatening—mother.

Despite the compromise which informs Helene's character, Weimar women readers were likely to have experienced, albeit vicariously, certain transgressed limits and new possibilities for women's lives by reading her story. The same can be said for many other popular novels whose female protagonists are single and operate independently of men, at least in part. New ways of looking at heterosexual relationships appear frequently in popular fiction of the twenties, and although female characters seek such relationships, they—sometimes due to education—do not always need them to survive. In Kästner's novel, *Fabian*, a woman with a law degree is viewed askance by the title character when she jilts him in favor of stardom. Just the same, some independent women who inhabit texts by women writers show a different attitude. They fall in love and have emotional and sexual relationships, but they do not necessarily equate heterosexual relationships with marriage. Marriage is not their only criteria for social respectability and sometimes not even for financial survival as long as the economy is good. Although women, in reality, were as likely to marry as to remain single, the important thing to note in this context is that neither they nor their fictional sisters any longer considered themselves choiceless in the matter.

The interwar years marked the first time young, unmarried, middle-class, German women could move about in public unescorted. It is therefore not surprising that many fictional women from that time convey the contemporary zeal for independence. Keun's *Gilgi* constitutes a particularly poignant illustration of the single, lower-

and middle-class woman. To Gilgi, independence is primarily economic and she dreads giving work up to spend more time with her lover. Nevertheless, she leaves her job hoping in vain that love and nest-making—that is, house-keeping—will take its place. The novel conveys clearly that Gilgi's new life-style is more nurturing for her man than for her and she realizes slowly and painfully that her autonomy is vanishing. Some readers may have agreed with her girlfriend's advice: "Make sure you're independent—then you can have a man and keep love going." (138) Other readers would have understood the remark as a signal of the trap that catches women in a double bind: being employed and having a man meant doing the work both in the office and in the home, a hefty price to pay for both love and employment.

There were alternatives, however, and in fiction, Vicki Baum's character, Flämmchen, from her 1929 novel, *Grand Hotel,* incorporates these. Lasting relationships or jobs are not what Flämmchen seems to care about. She harbors no marriage plans, but the quality of her life depends on men inasmuch as they reward her sexual favors with money, momentary pleasure, or temporary security. For Flämmchen to remain desirable, it is crucial that she retain emotional autonomy. Her success in this endeavor may be measured by her statement: "You'd make acquaintances the way you'd light a cigarette; take a couple of drags as long as it tasted good, then extinguish it, making sure all the little sparks were out."[56] Flämmchen's character is emblematic of a modernity that has turned away from utopian dreams. In 1929, Weimar citizens were already experiencing an economic downswing that would only worsen with time and women's jobs were the first to go when the economic screws were turned. Pleasures had to be taken as they came; they were intense and short-lived, like a cigarette, but not to be missed.

Those kinds of measures of independence were very new to German women and may have sounded cynical to readers then. The "new" woman was exploring novel territory, and for a short time she marked that territory as hers. Flämmchen is a particularly luminous example. Her low-key emotionality in sexual relationships has a startling effect on men and she leaves a trail of desire behind her. Still, she is not the archetypal 1920s vamp or *femme fatale*. She is too poor and too low on the social ladder for that. Rather, she is a wild spirit, a (short-lived) new phenomenon, exhibiting the characteristics of an undomesticated female. Not only is she uninterested in lasting relationships, she has also escaped equating sexuality with reproduction. Although her character is young, she is outside the 1920s trend of female adolescent sexuality, and as such deviating from what was considered normal "feminine'" development.[57] In fact, her sexuality is very much in line with patriarchy's worst fears of immodesty, perversity, and degeneracy, since it is subservient to no master but rather overt, volatile, and unrestrained. Granted, she, too, is caught up in dreams of stardom that would ultimately give her over to exploitation, if she were to reach her goal. It is also true that she, as all commodities, is subject to the rules of economics and that men determine the extent of her fun and yet, she is an indomitable, free spirit following her own moral code.

It is not education that makes Flämmchen disobedient to patriarchal codes of behavior. In some fashion, she appears untamed, even untameable, according to the cultural totems and taboos that act as society's superego. Because she acts instinctively on her own desires and is often instantly gratified, she furthermore disrupts attempts at a single reading of her character as either victim or vamp. She can be read as a locus of the many discourses on women: modernity, experimental sexuality, emancipation, class, trivial pursuits. In another manner of speaking, Flämmchen is also the ultimate commodity, for as she puts her sexiness to work (for her?), it in turn exposes the economy of sexuality and the specific commercial value of female sexuality. In a scene, examined in more detail in another chapter, Flämmchen's body is clearly set up to be a linguistic spectacle, to be consumed, and consequently, also tamed, by the (male) customer.[58] Finally, Flämmchen is the "new" woman whom Elaine Showalter describes in *Sexual Anarchy* as "an anarchic figure who threatened to turn the world upside down and to be on top in a wild carnival of social and sexual misrule." (39) For a short time, Flämmchen glows, in her own right, as a star image of an unfettered, free-floating libido.

There is, of course, another side to the euphoric view of the liberated woman, one that is seen all too clearly by Irmgard Keun and mediated by Doris, an 18-year old typist and the protagonist of Keun's novel *Das kunstseidene Mädchen* (1932). She, too, thinks only of the moment and her image. As for so many of her living contemporaries, appearance was the overwhelming priority. In all probability, her way of life reflects the increasing influence of the media such as daily or weekly magazines, advertisements, and movies. Doris also wants to be rich, glamorous, and pampered. She seems to be carrying the subconscious sense of doom that underlined Weimar culture, her sense of *carpe diem* forcing her to race along the surface and to demand instant gratification without any thought for tomorrow. In Doris's own words: "These are terrible times, nobody has any money and morals are in flux." (28) The text emphasizes Doris's prolific sexual activities which seem so compulsive that the 1990s New Age pop psychologists would call her a "sex-addict." But Doris is a child of her times, whose hunger for excitement and glamor is matched only by that for food. The novel leaves her penniless and loverless without much hope of survival other than that of joining the ranks of the multitude of prostitutes she sees everywhere in Berlin's urban landscape.

Although sexual and economic independence seem to have been accessible to women for a short time in the interwar period, the Weimar years did not usher in a new millennium for women. Rather, in the late 1920s, another message rang out clearly: in spite of the profound changes in German society after the First World War, truly secure survival for women was to be found in matrimony. Indeed, both Flämmchen and Doris rely on their youth and sexual desirability to men for their material survival which only confirms that it is male rather than female privilege that is the final arbiter of the discourse of female independence. Women's sexual behavior no longer moved society to brand them immediately with a scarlet letter, but there was no security outside marriage for women once they lost their youth and first beauty.[59] The thousands of prostitutes on the streets of Berlin, increasing in number as the depression grew worse, testified to this.

Maria Tatar notes that a "settled existence is a corollary of desexualization" and in the fictional marriages examined for this work, the element of sexuality is indeed missing (141). All the eroticism and sexual attraction, explicit or implicit, occur in alternative or premarital relationships. We have seen that women characters have their fair share of sexual experiences but most wives in Weimar popular fiction are de-eroticized. This cannot simply be attributed to the notion of marriage as being founded on the rock of motherhood and family values, although this was (and is) a much treasured fantasy among bourgeois and conservative groups; nor does it simply reflect the domesticating effect that marriage is said to have on female sexuality.[60] The puzzle seems also to have its foundation in reality: one of the major issues at the time, borne out by the rising number of divorces, was the extent of "female frigidity." This phenomenon apparently occurred often enough to constitute a major problem, particularly for married couples. If Western culture, patriarchy, and population growth were not going to come to a grinding halt, something had to be done. Consequently, we see progressive sex-reforms working in the service of the conservative idea of "family values." Regardless of the politics of the particular organization, the consensus of the sexual reform movement was that it was better to regulate sexuality than to repress it.[61] An interesting, active sex life was no longer just a prospect for the young and unattached, for if the housewife and mother could be kept happy in the conjugal bed, she might stay in it, as it were. With an improved knowledge of how to satisfy his wife sexually, the husband might prevent her infidelities, lesbianism, "self-abuse," and even divorce. Thus, in permissive Weimar Germany, orgasmic pleasure and motherhood combined in a previously unimaginable alliance. But as far as the conservative desire for a baby boom went, it was all to no avail. It may be that married Weimar women learned to experience pleasure in their conjugal duties, but this did not translate into a higher birth rate.

* * *

It is obvious that popular works from the Weimar period actively participated in the vigorous debate about family values. Fictional voices resounded with the dilemmas of modern women. Questions of motherhood, marriage, and sex were articulated in popular fiction through many women characters, whose situations mirrored those of their living Weimar sisters. A paradigm of a "new," urban woman was becoming visible, accompanied by the frictions and dissensions that could not but attend such a construct. The majority of popular urban writers tended to voice the opinions of lower- and middle-class, liberal women, but even so, the contradictions of Weimar culture are clearly present. The various fictional negotiations of marriage are as ambivalent as those of material Weimar. Perhaps Frau Persenthein from Baums's *And Life Goes On* says it best: "Marriage is a curious affair. It is old ... and in need of repair ....A house of cards, at its best; at worst, the life of a galley slave for its willing victims ...." (290)

It has been argued that emancipation is not reflected in the women characters featured in Weimar middle-brow literature.[62] If we examine closely the characters of the women discussed in the present study, however, it becomes much more difficult to be so categorical. The nature of emancipation is complex, since it is specific to so many categories, among them culture, race, class, historical period, and, of course, gender. Arguably, then, any negotiation of emancipation in fiction—except in utopian fiction—requires at least an approximation of such emancipation in reality. Then, as now, popular fiction had to make compromises in order to please as many readers as possible. The novels examined here were written for popular entertainment, and with a certain realistic aesthetic in mind. As we have seen above, many of the women characters are light years ahead of their mothers' generation, politically and economically. At the same time, let us not forget that popular fiction is a commodity, dependent in varying degrees on the frequently conservative market place.

The attempts to regulate women's reproductive and sexual bodies were clearly high on the list of priorities in Weimar Germany. If, on the one hand, the impact of popular fiction on readers is difficult, if not impossible, to gauge, the great frequency with which the themes of marriage, sexuality, and reproductive issues occurred in popular works of the time bears witness to the urgency of the questions that accompanied them. The currency and frequency of these issues added to the intensity of the debate and undoubtedly also helped shape opinions on these issues for many readers. I contend that these very texts provided yet another venue for utterances on issues crucial to women's lives. The texts are extraordinary in their topicality and constitute an important female public sphere where, perhaps, for the first time, women, on a mass scale, experienced and participated in the making of their own destiny.

Notes

1. Rudolf Braune, *Das Mädchen an der Orga Privat. Ein kleiner Roman aus Berlin* (Frankfurt am Main, 1930), 133. Further citations are noted in the text as *Orga Privat*. All translations are mine.
2. Ute Frevert, *Frauengeschichte zwischen bürgerlicher Verbesserung und neuer Weiblichkeit* (Frankfurt am Main, 1986), 179.
3. Christa Anita Brück, *Schicksale hinter Schreibmaschinen* (Berlin, 1930), 22. Further citations are noted in the text as *Schicksale*. All translations are mine.
4. Lola Landau, "Kameradschaftsehe," *TAT* 20 (1929) as quoted in *The Weimar Republic Sourcebook*, eds. Anton Kaes, Martin Jay and Edward Dimendberg (Berkeley and Los Angeles, 1994), 702–3.
5. Heinz Bernd, *Vergessene Schuld und andere Sittenromane* (Dresden, 1921), 51. All translations are mine.
6. Frevert, *Frauengeschichte*, 181.
7. *Statistisches Jahrbuch für das Deutsche Reich* as quoted in Jill Stephenson, *Women in Nazi Germany* (New York, 1975), 51–52. Also Detlev J.K. Peukert, *The Weimar Republic* (New York, 1992), 7–8.

8. See also Cornelie Usborne, *The Politics of the Body in Weimar Germany: Women's Reproductive Rights and Duties* (London, 1992).
9. Karen Hagemann, *Frauenalltag und Männerpolitik: Alltagsleben und gesellschaftliches Handeln von Arbeiterfrauen in der Weimarer Republik* (Bonn, 1990), 25. All translations are mine.
10. Vicki Baum, *Helene*, trans. Ida Zeitlin (Garden City, 1933). The English translation is used in this text.
11. For a traditional critique of Baum's resolution to these conflicts, see also Johann Holzner's article "Literarische Verfahrensweisen und Botschaften der Vicki Baum," in *Erzählgattungen der Trivialliteratur*, eds. Zdenko Skreb and Uwe Baur, vol. 18, Innsbrucker Beiträge zur Kulturwissenschaft, Germanistische Reihe (Innsbruck, 1984), 233–50.
12. George Mosse, *The Culture of Western Europe* (Boulder, 1988), 285.
13. Frevert, *Frauengeschichte*, 122. US historian William Chafe points out that the "first two decades of the twentieth century witnessed in America a "1000 per cent" increase of women's enrollment in public colleges and a "482 per cent" increase of female enrollment in private schools." As quoted in Sandra Gilbert and Susan Gubar, *No Man's Land: The Place of the Woman Writer in the Twentieth Century*, vol. 1 of *The War of the Words*. (New Haven, 1988), 33.
14. Erich Kästner, *Fabian: Die Geschichte eines Moralisten* (Zürich, 1931). Further citations are noted in the text as *Fabian*. English Translation: Cyrus Brooks. Evanston, 1990.
15. Irmgard Keun, *Das kunstseidene Mädchen* (1932; reprint Bergisch Gladbach, 1987). All translations are mine.
16. Tim Mason, " Women in Germany 1925–1940: Family, Welfare and Work," part 1, *History Workshop* 1, no. 1 (1976): 77.
17. I thank Susan Hanson for bringing up this point in a conversation.
18. *The Book of Marriage: A New Interpretation by Twentyfour Leaders of Contemporary Thought*, ed. Count Hermann Keyserling, (New York, 1926). Among works that appeared in Germany, Theodor van deVelde's *Ideal Marriage* (1926) was counted among the most popular. A very similar trend was pursued on this side of the Atlantic where the most famous work undoubtedly is Margaret Sanger's *Happiness in Marriage* (1926).
19. Leonie Ungern-Sternberg, "The Marriage of the Future," in *Book of Marriage*, 264.
20. Thomas Mann, "Marriage in Transition: An Open Letter to Count Hermann Keyserling," in *Book of Marriage*, 257–58.
21. Wolfgang von Lengerke, *Die Amazone Gloria* (Berlin, 1928), 33. Further citations are noted in the text as *Gloria*. All translations are mine.
22. The population figures for men in 1910 were: 32,040,166 and in 1919: 29,011,216. The corresponding figures for women in 1910 were: 32,885,827; in 1919: 31,887,368. Stephenson, *Women in Nazi Germany*, 52.
23. Ibid., 52.
24. Keyserling, *Book of Marriage*, 47.
25. Frevert, *Frauengeschichte*, 181.
26. Vicki Baum's depiction of housework stands in sharp contrast to that of another Weimar woman writer, Anna Seghers. The latter communicates housewives' duties as being valuable, skilled, and worthy of the effort. Cf. the character of Liesel in *Das siebte Kreuz* (Neuwied, 1979), 194-95.
27. Vicki Baum, *And Life Goes On*, trans. Margaret Goldsmith (Garden City, 1932).

28. See also Wassermann's *The Gooseman* and Berend's *The Captain of Bodensee*. The synopses of the novels mentioned in the main text can be found in the appendix.
29. Vicki Baum, *Secret Sentence* (London, 1932), 43. The English version is quoted here.
30. Hans Fallada, *Lille Mand—Hvad nu?* trans. Sonja Heise (Copenhagen, 1933), 7. All translations are mine.
31. It is difficult to determine whether the visibility and the more permissive discourse about unwed mothers encouraged reporting such incidents. It is possible, as has been suggested by some historians, that the numbers were as large earlier, but that women just kept quiet about it.
32. Atina Grossmann. *Reforming Sex: The German Movement for Birth Control and Abortion Reform 1920–1950* (New York & London, 1995), 15.
33. Atina Grossmann, "Abortion and Economic Crisis: The 1931 Campaign Against §218 in Germany," *New German Critique*, no. 5 (Spring 1978): 130. See also Grossmann, *Sexual Reform*.
34. Grossmann, *Sexual Reform*, 47–56.
35. Kathy Peiss, "'Charity Girls' and City Pleasures: Historical Notes on Working Class Sexuality, 1880–1920" in *Powers of Desire: The Politics of Sexuality*, eds. Ann Snitow, Christine Stansel, and Sharon Thompson (New York, 1983), 83. See also Hagemann, *Frauenalltag und Männerpolitik*.
36. Wilhelm Reich, *The Mass Psychology of Fascism* (3rd ed. New York, 1988), 89.
37. Hans Franck, "Mamschka," in *Recht ist Unrecht. Neun Novellen um eine Wahrheit* (Leipzig, 1928), 14. All translations are mine.
38. Grossmann, "The New Woman," 124.
39. Stephenson, *Women in Nazi Germany*, 58.
40. Although women oftentimes replaced men on assembly lines, they worked for subsistence wages. At the same time, unions, which primarily looked after the working *man's* interests, renewed the debate over working women's physiological and psychological fitness during times of economic crises. See also Renate Bridenthal, "Something Old, Something New: Women Between the Two World Wars," in *Becoming Visible: Women in European History*, eds. Renate Bridenthal, Claudia Koonz, and Susan Stuard (Boston, 1987), 480–82.
41. Atina Grossmann, "The New Woman and the Rationalization of Sexuality in Weimar Germany," in *Powers of Desire*, 157. The figures have been contested as approximate at best since abortion was a crime in the Weimar Republic.
42. Irmgard Keun, *Gilgi—eine von uns*, 1931 (3rd ed. Munich, 1990). Further citations are noted in the text as *Gilgi*. All translations are mine.
43. King, *Best-sellers by Design*, 32, 101.
44. Erich Fromm, *The Working Class in Weimar Germany: A Psychological and Sociological Study*, 1929, trans. Barbara Weinberger (Cambridge, Mass., 1984), 176. This study was done in 1929 and parts of it comprise an analysis of 584 answers to Fromm's questionaires. Originally he received 1,100 responses but only 584 survived his move into exile in the US. Although the paucity of responses impairs the validation of his findings considerably, one can get some general indications of how the working classes thought of certain issues.
45. Grossmann, "The New Woman," 161 and *Reforming Sex*, 57.
46. Marilyn J. Boxer and Jean H. Quataert, eds. *Connecting Spheres: Women in the Western World, 1500 to the Present* (New York, 1987), 210.
47. Stephenson, *Women in Nazi Germany*, 59.
48. Ibid., 52.

49. Grossmann, "Abortion and Economic Crisis," 123.
50. Stephenson, *Women in Nazi Germany*, 60.
51. Grossmann, *Reforming Sex*, 7.
52. Grossmann, "Abortion and Economic Crisis," 129.
53. Bruce Murray, *Film and the German Left in the Weimar Republic: From Caligari to Kuhle Wampe* (Austin, 1990), 172.
54. Grossmann, "Abortion and Economic Crisis," 121, 125.
55. Ibid., 125.
56. Vicki Baum, *Menschen im Hotel*, 1929 (Reprint, Frankfurt am Main, 1986), 111. Further citations are noted in the text as *Grand Hotel*. All translations are mine.
57. Patrice Petro, *Joyless Streets*, 45.
58. Lisa Mizejewski, *Divine Decadence: Fascism, Female Spectacle, and the Makings of Sally Bowles*, (Princeton, 1992), 42, 77.
59. According to Renate Bridenthal, the vast majority of women in the service sector were under thirty. "Something Old," 485.
60. This notion was greatly facilitated by Pope Pius XII's 1930 encyclical on Christian marriage which denounced sex in marriage without the intent to procreate. The character of Nick Persenthein in Baum's *And Life Goes On* presumably shares similar notions about marriage when he insists that the child is the foundation for his and Elizabeth's relationship.
61. Grossmann, *Reforming Sex*, 14–15.
62. Cf. Lynda King, "Probable or Possible? The Issue of Women's Emancipation in German Literature of the 1920s," *Rocky Mountain Review* 35. 2 (1981): 138–52 and Renny Harrigan, " Die emanzipierte Frau im deutschen Roman der Weimarer Republik," in *Stereotyp und Vorurteil in der Literatur*, eds. James Elliot, Jürgen Pelzer, and Carol Poore (Göttingen, 1978).

Chapter Three

WORK AND PLAY

My initial aim in writing this chapter was to examine and comment on the tension between the body regulated through work and the apparently non-regulated body at play. In the works I will discuss, the body at play appeared, at least at first, to be liberated, at times almost excessively so. But a paradigmatic shift occurred as I read on. I began to suspect that perhaps the playful physical activities which, at first glance, appeared to be antithetical to those required of workers by industrial capitalism were, in fact, adhering to the same set of principles.

It should come as no surprise that discourses concerning our physical selves are formed within and according to the ideologies of a given historical moment. Still, until we investigate the connections between movement (and here we mean the term in its widest sense) and capitalism, the connecting links will remain hidden under layers of assumptions. According to Janet Wollf, the factory, office, and government department have been marked as the prime sites of rationalization.[1] Intriguing links can be seen between rationalization of labor and how it permeates "forms of perception, representation and experience" as exemplified in Max Reinhardt's synchronized stage choreographies and the choreography of the mechanized workers in Fritz Lang's film, *Metropolis*.[2] Thus an investigation is called for to explore sources and impulses that suggest how and by what means the employment and inscription of rationalization onto the human body occurs.

What is of particular interest for this examination is that the fascination with "modern" technology comes to be inscribed onto and enacted by the human body in Weimar. Not only is the body regu-

Notes for this section begin on page 70.

lated and made re/productively efficient, but the body-as-machine is also apparent throughout the Weimar period. Is there such a phenomenon as the un-rationalized, playing or resting body? Are there among the numerous physical activities in Weimar any attempts at all to free the body from its cost-effective modes of movement or is the hegemony of industrial-technological efficiency total? To what extent do early cybernetic notions of the body play into recreational views of the body, that is, that the body was capable of doing everything one wanted it to do if the owner simply followed the manual? In pursuing these questions, I do not expect to find clear-cut answers; rather, my investigation will only add complexity to our understanding of Weimar cultural discourses and the ways they become manifest in material as in fictional lives.

Since the Enlightenment, science had gradually replaced theology and metaphysics in popularity, but after 1918, in the public eye, the romance with science had suffered some severe set backs due the almost exclusive application of science to the manufacture of arms and the consequent death and destruction during World War One. Nonetheless, many scientific paradigms still held great promise. Such promise fascinated the scientific and industrial-commercial communities in the West. Among them was that of scientific management, characterized by efficiency studies, as proposed primarily by Frederic Taylor, which was gaining increasing popularity. Taylor envisaged applying standards of efficiency (signifying the energy input-output ratio of a machine) to the working human body in order to secure maximum production, higher profits and, consequently, higher wages.[3]

His goal of maximum physical efficiency was to be achieved, he hoped, through harmonious—or at least measured—use of the body, which, in its microcosm, is a traditional signifier for the broader body of society. In a time of social upheaval and amid attempts to up-end the traditional class system in Weimar, the discipline that scientific management imposed on the body might certainly serve more than commercial ends. Social harmony and responsible citizenship ranked high on most Weimar Germans' wish lists and taken a few steps further, this could be grafted onto a wider agenda that included social control and the rush for industrial efficiency, each of which could further the other.

Taylorism is imprinted not only with the public characteristics of its historical context but also with the private pathologies of its inventor. Taylor's personal story exhibits an extreme desire for controlling the uncontrollable, his personal subconscious. An indication of this was his preoccupation with sleep and oppressive dreams. In order to prevent nightmares, which he thought arose from sleeping on his back, he would wear to bed a self-designed harness with wooden points or other devices that were meant to force him to sleep in a sitting position.[4] Consequently, his program for regulating the factory can well be viewed as extending into the public sphere his will to regulate, i.e. restrain, categorize, and make predictable, his world, including his own most intimate life. The spirit of Taylorism was often found in the office where clerical work was strictly categorized and hierarchized, meaning, to take one example, that young women now sat at typewriters for hours on end typing invoices. Similarly, we find it in the growing obsession with sport excellence and its growing professionalization. As we shall see, it is perhaps most visible in the chorus line where the body-as-machine exhibits mass efficiency and precision. In Weimar, a republic oftentimes perceived as a chaotic one, supposedly benign scientific mechanisms to discipline and contain the social body gained an easy foothold.

Work in the City

A discussion about modernity, the female workplace, and the labor market is not invariably cheerful or upbeat. Surveys of the interrelated histories of women, work, and leisure in the twentieth century often tend to assume that once enfranchised, women would necessarily have become assured of a steady, positive progression in their quality of life and autonomy. Such a sweeping generalization regarding the apparent gains of women during the last century may be acceptable on some points, but it glosses over particularities of specific groups as they are played out at various historical junctures. Such an undifferentiated perception of the variety of women's experiences reverberates with uncanny echoes of the by now acknowledged yet nonetheless injurious non-recollection of women's pasts, both collective and private, which led to an almost global erasure of women from official historical records. The systemic predisposition toward excluding women from the past may have worked in favor of homogenizing—and thus rendering monolithic—all working women's stories into one: that of middle-class women's experiences of the labor market. In so doing, all particular and contradictory experiences disappear and are instead collapsed into a formula that equates female visibility on the labor market with unmitigated progress for all women.

Expressly in regard to the present work, such a hegemonizing memory can be seen as leveling, even ignoring, the many texts by Weimar inhabitants which testify to an often contrasting view of their "liberation" through work. Among them, Brück's *Schicksale hinter Schreibmaschinen* may serve as a case in point. "I earn 110 marks now and I don't have to be cold or go hungry anymore. Instead, poverty has now crept inside me." (24) The protagonist, typist Fräulein Brückner, has arrived at this material and spiritual niveau after three years of employment, and her statement is far from a celebration of life. Although her wages keep starvation at bay, the long work day in an unventilated office, the repetitive functions she must perform, and the intense competition for the few promotions among female colleagues are among the things that work to render her existence joyless. As a matter of fact, Brück's novel, a scantily disguised autobiography, exposes the workplace for women as a nightmarish walk on the tightrope of ageism, gross sexual harassment, exploitation, hopelessness, and physical and spiritual deprivation.

Flämmchen from Baum's *Grand Hotel* dreams of fame and fortune, which she hopes to gain through the medium of film. Yet, aware of her position in the economic system, she, too, harbors few illusions about her future as a white-collar worker. As Ute Frevert has pointed out, the well-paid and powerful positions in the business sector, such as management, were unavailable to women; they performed the manual jobs like stenography, typing, or filing.[5] Like *Schicksale*, *Grand Hotel* was conceived and published at the beginning of the economic downturn when the return of despair and pessimism to workers' lives resonates in both young women's unease with and dislike of their work.

From this point of view, Brück's and Baum's narratives contrast with that written by Rudolf Braune. *Orga Privat* is carried by a call for solidarity against class and sexual oppression. In Braune's novel, the protagonist is a young working-class woman, Erna Halbe. She is the fourth of eleven children, trained in shorthand and typing, and comes to Berlin from the provinces to work. Her experiences in the workplace encompass the death of a colleague resulting from an illegal abortion; a subsequent spontaneous strike, significantly not backed by the local union; and finally, her own dismissal. And yet, Braune's Erna wanders bravely into the Berlin cityscape, drawing on her inner strength and knowing that she will prevail.

Few working men or women in Weimar lived under what we today would consider decent conditions. Where women were concerned, the oppression was not only class- but also gender-specific.

It is therefore easy to understand why neither Fräulein Brück nor Flämmchen have reason to sustain a positive outlook. Yet Braune appears to have applied a different paradigm to the text, possibly one less realistic but evidently governed by utopian socialist thought. His narrative exposes the sexual abuse of female office staff by (almost exclusively) male management as being widespread in the Weimar workplace: "[Erna's supervisor] just stands there and ogles her from top to bottom. His eyes move over her slowly and carefully and Erna's eyes grow small and narrow, she is furious." (49) Braune also includes an implicit criticism of questionable union practices, where the interests of male workers are met at the expense of those of working women. This sort of gender bias was particularly conspicuous during the recession, when women's physiological and psychological fitness was a matter of intense debate.[6]

Finally, Braune's text condemns the unavailability of safe and legal abortions, textually indicated by a young woman's death from complications after one such operation. It is often difficult to understand the origins of Erna Halbe's optimism since the above issues in and of themselves would be enough to dishearten even urban diehards. The reader has to ask whether what is at issue here is in part gender: that of the writer and also the gender blindness of the utopian socialist ideology that warrants such optimism regarding the capacity of young (working-class) women to succeed, despite the harsh conditions, with verve and vigor. Or is it indicative of the fact that the novel was written in 1925, a period of relative economic stability? Perhaps a clue can be found in Braune's implicit faith in the ultimate success of socialism. This becomes evident in the way Erna's background is described: "[She has] grown up in a strict, clear, working-class world where personal ambition was not aroused but where everything had to be subject to the momentous laws and the unlimited will of class." (55) Although she is away from home, Erna is nonetheless subject to inevitable historical laws that are to propel her and her class to victory. Individual fate is thus of importance only insofar as it contributes to class experience and to the improvement of class and the community's sense of identity and purposefulness. Be that as it may, it is strange—indeed, it is somewhat of a contradiction—that an unemployed individual is able to rise above the economic and cultural conditions of her society, hoping against experience that she will find the pot of gold at the end of the rainbow. Particularly when read together, these individual texts expose the complexity of this subject and its many interwoven discursive strands, thwarting any attempt at a tidy, sutured perception.

The Weimar years were a period of "intense and rapid transition in the employment patterns of those women who did work outside the home."[7] This transition comes to light in Baum's *Helene* where the desires of two young girls are described in the following fashion: "[O]ne wanted to be an infant's nurse, the other was indulging in dreams of the polytechnic academy." (120) Among the cultural discursive strands woven into this quote, is one recalling the orthodox gender categories of occupational fields: nursing (female) and engineering (male). Simultaneously, the transgressive desire of one girl to enter the gender-demarcated career of engineering represents a new and startling vista for women's futures. Yet, the words "indulging in dreams" indicate a wistfulness, as if the wish to become an engineer and construct in the world unrelated to the female body were unreasonable and excessive: a whim impossibly doomed for a young woman. Finally, it is not irrelevant that both futures are represented in the context of *Helene,* whose protagonist—a scientist—emulates the famous woman scientist, Marie Curie. Madame Curie received the Nobel Prize twice, in physics in 1903 (with her husband) and in 1911 in chemistry. Her genius obviously disproved prevailing prejudices about women and science and served as a role model for generations of women, not least for Baum's "new" woman, Helene.

The "new" woman and her lower middle- and middle-class representations are dealt with extensively throughout this work; Chapter Four will examine why so few other types of women, for example, young working-class women, are represented in popular fiction of the time. The novels we are examining here make it clear that the "new" woman was an urban phenomenon. Nevertheless, there were "rural" novels as well and what follows is a discussion about representations of women's rural work and their use in and relations to discourses about womanhood and the nation.

Work on the Land

Many factors come into play when we consider the diverse notions of work and leisure that hold sway throughout Weimar fiction. Among them are differing ideological paths taken by writers of urban and rural novels, for it would appear, in grossly generalizing terms, that the texts move us from a modern perception of work and play to a traditional, at times even reactionary attitude toward them. This is far from suggesting that all urban novels are progressive; this work has repeatedly pointed out backward-looking and dystopian features in urban novels. Nonetheless, a certain fascination with technology, modernity, and the break with traditions permeates texts that are situated in the city. When such an intense interest in these matters appears in rural novels, it is frequently in reverse, so to speak. Here, traditions are revered and their rupture is seen either as a bad omen for both a present and future state of civilization or as an already present manifestation of a national, even international, degeneracy. As the narrator in *Die Buben der Frau Opterberg* states, musing about the city, "it could be so rich in the creative powers of art and science … but then again it is so poor in the necessities of life for large herds of people."[8]

The novels are, of course, already embedded in a set of material discourses that indicate an important shift in the nature of rural employment. An article written during the Weimar years, entitled "The Labor Market for White-Collar Workers," spells out an overall 50 percent decline in white-collar employment in rural public offices between World War One and 1924, with Prussia alone accounting for 30,000 newly unemployed.[9] Evidently, material conditions supported conservative perceptions of the decline of the good, traditional life. When such a disquieting development enters into a psychic interaction with a long-standing suspicion of urban matters and when they are furthermore coupled with the indisputable scapegoat of modernity, the outcome surfaces in many rural texts as a heightened nostalgia for a better—i.e., predictable and controllable—past. Alice Berend's novel, *Der Kapitan von Bodensee*, exhibits an unbounded nostalgia for a time of hard work, good humor, innocence, love, and practical marriage arrangements.[10] In the bucolic setting of the Lake Constance area, physical work is done largely by women according to the decisions made by men in the community. The beautiful natural surroundings appear to call forth an innate ability for and willingness to engage in hard physical labor on the part of women. And they, particularly Josefa, the housekeeper, and Balbine, the motherless daughter of the farm, are always portrayed in some activity that serves to support life on the farm in a significant manner. It is not the unrelenting work that worries Josefa but the fact that it has never facilitated her traveling "the short distance to the altar [and] … to the hearth and other warm places in the house." (88) For Balbine, there are no coffee houses, cinemas, restaurants, or dance halls but an unimpeded access to nature wherein she takes up both her work and leisure actitivities.

Whether fascinated by an increasingly technologized modernity or rejecting the same in favor of well-tried traditions, both urban and rural novels have something in common: the work undertaken and narrated in them is almost always stratified according to gender, albeit with varying measures of critique of the gender division of labor. There must have been a resounding shift, dating from World War One, in the ways women imagined themselves in the world. They went from confinement to house and hearth or dark factories to going to work with thousands of other women in typing pools and to moving unaccompanied through lit-up city streets at night. Naturally, such an enlargement of accessible space had far-reaching consequences for women's identity formation and self-definition. Like rings in the water from the stone thrown into a pool, the effects of this change in women's space do not remain local. The fact that women were literally moving away from their assigned places in society added momentum to the already extant wobble in Weimar society. The so-called balance had disappeared, and although the deeply gendered world continued, many of the historical divides were shifting.

In view of the fact that 1925 saw three times as many women white-collar workers as in 1907 (almost 1.5 million), things were not the way they used to be. Such a feeling was strengthened by a media representation of working women that as a rule falsely glamorized the working life of the "new" women. Some of the novels examined in this chapter all too clearly show the reader a different aspect of the issue. Moreover, it should not be forgotten that the largest single group of women in the labor force in 1925 (4. 63 million) consisted of farm family assistants and agricultural laborers.[11] Nonetheless, they were not nearly as visible in Weimar popular culture as the urban working woman, the new caste of office workers and sales clerks, who captured the imagination. Hence, it is easy to understand the perception common at the time that a state of chaos existed in the arena of gender roles. Consequently, some of the malaise of the German national body was traceable to gender trouble.

The *Volkskörper* (loosely translated as the body of the German nation and its people) and prescriptions for its health appear to be written on representations of the rural female body. Quite germane to the tenets of nationalistic writers of *Heimat* or *Blut und Boden* novels is the notion that the rural community occupies the site where work toward a healthy national identity is performed. Here, men and women share a rootedness with their region and the soil they till; women do physical labor along with the men, "keeping their muscles hard."[12] Balbine does her normal work during the week and, on Sundays, tends to the small piece of land her father has given her—

with a smile and a song. All her hard work notwithstanding, Balbine never trespasses upon the arena of masculinity; instead she remains traditionally feminine and desirable throughout.

The blacksmith in Berend's *Der Kapitan von Bodensee* represents a different and very ambiguous paradigm of body, masculinity, and femininity. The quintessentially masculine profession is here occupied by a woman, the "blacksmithess" (*die Schmiedemeisterin*), as she is pointedly called throughout the novel. "The blacksmithess knew how to swing a hammer better than most women knew how to hold a crochet hook." (51) "[The] blacksmithess appeared in front of her smithy, no longer in her leather apron but tidied up neatly and femininely" (106-7); and finally, "[w]e can believe her well-rounded, firm arms fully capable of swinging the blacksmith's hammer even if she is dressed as elegantly as a city woman." (117) Ironies struggle with and perhaps against anxieties in the above quotes. The constant use of the feminine ending alone brings out the tension between professional expectation and the female occupation of that terrain. The irony of this character would not be lost on contemporary readers, particularly rural readers, where muscles and well-rounded female bodies were not anomalies.

The elongated shape of the "new" woman was of little use to a population that lived by the sweat of its brow. Moreover, that this particular blacksmith, as a woman, was better at a man's occupation than most women were at theirs is a complex rejoinder to the necessity for corporeal energy and strength, regardless of gender. In fact, this was a notion that the Nazi-regime (but also other industrialized nations) struggled to shape and incorporate into their ideology in view of the need for both a larger birthrate and increased demands for labor. Here it must be mentioned, however, that the last thing Berend, a Jewish woman, wanted was to further Nazi ideologies. Her works were among those burned in 1933 and she died in exile, impoverished, in 1938.

In spite of the fact that there may be contradictory notions inherent in the idea that a woman working in a man's sphere is a better woman than those working in traditional female occupations, in this instance, it seems to be a way of introducing the notion of the social construction of gender into the novel without making it a straightforward thesis. It is worth taking note of the fact that the comparison is made to women and not to men. In this fashion, the character is not a confrontational or adversarial challenge to contemporary masculinity. Rather, the presence of such a female protagonist aids the popular, albeit erroneous, understanding of rural gender division of labor as equal in kind, while, at the same time, it expands the received construction of femininity with gentle irony. Add to this the tongue-in-cheek tone used to demonstrate that although the smith does exert muscle power worthy of a man, she, too, can be a woman when her work is done. However, should we think that gender divisions and characteristics are fixed once more firmly in place, the final quote reminds us that the urban elegance worn by this rural woman does not diminish her strength, for behind her apparent femininity there lies a masculine strength. The last citation is particularly thick with resonances from Weimar cultural discourses. The notion that it signifies superficiality, idleness, and deceit is strong, since "city woman" is translated from *Stadtmadame* which calls forth an image of prostitution and commodified female sexuality. Here, Döblin's epithet in a similar vein about Berlin as the "Whore of Babylon" springs to mind.

The female character of the *Schmiedemeisterin* constantly insists upon transgressing gender lines and reader expectations. The heterosexual bent of the novel and the fact that she marries Lorenz, Balbine's father, a very well-heeled local vintner, at least determines her sexual proclivity. But the reader need not have feared; sexuality in *Der Kapitan* is strictly "natural," i.e., heterosexual, through its apparent link to the earth and farming. Whatever extramarital sex we may sense having taken place did so somewhere in the past between Josefa, the housekeeper, and her "master," Balbine's father; and that, in turn, is embedded in the text as a matter of course, almost as if it were Lorenz's *droit de seigneur*.

Berend's novel lends itself directly to analysis of issues in Weimar culture relating to gender, work, and their traditional frameworks. The blacksmith's character swings like a pendulum from one gender expectation to the other, calling attention to this novel's construction of gender as social. This is not done in the manner of a city novel through use of the often androgynous *Bubikopf* (the flapper's boyish haircut which quickly came to stand for the flapper herself). Here, each swing of the character seems to strike the circumscribing walls of gender-role specificity and push them further out, creating more space inside the gender frame in order that a larger array and mix of femininity and masculinity might be legitimately exhibited. In other words, the representation of the "blacksmithess" refuses to substitute one gender perception and expectation for another, as we have witnessed in the representation of urban "new" women, even if this were done only reluctantly. Instead, the coming and going of gender traits opens a possibility for the reader to imagine femininity not so much in binary terms but rather in ways that far surpass the traditional range. Intentionally or not, *Der Kapitan* has used the conservative genre of the rural novel to transmit an untraditional announcement about gender as an unstable category.

Lena Christ's novel from 1920, entitled *Madam Bäuerin,* similarly subverts traditional expectations of the genre in its direct comparisons between urban and rural sensibilities, mores, and quality of life. Here, the female experience of independence, elsewhere so readily defined as an urban existence, is turned upside down as well as modified. The female protagonist, Rosalie, an urban young woman from a once well-heeled, "good family," comes into her own in the country through hard work and good humor and, importantly, through the love for and marriage to a good but powerful and wealthy farmer. The novel contains few if any *Heimat* clichés about soil and blood. In contrast to that genre, Christ's notion of "homeland" is not where you were born but where you feel happy, are productive, and sense an almost organic belonging. In other words, happiness and productivity are the important goals in life and the arena where those goals are met is considered your "homeland." It appears that rural life alone can provide such clear goals and the means to meet them. The story unfolds against the backdrop of constant hard, physical, but satisfying, labor, and the willingness and ability to perform it qualify people as worthy members of the community. Work is an instrument for building community and happiness rather than an overt metaphor for national character, and although the local community logically extends to the national community, a mention of the larger nation has been avoided throughout the novel. This strategy enables the exchange of traditional customs—here considered useless and harmful—with newer, more modern ways of life, at least on a local level. To be sure, country life is confirmed as the worthwhile life, offering invigoration and the tangible results of honest labor, but one may also read the novel as castigating the old while it praises the bastardized new. This complexity foreshadows one of the dilemmas the National Socialists would face in the years to come, namely that of "retaining" and combining mythical traditional customs with modernity in the shape of a technological nation equipping itself for war.

How different this novel is from Herzog's sense of work, belonging, customs, and gender as manifested in his strong woman of the land, Christiane Opterberg from *Die Buben der Frau Opterberg* (1920). She, the true hero of *Die Buben,* possesses the "bright and shiny sobriety of the feminine spirit." (43) Christiane's indomitable will rules the upbringing of her boys while her husband, Arnold Opterberg, an artist and, needless to say, therefore also a weakling and an alcoholic to boot, spends time entertaining other artistic and intellectual *Hochstapler*—poseurs—in a small town nearby. Her hard work in the house and on the land saves the ancestral farm and makes it prosper. The effort to preserve an inheritance for her boys even brings her to speculate on the stock market. In fact, Christiane Opterberg possesses all the intelligence and fortitude of a traditional male character in a rural novel. This is not surprising since the novel is deprived of its customary center of gravity, the father, whose artistic and consequent weak character is the novelistic metaphor for the damage done by World War One. The novel makes clear that the war can only damage those who are not sufficiently rooted in the glorious German nature and soil because the Opterberg boys, Martin and Christoph, the latter adopted, grow up to be strong German men of action and industry through precisely that tradition. They are introduced to the reader in the very opening lines of the novel in the following manner: "An eagle's cry—from the peak of the mountain—An eagle, mother! There! Can you see it?" (7) A confirmation of this national imagery follows the boys' outcry, as they elaborate upon it in a clearing of the woods:

> "The sun is over the South; mist covers the North. What do you want to do?"
> "The long road, mother. Struggling, laughing, singing. Through the mist."
> "The long road ... Creating, working." (13)

Here we not only recognize the stereotypical elements of a *Blut und Boden* text. We are also alerted to the spectacularity of the text, its visuality, as it were, which points towards the later Nazi penchant for privileging the spectacle over language.

The issues in *Die Buben* are a far cry from those that concern the women in Baum's, Bruck's, or Keun's novels. Christiane Opterberg's true work lies in bringing up Martin and Christoph and pedagogical knowledge such as hers seems to well forth naturally from good, German women, or so the text would have us believe. Hard work is part of the measures of both "good" and "German," and Christiane does more than her share of it. As a matter of fact, she is so quietly efficient that her many tasks are seldom mentioned. The hard work of the "strong-as-an-oak woman" and her assumption of full responsibility for and management of the property, are for the sake of the boys, not for herself. Stated somewhat differently, Christiane's moral imperative and inner voice are really her sons' and so, many of her strong deeds are tempered by her own words. She preempts her opinions and de-rationalizes her striving toward the goal of a university education for both sons when talking to them about it: "That is a man's issue ... and a woman can only let her feelings speak to it ... . That's at least my opinion as a woman and mother." (91)

Such descriptive and prescriptive novels were very popular, a fact which may be ascribed to their representations of women characters who, at least on the surface, settle for hard work in customary settings. One may ponder the very few direct addresses to nationalism in urban novels when compared to its presence in their rural counterparts. It may be due to the uprootedness from the soil and consequently the nigh foundationless existence of the urban dweller as well as her exposure to non-parochial, even international discourses and influences. After all, is it not urbane to transcend nationality and to be at home anywhere in polite society? Moreover, the "new" woman was an urban phenomenon and on her body is capitalism writ large—not nationalism. The media creation of the desirable, tall, slender, and non-curvaceous body of the *Bubikopf* was unsuitable as a model of strength, fecundity, and German-ness. Her sexual mores, independence, and consumption of mass culture and other fashionable commodities were characteristics considered beyond the pale for models of both German womanhood and a nationalistic discourse. Instead, those qualities made her a site for pent-up anxieties. Consequently, even if Taylorism in the factory and the office worked toward at least disciplining her body in the workplace, the "new" woman still constituted the negative parameters of German-ness, all that German-ness was not.

In contrast to today's culture shaped by international capitalism, Weimar culture still harbored notions of a *national* culture and in its popular fiction it is often female characters who embody those notions. Christiane Opterberg is no "new" woman. She has all the physical markings of the right kind of femininity, she is tall with long, blond braids and blue eyes and her career is to nurture and be the custodian of Germany's future. This is experienced as a labor of love that she cannot refuse, even if she wanted to. Such an endeavor is assumedly "instinctual" for women like Christiane, thus making this her "real" work, the crucial constituent of a true femininity. In other words, not only are Christiane's properties those of true German women, they, in fact, define true German womanhood. The qualities and definitions of Herzog's heroine foreshadow those that The Housewives Union and Magda Goebbels were to promote in 1930, ten years later. Then there would be much talk about housework being if not quite a calling, then at least a vocation that called for self-sacrifice, renunciation, and service.[13] In the words of the skeptical narrator in Baum's 1931 *And Life Goes On*: "[I]t was [the] wife's daily and hourly duty to remove ... unpleasant details of daily life from ... [her husband's] path." (240) The need in the late years of the Weimar republic to reinstate order, or at least to appear to do so, entailed categorizing abilities and affinities according to gender, particularly in a way that met the nation's economic and demographic needs. According to an article by Magda Goebbels in *Die deutsche Hausfrau*, nurturing activities such as welfare and teaching were tasks inherently feminine due to women's nature. It was therefore incumbent upon women to perform such duties. There were, however, also duties outside the home that were perceived as congruent with women's nature, and factory and office work were among them.[14] Such examples exhibit an urban bias in the conception of women's work, but the many duties traditionally linked with rural women fit well into the definitions used by Frau Goebbels. This is particularly true with regard to nurturing the ancestral farm as the sons' inheritance (*Blut*) with a closeness to the German nature and the paternal soil (*Boden*).

Despite the many attempts to define and thereby circumscribe femininity through work, work was, as we have seen, also a part of the era's exhortation to patriotism. And the call was not directed solely to women. Martin Opterberg's plan for keeping his factory solvent during the depression is formulated at a meeting with workers and the loyal foremen. In his speech he urges "his" workers "to increase performance ... through increased joyousness over work." (361) It is easy to recognize this rhetoric regarding joy and work. It constitutes a quasi-feudal appeal to worker fealty or loyalty to the employer which assures his investment and continuing wealth as well as the workers' own employment. In this discursive context, with Martin as stand-in for the fatherland, his appeal to work as joy becomes a measure of patriotism; inversely, the lack of joy indicates a nearly treacherous and unpatriotic stand. The ideological tenure that marks work as a site of patriotic behavior simultaneously hides some work issues of a material nature. Work "enjoyment," "joy," and "readiness" were in fact terms often used to facilitate the exploitation of workers by preventing unionization and fixed hours. This can be seen, as an attack on the liberal strand of German cultural thought and as Bridenthal puts it, "as an assault on labor in general."[15]

Play

"He who neglects to train his body, neglects the health of his country."

—Jean Giraudoux, "Der Sport."

In his analysis of spatio-temporal movement, Siegfried Kracauer admits to the thrill of dance and travel, but condemns it for being a substitute for "real" life: "It almost seems as if what is being called for is the very activity of spatial and temporal indulgence as such. The adventure of movement as such is thrilling, and slipping out of accustomed spaces and time into as yet unexplored realms arouses the passions. This spatio-temporal double life could hardly be craved with such intensity, were it not the *distortion* of real life."[16]

This critique of *Ersatz* aesthetic and sensual experiences, which Kracauer perceived in the growing mass cultural industry, is familiar to today's readers. We find later, similar observations in the writings of Adorno and others of the Frankfurt School. Such incisive critics and critiques notwithstanding, discourses like the above nonetheless posit a universal subject, and as Rita Felski observes: "[g]ender affects ... the philosophical assumptions underlying our interpretations of the nature and being of social processes." (1) Therefore, once Kracauer's universal subject is replaced by a gendered and/or classed subject there is more to the movement of which he speaks than meets the eye. Indeed, "spatial indulgence," for its own sake may very well be precisely what some female subjects of the day undertook. The immobility of traditional middle- and upper-class women had long been secured through rules of fashion, morality, and the legal system. One thinks here of the bodily confinement afforded by corsets and bustles; women's physical confinement to the household; the chaperoned traversing of public spaces—not for leisure but in pursuit of a clear purpose—and the legal ban in Germany against women attending public meetings in force until 1905. The thrill of moving freely "out of accustomed spaces and time into as yet unexplored realms" is applicable here, not only to local or distant geographies but also to the female body as an unexplored arena and a locus of power. Indeed, such discoveries could not fail to "arouse the passions."

Working-class women, whose confinement was other than spatial, had generally had to leave their own homes to perform their wage-earning labor, often traveling to the confines, i.e., homes, of their middle-class sisters. For most of them the traveling that Kracauer criticizes would remain an unobtainable dream. Even for the petty bourgeoisie, visiting the world outside one's own daily life was part of a fantasy like that which Irmgard Keun's character Gilgi harbors about the five continents: "Everywhere was beautiful, everywhere was new, and everywhere life held new surprises." (50)

Billie Melman writes: "Travel ... became in the twenties [*sic*] a metaphor for freedom and flight." (95) Writing about women in the 1920s and, in so doing, gendering or classing the moving body, Melman restores psychological and spiritual qualities to the act of traveling. She transcends, therefore, Kracauer's definition of modern travel as simply signifying being somewhere else than where one normally is. Similarly, geographical movement, be it across a foreign or a purely local landscape, engages in a different discourse as it evokes a stark contrast to the immobility of First World War veterans. As I have discussed elsewhere in greater detail and in a different context, 2.7 million First World War soldiers with permanent war injuries formed a visibly disabled and thus circumscribed segment of the social body. In light of that ubiquitous public display of restricted corporeality, traversing physical spaces becomes an activity bound up in a network of meaningfulness that is highly charged. It is easy to imagine, although it may be difficult to establish, that able-bodied women of all classes experienced some guilt-mixed feelings in the face of so much bodily breakdown; this in itself may have constituted a psychological encumbrance to the joy of free movement. Thus the complexities of movement of class and gendered subjects at this particular historical juncture reveal themselves as irreducible to a singular and easily defined phenomenon. What can be established, however, is that the pleasures of movement are scarcely trivial even as its privilege of physicality ironically shifts, at least in part, from the province of one gender to the other.

According to some sports sociologists, for an activity to be play, it must be devoid of utilitarian value, spontaneous and free. In other words, it must be "bracketed off from the realities with which the individual must contend in [her] ... daily life."[17] According to this definition, it soon becomes obvious that "play," as I mean it throughout this chapter, is a much looser concept than the first one evoked—a concept we will consider as a metaphor for activities which presumably stand in contrast to work. Rather than being restrained by the increasing compartmentalization of sport, athletics, physical exercise, and other free-time locomotion, I have placed a medley of (mostly) pastime activities under the rubric "play." Solely for analytical purposes, the liberty I have taken with the category of play of course blurs the differences between the great number of the activities undertaken by people who are not at work. I contend, however, that these differences are already unclear depending on the intensity and the purpose of both the exercise and those who engage in it.

As the examination proceeds, it becomes clear that the boundary between play and work is not as fixed as we perhaps would expect. Many activities one could call play espouse a creed concerning their goals that lends them a gravity and zeal that consequently render them almost parallel—rather than contrary—to work and career. In fact, concepts such as competition, prizes, and (semi-)professionalism at times render the distinction between the realms of play and work one of mere nuances.

Nonetheless, there can be no doubt that Weimar citizens played. Berlin derives its fame in the 1920s from being the heir apparent to the "gay Paris" of the 1890s. And not only Berlin had decided to be jolly. In the mid 1920s, Munich, for instance, was the second-largest center for the production of feature films.[18] Cities and towns throughout the republic found a war-weary population eager to visit shops, cafés, bars, theaters, concert halls, and amusement parks. For the adoration and exhibition of themselves and others, citizens showed off their bodies on hiking trails, tennis courts, and beaches, in boxing rings, and dance halls, by means of gymnastics, Wigman- or Duncan-inspired dance, nudist camps, and in films. Prescribed dress for the fashionable young included pull-overs, and pleated skirts for women and white slacks and loose-fitting shirts for men.[19] This was the era of *Körperkultur*—body culture.

This preoccupation with and cult of the body must be understood as a means of writing one's "own" body. Most of the desires and utopias of Weimar culture were expressed through *Körperkultur* which in return became a vehicle for self-realization and fulfillment, also in a national fashion. This is amply demonstrated by Hans Suren, a Weimar contemporary, who, in the preface to the 61st edition of his 1925 book, *Der Mensch und die Sonne*, claimed that it "reflects the aspirations of the true German race." Promoting nudism, Suren goes on to comment on the photographs in his book, saying they "display people as symbols of strength and health. Their bodies, governed by firm character, assure a better future. It is the duty of those with high aspirations to steel and train their bodies in such a manner."[20]

In another era and with another goal in mind, former Olympic athlete and noted sports sociologist, Harry Edwards, notes that "sports ... is strongly marked by non-utilitarian loyalties and commitments ... by expressive symbolism, and by ideological creed justified in terms of "ultimate" values ... ." (90).This was also the case in Weimar Germany. During that period and beyond, the training and "steeling" of the individual body transferred easily to the *Volkskörper*, the "national body." Suren's prescription is plain: the fate of the nation relies upon well-trained and "steeled" bodies. By the same token, his comment also makes clear a certain reciprocity: not only were longings inscribed on the body and prescribed for it via particular activities, the body itself is identified as a legible text. As Ludmilla Jordova has pointed out, the importance of "reading the body" lies in the fact that this undertaking sanctions the linking of visible surface indicators with invisible traits that are "deeper," i.e., inside the body (51-52). It is this notion that makes it possible to render the body the symbolic site for reading, presenting, and inscribing the nation's character, strength, and future on the body of its citizens. We may now read that a nation of trained and "steeled" bodies symbolizes a steadfast, strong, and steeled German nation, now and in the future.

One of the most generally approved pastimes, one that affirmed one's patriotism while strengthening the body, was hiking in nature. "It makes me happy to think ... that people would hike through the German magic woods ... to experience great joy" exclaims a character in *Die Buben* (381). Hiking, or *wandern*, was (and is) enormously popular in Germany. During the Weimar years hiking became the most popular form of exercise among German adolescents, and in 1931 a total of 4,322,026 participated in overnight hiking trips—that was up from 3, 000 in 1911.[21]

Wandern as a movement was initially conceived with the aim of unfolding young male souls in the realm of nature, and during the 1910s, the thought of girls' participation caused much consternation and much dissension in the movement. The ever-present question of sexuality, which lay at the root of the turmoil, was cloaked—as were its answers—in a multitude of ways. One statement vowed that while strenuous exercise would not hurt men it would prematurely age women and make them ugly.[22] Among the works of popular fiction examined here, the appeal of hiking appears to be limited to stories and novels of the *Heimat* genre. Considering the intended gender specificity of *wandern*, it is interesting that by 1920, *Die Buben* can present both of its strong women characters as nature-sensitive and powerful hikers. We may also consider the female protagonists to be mediators of the highly charged German nature for the boys and, later, men in the novel. The special connection women presumably have with nature makes them the perfect tool for facilitating men's conquest of nature and, by extension, of women themselves. Putting women and nature on the same footing is, of course, not new. But then again, recourse to time-worn images or clichés is part of what makes popular fiction so appealing to the readers.

It is not surprising, then, that an activity as popular as hiking was quite consonant with the dominant culture's ideological exhortations to its people. The movement that had started as an expression of spiritual freedom for German youths through communion with German nature went through a metamorphosis. By the late 1920s the perceived benefits ranged from sublimating sexual desires, to substituting for military service, to diverting youth from urban vices, to teaching "love of and willingness to serve the Fatherland and the people."[23] *Heimat* texts like Herzog's propose hiking as a means of appropriating nature as a specific German realm, the ultimate arena of patriotism, as the term "German nature" implies. This becomes apparent in Martin Opterberg's declaration that Germans "spring from the *ur*-forests of Germania whence we ... strove in combat toward our faith." (38) The forest has become synonymous with what is German, an equation that is conceptually employed also by Fritz Lang in his famous shot of Siegfried, the Germanic *ur*-hero, on his horse in the forest in the film of the same name.[24] Martin's remark moreover expresses what Alfred Rosenberg would later theorize in *Der Mythos des 20. Jahrhundert*, namely, that "the peoples of the Nordic race have not developed but have either stood their ground, been destroyed or enslaved."[25] Both these citations call our attention to the links between pugilism, nature, faith, and German-ness almost as part of a ritual. They furthermore incorporate World War One and Germany's defeat in a manner that transforms the conservative desire to avenge the perceived betrayal at Versailles into a "manifest destiny," a natural, inevitable claim on behalf of the German people that they will return to their rightful place in the world.

Of course, sport was not an obsession only of the nationalist right, nor were all sports or recreational activities summoned to stand as codes for the state of the nation. Dance, for one, was a highly ambivalent and contested field. Artistic dance was acclaimed as the highest and most splendid expression of movement, although it more recently has been criticized by one scholar as a commitment of the female body to an "ethereal presence rather than real corporeality."[26] Even though such a reading could not appear until long after the demise of the first German Republic, Weimar high culture's preference, and reverence, for such an unearthly and unrealistic female body must have appeared to some to contradict if not deny the legitimacy of the very materiality of the "new" woman. She, however, tended to dance the Charleston to the music of jazz bands, refuting through this very activity her own disembodiment. Moreover, the connotation that jazz bands bore in the eyes of society with "Americanization," Africa, eroticism, and thus a decided non-Germanness—all rendered this kind of dance a sexual sport.[27] Of interest in this connection is an anonymous observation from 1934 which states that the style of dancing recommended by the Nazis in that very year strips it of all erotic tension: as if specifically to counter the movement of the Charleston and dances of that ilk, citizens were enjoined to dance "as if a rod went through the entire body, from the feet to the head!"[28]

Dance *per se* was part of a set of national barometers of decency and morality. Dancing that upset delicate sensibilities, and in particular the kinds that were popular with "the masses," was not included in positive considerations of national identity. Instead, the Charleston and other sorts of dancing to jazz music were negatively perceived as expressions of identity of precisely those groups whose obverse but corresponding characteristics shored up the positive traits of German national identity. In other words, the very un-Germanness of those sorts of dances underscored the patriotic and national character of more traditional or conservative modes of corporeal movement.

Siegfried Kracauer remarks that dance clubs during Weimar were "no less numerous and no less important than churches ... in previous centuries."[29] Weimar popular fiction bears this out in its emphasis on the importance of dance. Flämmchen, in Baum's *Grand Hotel*, dances "a relaxed version of the Charleston, something new, where the knees snapped to a syncopated beat to which the bodies of both dancers agreed." (296) Significantly, she teaches the parochial, self-effacing bookkeeper, Kringelein, how to dance. Although she serves as the novel's metaphor for vice—albeit redeemable vice—she becomes the instructor of Kringelein, the novel's virtue. When she introduces him to one of the important physical gestures of the Weimar Republic, dancing, she facilitates Kringelein's exit out of parochialism and entry into what, at least in the eye of the novel's narrator, constitutes the exciting modernity of city life.

The urban landscapes painted in popular fiction constitute another novel phenomenon, namely a burgeoning youth culture. The ubiquitous and clichéd streams of pedestrians hurrying toward their goals are frequently depicted as made up of young people. More often than not, such general mood-setting vistas contain references to young women's fashionable clothing and their bright make-up, and almost always their goal is music and dance: "[The young girls] meet with the city's young men, they disappear into cafés, from the cafés come the sounds of dance music ... ."[30] Understandably, dancing becomes the activity that expresses an existential urge to live in the now; travel and dance are thus well suited to "brand the transformation of space and time itself as an event."[31]

Alongside individual enjoyment and execution of dance, dancing was also performed *en masse* for a paying public outside the artistic stages of High Culture. The chorus line, then embodied by the Tiller Girls and the Chocolate Kiddies, was—and still is—a curious hybrid of *joie de vivre* and the age of mechanical (re)production. This quasi-militaristic linear formation of scantily, but uniformly, dressed women performed drills on the stage. Their symmetrical patterns and uniform repetitions, stunningly executed, were prime examples of an efficient use of bodily movement to create a purposeful image of physical harmony. The view of a chorus line therefore stands in sharp contrast to a view of individuals dancing the Charleston in a dance club. Strict order rules on the stage, whereas an amiable chaos can be observed in the dance club. This contrastive juxtaposition of order and dis-order carries over into the audience, where, according to Kracauer, the chorus line is applauded by the masses "themselves arranged by the stands in tier upon ordered tier."[32] It should also be pointed out here that the creation of such a line, as was suggested to me, was hardly imaginable until an audience was sitting or standing in a similar line watching it.[33] Be that as it may, such linear arrangements seldom exist in dance clubs, where the constant coming and going of servers and patrons disrupts even the hint of a formal pattern, if such were to be found.

The orderly symmetry formed and experienced in the variety theater is in some respects an expression of the ideal military patriarchy, manifest in most Western industrialized countries. In the first German Republic, the militarism of the Second Reich and the marching columns of World War One made such formations familiar. But further implications present themselves once we seek to articulate the obvious appeal of the chorus line and the complexities that the columns of dancing women convey to the audience. The dissolution of individualism in the mechanized collective might, for example, remove the need, both on a subconscious and a material level, to face the "new" woman whose refusal to "toe the line" constitutes a very real rebellion.[34] Dancing drills may, then, be seen to modify fear of chaos while they nurture love of order. They can be seen as holding women together as a single entity, thereby creating one manageable body with fixed borders; a single body that, according to Theweleitian theses, could stem the tide of anarchic streams or masses. One might even say that the chorus line is a manifestation in space of patriarchy's struggle against (feminized) masses and the uncontained female sexuality that threatens its own identity and order. Taking this notion one step further, one might even read the chorus line as a manifestation of patriarchy losing the struggle with the inherent licentiousness of the spectacle and the mass pleasure in the same.[35]

If we return, then, to examine the hybrid of enjoyment and disciplinary order in industrial Weimar, the link that Kracauer pointed out between the scientific management of Frederick Taylor and the arena of dance appears unavoidable. The discipline that scientific management sought to impose on the industrial or working body appears to serve more than economic and commercial ends. Taylor's ideology of efficient bodily movement was apparently able to invade social spaces outside the factory and to align itself with militaristic ways of seeing. But while marching columns of soldiers and the chorus line of dancers both tapped into a public scopophilic pleasure in mass harmonies, the latter formation, exclusively female, instilled in the audience a definite notion of the exchangeability of woman and machine. A similar notion is evident in the character of Maria, the female robot in Fritz Lang's film *Metropolis*. While the paradigm may carry with it some relief from modern *Angst* by way of its de-eroticization of the performance and the de-subjectification of women, it, at the same time, makes the nature of technology problematic by giving it over to female embodiment. Thus, to some degree, the chorus line serves as a site for some of Weimar's many cultural ambiguities.

The marriage of the national to the military body, expressed through movement, is not limited to Germany, despite the overshadowing presence of the twelve years of Nazi domination following the Weimar Republic. The way that industrial, military, and physiological discourses inscribe themselves upon mass movement is fascinating. The circulation of cultural scripts and their articulation is particularly apprehensible in choreography. The immense success of the Hollywood films of Busby Berkely and his chorus girls, the lasting popularity of synchronized swimming even into the 1990s Olympic games, as well as the monumental international success of the dance show *Riverdance*, all indicate the appeal of highly choreographed mass movement. The will to regulate our world, that is to synchronize, to restrain, to categorize, and to make it predictable, is evidently still alive and well.

During the first couple of decades of the twentieth century, it became possible to identify a mass market of consumers for a broad-based public entertainment and leisure industry.[36] A plethora of activities from car racing, hiking, and tennis to movie watching and reading was available to Weimar citizens, occupying the amount of leisure time that had been slowly on the increase, particularly for the middle classes. It followed that young women who were working in repetitious jobs as stenographer/typists or sales clerks and who struggled to keep their (economic) independence, also wanted to play after work. What they did in their leisure moments appear to be determined by how much visibility the enterprise offered them or how much glamour they could share in vicariously. Irmgard Keun's protagonist, Doris, from *Das kunstseidene Mädchen* is an outstanding champion of the pursuit of glamour. "I want to be glamorous, at the top. With a white automobile and a bath smelling of perfume, everything, just like Paris." (45) Doris is adamant in saying that her most important influence is the movies, a dream source which she shares with most of her generation. In 1932, a survey questioned 10, 000 Berlin youths and found that two-thirds of them went to the movies once a week.[37] Even if reading was the most frequent everyday leisure activity in Weimar, Abrams' remark that cinema was considered by many nothing but trash novels in picture form[38] finds its direct articulation through Doris: "And later, when I read, everything is like in the movies—I see ... in pictures." (8)

Like all other enterprises, those of leisure were (and are) hierarchized according to income and class. As an examination of popular fiction of the time demonstrates, it was members of the old leisure class who effortlessly swung tennis rackets or adopted new sports like car racing. Boxing, however, held a great allure for Weimar citizens and cut across class lines. Bertolt Brecht wrote a poem to boxing, George Grosz painted heavy-weight Max Schmeling's portrait, and periodicals, journals, and magazines featured essays and stories about the sport. Boxing was "hip." And yet, since only a fraction of this particular fascination is represented in the popular fiction examined in this work, this suggests that a measure of gender specificity was attached to the it. *Orga Privat* contains a passage that supports such gender preferences: "After dinner ... young men would talk about soccer and boxing matches while young woman discussed cafés where one could dance." (45)

Vicki Baum's Weimar novels are exceptions (Baum took boxing lessons). They are full of examples of and allusions to boxing. One of her heroes possesses "boxer shoulders" and a croupier in a casino is described as having "no bone in his nose. He had either been a boxer or was suffering from syphilis."[39] The light-handed acknowledgment of the presence of venereal diseases in Weimar is here linked with gambling, a *risqué* leisure activity, and boxing, a potentially maiming but, at the moment, sexy sport. The association of boxing with syphilis effectively marks the sport in ways that emphasize its physicality, i.e., the fact that both winning *and* losing in fact leave visible tracks on the body. Moreover, although boxing might mean upward mobility for a few males, the middle-class's, and in particular the Left's, interest in the sport indicates a fashionable fascination with a "proletarian" activity. On the other hand, long before the era of Native American gambling casinos in the United States, casino gambling was exclusively for the rich and powerful. European casinos, particularly those in Monte Carlo, held out the promise of fabulous wealth and elegant intrigues. Thus, the addition of gambling to the roster of leisure pursuits suggests a class promotion to the upper echelons of society and unexpectedly lends an almost roguish quality to both boxing and, strangely but by association, to venereal disease.

This fascination is particularly obvious in *Grand Hotel*, where the sexuality and eroticism of the nobly-born hotel thief, Gaigern, is heightened through constant reference to his athleticism. Whether on the street where he "walks friskily like a boxer" (69), or dressed in pyjamas in his private rooms, where he displays a magnificent body with a perhaps "little too barrelled rib cage of a boxer" (120), boxing again surfaces as the peerless athletic activity and the ultimate shaper of masculinity. Gaigern is (of course) also an avid boxing fan and in this, too, he distinguishes himself from Kringelein who, in his quest for cosmopolitan life and culture, looks down his nose at boxing; he "certainly is not at all interested in boxing." (277)

It is nevertheless a boxing match that provides the key to unlocking the provincial clerk's libido. Here, Kringelein discovers the mass spectacle as arousal. As he watches and hears the thump of the blows, he is filled with "a sweet and feverish satisfaction" that comes "from deep in his blood." He desires that the match go on for much longer and considers the clinches to be as "passionate and earnest" as "love" (311-16). These passages establish a clear link between male sexuality and male violence, which appears to be encouraged through the high esteem of boxing held by the novel's sophisticated characters. Kringelein, sickly and fearful, is one of Weimar's many functionaries, a lowly white-collar worker in whose life nothing happens to make him feel alive. But like other boxing fans who come to the ring to get their excitement and suspense, once Kringelein is in the boxing arena, the sound of blows, of pain, the sight of bloody flesh, and the spectacle of struggle excite him making his heart beat faster. The words of the text in effect act as an erotic stimulant, one that is punctuated by a textual presentation of clichés constitutive of both passion and love.

The melding of male sexuality, sport, violence, and love in a mix whereby they co-exist comfortably is a conceit that readers of popular fiction come across frequently. The combination of violence and sexuality is disturbingly familiar. In this novel, the introduction of another element, love, may signify, however, a modern woman writer's unease with the mixture and her awareness of its dangerous potency. At the same time, the very addition of love to the duo of sexuality and violence in this case tends also to neutralize the traditional combination; in rendering it harmless, an integral constituent of patriarchy, the combination of male sexuality and violence, seems somehow permissible.

In a distortion of the expected scenario, Joseph Roth's novel *Zipper und sein Vater* also makes mention of boxing: only this time it is ladies' boxing: "Arnold Zipper was now a member of several associations. Not charity clubs like his father! There was an association for the erection of an Asta Nielsen memorial, some journalist clubs, an association that put on yearly film festivals with beauty contests and women's boxing. Arnold was an active member in all."[40] The phenomenon is set in the context of the superficiality of the Berliner film world which facilitates the novel's deep pessimism regarding the relationship between modernity and humanity. The perversity of ladies' boxing is syntactically underscored by appearing one word removed from "beauty contest." Whereas the latter expresses the passive exhibition of female beauty, ladies' boxing, in this context, connotes a semi-pornographic scene, where half-naked women actively participate in their own self-inflicted ritual of disfigurement for the erotic titillation of the (supposedly mostly male) audience. One is tempted to speculate that this is staged as a piece of men's (sub)conscious retribution against women for the terrible bodily harm men sustained in World War One and from which women were largely spared.

The underlying violence of the Weimar years which can be clearly seen in the films and pictorial art, of the time, has been noted by scholars. In *Lustmord: Sexual Murder in Weimar Germany*, Maria Tatar speculates that World War One may have functioned as a legitimized release of creative violence which, after the war, is deployed against women on the domestic front and no longer against "male adversaries on the military battlefield." (68) No one can doubt the brutalizing effects of war on its participants and it is therefore highly plausible to consider World War One as instigating if not legitimizing violence. Earlier discourses of violence had been re-channeled through this war, finding there both the atmosphere and the cultural space for their varying expressions and representations. The carnage of World War One and its representations permeated life and were visible both on Weimar streets and in cultural representations throughout the Weimar period. Therefore, views with regard to the material body were represented with as much complexity and contradiction as belongs to the era itself. For example, adoration of the body is manifested both by the fashion industry and its main denigrators, the nudist cults; the artistic use of the body is expressed in new notions of dance; the various disciplinary movements to "steel" the body in a masculine and nationalist sense, such as in the *Wandervögel* and gymnastics is also found among them; the corporeal violence of Weimar political parties; Taylorism, and the many forms of athleticism—all of these collectively constitute a "body" of discourses on the physical being, real and metaphoric, which deny the attempt at easy categorization.

Both work and play have more in common than the obvious physicality involved in either activity. In fact, a great number of sport and other forms of exercise rely on or promote the most precise and efficient bodily movement in order to achieve one's goal most effectively. A series of moves, strategically planned in advance, as well as optimal use of muscle to ensure minimal waste of physical energy, play a large role in competitive sports and exercises. Modern sport is marked by a fascination with order, rationalization, measurement, and purposefulness that has created, among other things, written rules for most games.[41] Although a sporting body may not *produce* an obvious, marketable commodity, it has in fact *become* one through the professionalization of sport. Even in amateur sports, sports bodies effect community prizes which have other forms of value attached to them. In both cases, parallels between the body at work and the body at play emerge: both rely on regulation for maximum performance and profit.

Work and sport are linked inextricably through the aims and practices of capitalism, and in Weimar Germany many sport-related industries were already visible. In addition, professional sport or, said differently, the capitalist mode of production of sport for profit, demonstrates even more clearly the connections between bodily movement and capitalism. The debate about sport as work was intense in Weimar, particularly among intellectuals. Willy Meisl speculated that modern specialization in sport—or "biceps culture"—must have a tedious effect on the athlete, similar to that which Taylorism had on the worker's creativity. He went on to declare that "[w]hen sport becomes an occupation, it is no longer sport."[42] The role of sports in capitalism and nationalism was, and is, crucial. Bertolt Brecht said that "I am for sport because and as long as it is: full of risk (that is, unhealthy) , uncivilized (that is, not collective) and an end in itself."[43] Already at the time of this utterance, however, the tide was turning, and Brecht's fondness for sport would indeed be very short lived.

Notes

1. Janet Wolff, "The Invisible Flaneuse: Women and the Literature of Modernity," *The Problems of Modernity: Adorno and Benjamin*, ed. Andrew Benjamin (London, 1989), 141.
2. Siegfried Kracauer, "Kult der Zerstreuung," as quoted in Patrice Petro "Perceptions of Difference: Woman as Spectator and Spectacle," *Women in the Metropolis: Gender and Modernity in Weimar Culture* (Berkeley, 1997), ed. Katharina von Ankum, 55 .
3. Samuel Haber, *Efficiency and Uplift: Scientific Management in the Progressive Era 1890—1920* (Chicago, 1964), ix.
4. Haber, *Efficiency and Uplift*, 4.
5. Frevert, *Frauengeschichte*, 309.
6. Bridenthal, "Something Old, Something New, " 482.
7. Mason, " Women in Germany 1925—1940," 78.
8. Rudolf Herzog, *Die Buben der Frau Opterberg* (Berlin, 1920), 166. Further citations are noted in the text as *Die Buben*. All translations are mine.
9. Fritz Schröder, "The Labor Market for White-Collar Workers," *Die Arbeit: Zeitschrift für Gewerkschaftspolitik und Wissenschaftskunde* I, no. 6 (1924):185, in *The Weimar Republic Sourcebook*, eds. Anton Kaes et al., 184—185.
10. Alice Berend, *Der Kapitan von Bodensee* (Berlin, 1932). Further citations are noted in the text as *Der Kapitan*. All translations are mine.
11. Mason, "Women in Germany," 80, 79.
12. *Die Buben*, 261.

13. Renate Bridenthal, "Class Struggle Around the Hearth: Women and Domestic Service in the Weimar Republic," in *Toward the Holocaust: The Social and Economic Collapse of the Weimar Republic*, eds. Michael Dobkowski & Isidor Walleman (Westport, Conn., 1983), 254.
14. Quoted in Bridenthal, "Class Struggle ... ," 256.
15. Bridenthal, "Class Struggle ...," 248.
16. Siegfried Kracauer, *The Mass Ornament: Weimar Essays*. Trans. and ed. Thomas Y. Levine (Cambridge, Mass., 1995), 68.
17. Harry Edwards, *Sociology of Sports* (Homewood, Ill., 1973), 46.
18. Christoph Stölzl, ed., *Die Zwanziger Jahre In München: Katalog zur Ausstellung im Münchner Stadtmuseum Mai bis September 1979* (Munich, 1979), 698.
19. *Orga Privat*, 81.
20. Hans Suren, "Preface to the 61st Edition," in *Weimar Sourcebook* , eds. Kaes et al., 678.
21. John Alexander Williams, "Steeling the Young Body: Official Attempts to Control Youth Hiking in Germany, 1913—1938," *Occasional Papers in German Studies* 12 (June 1997): 26—27.
22. Ibid., 14, 30.
23. Heinrich Hassinger, *Vom Weg und Wesen, vom Wollen und Wirken der Jugendherbergen und des Jugendwanderns* (Hilchenbach, 1931), 129, as quoted in Williams "Steeling the Young Body," 27.
24. See also Klaus von See, *Barbar—Germane—Arier: die Suche nach der Identität der Deutschen* (Heidelberg, 1994), 191.
25. Alfred Rosenberg, *Der Mythos des 20. Jahrhundert* (1933), 40ff. All translation mine.
26. Janet Wolff, *Feminine Sentences: Essays on Women and Culture* (Berkeley and Los Angeles, 1990), 136.
27. King, *Bestsellers by Design*, 192.
28. Anonymous quote in Jan Nederveen Pieterse, *White on Black: Images of Africa and Blacks in Western Popular Culture* (New Haven, 1992), 145.
29. Kracauer, *The Mass Ornament*, 296.
30. *Orga Privat*, 54.
31. Kracauer, *The Mass Ornament*, 67.
32. Ibid., 76.
33. I am grateful to Marc Keith for addressing this point in a discussion about this activity.
34. Erhard Schütz, *Romane der Weimarer Republik* (Munich, 1986), 163.
35. I want to thank Rick McCormick for his thoughtful comments when reading through this chapter.
36. Lynn Abrams, "From Control to Commercialization: the Triumph of Mass Entertainment in Germany 1900—1920?" *German History. The Journal of the German History Society* 8, no. 3 (1990): 279.
37. Williams, "Steeling the Young Body," 27.
38. Abrams, "From Control to Commercialization, 281.
39. Vicki Baum, *Leben ohne Geheimnis* (Berlin, 1932), 157. All translations are mine.
40. Joseph Roth, *Zipper und sein Vater* (Cologne, 1986), 81. All translations are mine.
41. Richard D. Mandell, *Sport: A Cultural History* (New York, 1984), 161-63.
42. Willy Meisl, "Der Sport am Scheidewege," in *Der Sport am Scheidewege*, ed. Willy Meisl (Heidelberg, 1928), 38, 56. All translations are mine.
43. Bertolt Brecht, " Die Krise des Sportes," in *Der Sport am Scheidewege*, 146. All translations are mine.

Chapter Four

Classed Genders and Sexualities

> There is not the faintest sign of fashionable life on the ground floor of a big hotel between eight and ten in the morning. No lights, no music, not a single woman to be seen—unless a charwoman in a blue apron sweeping out the lounge with damp sawdust were taken to represent her sex.
>
> —Vicki Baum, *Grand Hotel*.

Foucault's insights regarding class-specific efforts to organize and structure sexuality according to historical moments and the social body's specificity shed new light on issues concerning the intersection of class and sexuality. Despite the fact that the texts I examine below are only able to encompass a fraction of the various discourses on sex, gender, and class circulating in the Weimar Republic, this chapter offers a representative sample of sites in popular literature where those three defining categories converge. Since most of the texts presented here deal with the middle classes, I must emphasize that this study contains very few representations of working-class conditions and characters from a working-class point of view. That is material for another—much needed—study. As it stands, this chapter addresses the following questions: What particular images of men and women appear to have been represented by which class? How are men and women of the working classes represented in these popular texts, written mostly by writers from the middle classes? What are some of the working-class people's perceived attitudes toward sex? How are the various classes represented vis-à-vis their own sexuality? What sexual stereotypes and myths do different groups circulate about each other? What, if anything, do these political and cultural discourses add to our under-

Notes for this section begin on page 89.

standing of the roles of popular fiction in the imaginings and ideology formation of its women readers?

Un/Tamed Female Sexualities

Chronologically, Weimar Germany is separated from its previous "period," Wilhelminian Germany, by only four years: the four years of World War One. However tempting it may be to consider the war as the dividing line between traditional and modern Germany, many traditional attitudes persisted into the Weimar years and beyond. Although a burgeoning sex reform movement added a new institutionalized voice to the debate concerning sexual mores, the Weimar years entertained many contradictory and recurrent arguments. One notion that helped shape the debate on femininity, sexuality, and morality in the 1920's was the stubborn remains of a punitive sexual (middle-class) morality that focused primarily on circumscribing and repressing female sexuality.

During the nineteenth century, chastity and virginity had become synonymous with "a woman from a good family," thereby in effect aligning virtuous femininity almost exclusively with the middle and upper classes. Consequently, a woman's open display of carnal desire could, and often would, erode her status as an emblem of "true" femininity. It would not only debase her in the eyes of good society but also mark her as belonging to the so-called lower classes. If she affirmed the desire and sensual pleasures that historically had been denied any place on the bourgeois woman's morality scale—"brutal lust" as one author calls it—she was considered at best a femme fatale, at worst, a whore.[1] It was such a traditional perception of middle-class female respectability that struggled to define morality into the Weimar period and many of the novels of the time exhibit agreement, albeit to varying degrees, with these or similar definitions of femininity and respectability. It was traditional sentiments such as the above that made the new notions, that had emerged earlier, but did not come into full bloom until the 1920s, appear so daring and decadent.

In contrast, little of the restraining view of sexual mores that were invested in the middle-class woman seemed applicable to her working-class sister. Since the emergence of the industrial working class, the middle-class standpoint on the proletarian woman's sexuality was clear: she could not or would not restrain it, she was immodest, and she was not a virgin. Seen from the vantage point of working-class sexual morality, a loss of virginity and respectability were not necessarily at odds. As long as the couple had agreed to marry, a working class woman had no moral reason to abstain from a sexual relationship with her partner.[2]

It is clear that most perceptions of sexual morality were tied to a notion of morality that was far removed from the (sexual) reality of the working classes. In fact, one might say that the bourgeoisie had isolated itself, in that respect, from other estates with the emergence of the Enlightenment. According to the emerging morality of the late eighteenth century, "virtuous" essentially became synonymous with "bourgeois." As if to support such a notion, the growing individualization of urban, bourgeois living space promoted the isolation of discrete members of the household from exposure to sexual activities other than those they engaged in personally. Among the rural and urban proletariat, cramped living quarters not only got in the way of individualization and isolation of members of the extended family from one another, they also promoted close contact with a wide range of sexual manifestations and activities.

The middle classes had successfully pressed female sexuality into its only legitimate service—the production of children in wedlock, preferably sons. In keeping with the rules, if bourgeois female sexual behavior was perceived to have overstepped its bounds, its agent was relegated to the lower classes where the lack of moral fortitude in the face of brutal lust was well known. A child out of wedlock was a spicy plot element and some popular novels wove the action around a good woman with a horrible secret whose happily married life is in danger if her past is disclosed. As the righteous hero of Heinz Bernd's *Vergessene Schuld* (1921) says: "One does not marry 'something' of that sort." (3) In Ernst Georgy's 1922 *Der Konfektionsbaron*, Ilse Hansmann, a young ambitious university student, is the result of a illicit affair between a working-class woman and her upper-class lover. Baron von Flintschs, a member of the (once) landed gentry is attracted to the young woman but the circumstances of her birth cause him untold qualms. She invites him to pay a visit to her and her mother, a sales clerk, but at the thought of it "his class-consciousness, although vigorously disciplined during the last couple of years, soared."[3] Von Flintschs' code of conduct is assaulted on two counts: one, that he should consider paying a social rather than charitable visit to the house of a person whose station is below his own; and two, that a man of his background should be interested in a woman with a questionable pedigree. As a matter of fact, *Der Konfektionsbaron* is a modern *Entwicklungsroman* that charts a former aristocrat and World War One cavalry officer's reluctant and painful adaptation to parts of the loathsome and frightening world of Weimar democracy. Georgy's portrayal of life after the First World War and the attempted defeat of class privilege lends a sympathetic ear to the old world order. It is therefore no surprise that, in keeping with such sympathies, the novel makes no overt mention of sexuality unless in connection with artists or working-class characters.

In these cases, sexuality is, as Dan Spencer points out, "not merely an issue of private morality but a social power." (74) Textual sexual desires of the middle and upper classes appear contained to the point of invisibility. Class and sexuality are here at a juncture that confirms the older intertwined reciprocal definition of sexuality and middle-class womanhood: overt sexuality is vulgar and a working-class characteristic and therefore absent in decent, middle-class women. But this interconnection was and is unstable in modernity. Despite representations in which denial or lack of sexual desire are glaring, it should not be forgotten that one strand of experience for the citizens of Weimar indeed was the liberal sexuality that could be witnessed in many of Berlin's cabarets. There the beast of sexuality apparently had not been caged but was running loose, threatening (bourgeois) sensibility and order. And in reality, reproduction and marriage did not always go hand in hand, although there are fictional examples that combine them in a manner that makes matrimony a fiscally responsible act. A passage from Vicki Baum's *Secret Sentence* (1926) bears this out: "He and the girl who is going to have his baby were married ... today, so that she might at least get the maternity benefit." (46)

Working Girls

One of the defining markers of class is work. Until the time of advanced industrialization, women, regardless of class, had always had to work and assist their male relatives or husbands in product- or money-producing endeavors, be it supervising servants or actually engaging in physical work on the estate, the farm, or in the shop. While their experiences and the fruits of their labor varied depending on their circumstances, some kind of work could nevertheless be considered a common female experience, irrespective of class. Over the course of the nineteenth century, the concept of femininity became more sharply defined and that, in turn, bore upon the definition of class.

In its attempt to establish itself, the burgeoning German bourgeoisie concluded that the only conduct suitable for women of this class was to stay in the private sphere, running the household affairs and thus imitating the aristocracy. Moreover, in an attempt to outdo the aristocracy at its own game of exclusivity, bourgeois men insisted on chastity for their women, as we have seen. Compliance with this requirement was, of course, greatly facilitated by confining wives and daughters to the household, where they were left busy supervising the work of the household and its servants (who in and of themselves were an important representation of status). The division of labor into private and public spheres became synonymous with feminine and masculine spheres, respectively. A (publicly perceived) "inactive" woman became a new and important class marker for the bourgeoisie, one that drove a wedge into any remnants of the tenuous solidarity that had existed historically between working- and middle-class women in their struggle against the aristocracy. The dividing line would now run between the working class on one side and the middle and upper classes on the other.

One of the factors that put the crucial "working" in working class is precisely that women belonging to this group worked outside the home. The enforced leisure of large numbers of middle-class women created employment opportunities for rural and urban proletarian women. Rural day labor and domestic help were among the areas that during the latter part of the nineteenth century received the largest influx of female workers.[4] In other words, women of a certain class were seen to cross over into the public, masculine sphere, seemingly operating outside the definition of womanhood but in effect constituting its very negative criteria, namely defining that which was not respectable femininity. What occurred, then, during the nineteenth century, was that "femininity was being reconstructed as a class ideal which served to distinguish one level from another."[5] Women's experiences were molded by both gender and class, and the two categories were inextricably intertwined. As strange as these class and gender constructs may sound, (popular) cultural representations in the Weimar Republic supported and reinforced them, while they , at the same time, created a fiction of bodily dis/pleasures.

Class divisions informed Weimar popular culture, and millions of working class people appear to have been ignored by Weimar radio, for instance. Programs that dished up entertainment such as classical (and light) music, literary radio plays, readings, and discussions were aimed almost exclusively at the middle classes. This is a curious state of affairs because a very vivacious working-class culture existed in Weimar, as the following examples will bear out: the Workers' Education Institute in Leipzig was responsible for plays influenced by the young Soviet Union; workers' political parties, the SPD and KPD, extended their spheres of cultural influence by means of book clubs; there were workers' theater associations, workers' choral groups—some with between 250,000 and 500,000 members—and workers' sports clubs, all of which bear witness to a lively, alternative culture.[6] Nevertheless, it was not until 1927 that the educational program, Deutsche Welle, set time aside for its working-class listeners. This took the shape of a one-hour program "for workers" on Saturday afternoons.[7] The explicit designation of that program leaves little doubt as to who the intended audience was for the remaining hours of broadcasting. Such a bias was an integral part of a cultural production that persisted in most Western and capitalist cultures. The culture of the "lower" classes had been habitually ignored in German history and literature alike. But workers' spending power had increased due to rising wages between 1871 and 1914 and the working class was becoming more integrated into society as a whole.[8] In some instances, the growth of mass culture appeared to be wearing down the tradition of neglect, and gradually the scope and strata of intended audiences widened somewhat.

While bourgeois fears of the working classes might have been a primary cause of the invisibility of blue-collar workers in mainstream (read bourgeois) culture, their absence in popular fiction can also be attributed to a lack of interest on the part of the culture industry. Even Braune's 1930 working-class novel, *Orga Privat*, features office workers. Only one of the works examined for the purpose of this study, namely Leonhard Frank's *Karl und Anna* (1927), selects urban industrial workers as major—or even minor—protagonists.

Publishing houses played a crucial role in determining the sort of reader to whom a given book should appeal. Hermann Ullstein of Ullstein Press once suggested that Vicki Baum write a novel "with a hard-working girl as its central character ... someone like his secretary."[9] Here a stenographer is metonymously made to stand for the "working girl," and it appears, therefore, that this conflation of the working-class woman with the female clerical worker signifies the lowest position on the class ladder that Ullstein ever considered suitable for its literature. It is safe to assume that for him, and publishers like him, working-class workers were not acceptable characters in a novel plot. Reading audiences were asked to consider the office or sales clerk the role model of female modernity and economic participation. The inherent complexity in the "new" woman, the growing media icon that also encompassed elements of liberated, sometimes flagrant, sexuality, economic and emotional independence from men, and the narcissism of youth, is present throughout Weimar reality and popular fiction as are its real and textual attempts to contain and tame the entailed frictions. In addition, the conflation of all "working girls" into one archetype is one more indication of what was so ardently defended in many sections of Weimar society, namely that the German Republic was well on its way to becoming a classless society.

The demographic make-up of Weimar was one of the elements instrumental in erasing much of the overt class consciousness one might have expected to find in popular writings. In the 1920s, two German generations had their roots in two very different worlds. The older population had been formed during Bismarck's reign, his formation of the Second German Reich, Germany's expansion and growing industrialization, its race for African colonization, and the Wilhelminian ethos. All those factors enjoined subjects to revere the Fatherland, the family, and authority. Of the younger generation, women and men could trace their determining life experience—although to a differing degree—to the cataclysm of World War One, the ensuing (Russian) October Revolution, the various revolutions inside Germany itself, and the disintegration of central authorities.

The democratically elected governments of the Weimar Republic and the larger visibility of the working classes, both at the bargaining tables and as agents of their own cultural production, were taken as evidence by many (middle-class) citizens of the proletarianization of Germany and Germans. Georgy's *Der Konfektionsbaron* presents the readers with a large array of upper- and middle-class characters whose loathing of anything working-class is a testament to that fear. Others took it as a sign that they now lived in a democratic, classless society. Hermand and Trommler point out that these drastic generational differences appear to have justified the emphasis on generation as the watershed (90). The effect of such an emphasis was, however, to divert the discussion about Weimar society and its needs away from grim class realities with an unjustified optimism. Imagining age, not class, as the criterion for measuring differences in society, politics was removed from societal analyses by collapsing income, privilege, and power into a concept of age. Youth became the powerful image to which utopian notions, aiming for total democracy and the perfect society, were attached.

In some ways, popular works supported this notion of a classless society. The following passage comes from *Orga Privat* but could in fact come from a multitude of other popular Weimar novels. Reading that on the Berliner streets "sportily dressed young people, girls in jumpers and pleated skirts, men in white trousers and in shirtwaists milled around ..." (81), a reader gets the distinct impression that the visible world consisted largely of young people who expended much energy being fashionably dressed even if it made them indistinguishable from each other. Magazines and journals also seemed to point to a classless society. *Die Dame*—a weekly aimed at middle-class women—and, to a lesser degree, *AIZ* (*Arbeiter Illustrierte Zeitung*—a working-class periodical—both abounded with illustrations of tall, slender, boyish women, all seemingly from the same mould and all clothed in a style which featured an elongated and somewhat angular cut. A contemporary observer, Emil Lucka, comments that clothing of the "parallel erotic"—and with this expression he means the female androgyne—had become simpler and cheaper than previous women's fashions "thus softening the otherwise harsh class differences a little." (87) Ignoring class markers such as quality of material, manufacture, and design, Lucka contends that the contemporary fashion style that blurred gender lines would also help break down extant class markers.

But there is another aspect to Lucka's observation, namely the connection between class and gender. His remarks train our attention on cultural anxieties regarding class- and gender-specific dress codes, whose manifestations changed historically but which had been articulated through various power discourses. One need only think of the sumptuary laws in Jacobean England that restricted dress materials and styles according to the wearer's station in life. More importantly for Wilhelminian sensibilities, sartorial codes had been strict enforcers of dress that marked God-given sex differences thereby articulating institutional and cultural anxieties about blurred gender lines.[10] Such dress codes were flaunted by the young Weimar generations but not without a certain amount of ambiguity. If representations in the popular press and fiction managed to collapse classes through fashion, they stand in a curious and contradictory relation to representations of the generic proletarian woman, as we shall see later. At the same time, such conflicting representations support the notion of Weimar society as an arena of built-in contradictions.

Emil Lucka appears to welcome a disruption of class and gender categories and in his remarks resonates the phenomenon of the "new" woman that in turn led to a re-evaluation of femininity. If femininity in Weimar Germany, indeed, was reserved for the middle and upper classes, the "new" woman became the arena of an intricate play across the borders of both gender and class. In representations of her, women readers experienced a breakdown in established gender and class prescriptions. Femininity became less exclusive and was redefined: the "new" woman signified the crossover of femininity from the upper classes to the lower echelons of the economic strata and, in turn, class became less of a predetermined marker of femininity—or the lack of the same. Conservatives and their fictional twins such as Frau Babette Mierisch from Oskar Gluth's novel *Bayerische Himmelfahrt* (1933) reviled the phenomenon in her remarks that "modern depravities like vanity, bobbed hair, and silk stockings reign supreme." (115) To other observers, the "new" woman took on what might even be called a redemptive image: her apparently classless image became one icon of the new classless Weimar Republic.

Many women, particularly those living in the countryside away from urban centers, were not active participants in the passionate debate about current themes. Therefore, popular fiction served as a public arena where most of the issues pertaining to women in both urban and rural modernity were discussed. If women were unable to see real "new" women from their windows, popular culture, in the shape of radio, film, magazines, or books, made certain that her image was ubiquitously known. Moreover, acceptance or rejection of this image was often a deciding indication of one's position on the political spectrum. Herzog's *Die Buben*, a patriotic novel from 1922, comments in unflattering fashion on stockbrokers' wives who "wore short, rustling silk skirts, hardly reaching the knees and often showing strangely shaped legs always dressed in sheer silk stockings." (346-47) In a similar vein, Hans Franck's 1928 short story *Recht ist Unrecht* reveals a dislike of modern women in the following description: "The wife of the head of the family was a quiet, motherly, simple woman; the spouse of the city architect was a pearl-festooned diva, who, in spite of her forty years, dressed in bright and transparent clothes like a twenty-year old." (48) The other side of the picture may be found in Grete von Urbanitzky's anti-patriarchal novel, *Der wilde Garten* (1927), where the following describes two women in a cafe: "They looked like each other ... with the short skirts, lose-fitting clothes and short haircuts, all of which were manifestations of a hard-won outer freedom." (193)

Will the "Real" Woman Stand Up?

The quote used as the heading of this chapter reveals a particular cultural attitude toward the task of cleaning which, for the middle classes, was synonymous with proletarian women. Unlike the middle classes, working-class people seldom identify with their work but instead construct their identities through activities other than work.[11] Evidently such a notion has little bearing upon the representation of working people. Baum's charwoman is not only deprived of her sex through her work; here she is also an example of the way the middle classes think about work and individuals: the job is collapsed with the individual who performs it. We are thus left with a curious *reductio ad nihil*: the cleaning woman is not a woman because she is of the working class. Moreover, since the middle and upper classes draw *their* identities from their occupations, the char woman, who is thus not a woman, is consequently merely a desexed and de-gendered cleaning agent, no more, no less.

Compared to images of the so-called "new" woman, the lack of substantial representations of "those below" in middle-class cultural texts is conspicuous. It is as if the working classes were uncharted territory, an outer space, where middle- and upper-class writers and other artists projected stereotypical images alongside their fears. For example, the proletarian woman is generally typecast as a mother, usually of many children. Alongside this image of nurturing, we also encounter the middle-class projection onto the proletarian woman of insatiable sexuality. One only needs to think of the belief, widely held by the bourgeoisie, that servant girls were happy to serve male family members sexually, a willingness which in turn naturally made them morally suspect. The following lines from Jakob Wasserman's novel of 1922, *The Goose Man*, between the maid, Mela, and the novel's male protagonist, Daniel, conveys that very notion: "She made no more resistance. Perhaps she too was not without her fervent desire. Perhaps it was the time of day that made nature more insistent than usual … she yielded to him."[12]

As we have observed already, the few representations of the working classes found in this literature most often match the conception that the middle class has of them as a class. And yet, it would be wrong to claim that only bourgeois literature, popular or "serious," constructs or even limits its representations of workers according to a class typology rather than depicting them as individuals. Stereotyping according to class seems to be a time-honored practice performed also by working-class, class-conscious artists, and left-wing political and cultural organs. Socialists' view of sexuality and reproduction, for instance, did not focus on individual women. Rather, it tended to subordinate (female) gender issues under the broader rubric of the welfare of the working classes. Nor did *Arbeiter Illustrierte Zeitung* representations confer individuality on working-class women (or men for that matter). More often than not, the working-class woman was portrayed as carrying one child on her arm, holding the hand of at least one other while also being visibly pregnant. As Petro writes: "[E]ven the representation of the proletarian woman in the *AIZ* was intended to establish a class rather than a gender identification .... These images ... are clearly meant to serve as a point of identification for both male and female working class readers: as the symbolic victim of capitalist exploitation ...."[13]

In addition, the drawings and etchings of one of the most important artists of the time, Käthe Kollwitz, most often portray female subjects as proletarian mothers. Similarly Anna Seghers, whose award-winning *Die Fischer von Santa Barbara* was published in 1928, represents subjects that are all from the working proletariat, but they, too, are types, true to contemporary Socialist Realist prescriptions. We know that the artistic intention in these instances was to establish the working poor as victims of capitalist exploitation, but something happened in the process. The melodramatic representations of worn-out women and wide-eyed children in rags are icons of the needs and wants of poverty. But the teleology of those images strips women of any values other than the symbolic. Consequently they come to represent by association rather than representing themselves. Misery and want become personified in a female iconography similar to that employed in the symbols of liberty and justice; real women and their needs disappear conveniently into the metaphoric realm.

Material women stand to gain nothing through these representations. On the contrary, the female figure succumbs to yet another construction shaped by the imagination. Individuality, which we experience not least through our gender, is here cast to the wind, and we are left with a shell of "woman" waiting to be filled with ideological messages. Even those from whom one might expect a certain perspicacity with regard to marginalization, the class-sensitive artists, have victimized and sacrificed gender to class in order to drive home a point.

In/Visible Classes

There is only a modicum of divergence from stereotype in the personification of the "new" woman—the office worker. One of the most interesting ones is Flämmchen, the stenographer from Baum's *Grand Hotel*. Her body is not only an inspiration to male fantasies but also serves as a grand example of Joan W. Scott's gender definition, namely that gender is "the social organization of sexual differences." (2) Flämmchen's modern attitudes, sharp alertness to economic mores as they affect her, and awareness of her own sexual exchange value make her a paradigm of the independent "new" woman. She exhibits more sexuality and eroticism than overt traditional femininity and in this manner incorporates modernity's unsettled sexual behavior. Her image is often rendered in terms of a cat or a (race)horse, and this alignment with brute creation in turn characterizes her as a creature close to nature with the unfettered libido so threatening to patriarchal law and order. As stenographer she is a member of the petty bourgeoisie which apparently is what makes her respectable as a textual heroine, not only in the eyes of the House of Ullstein but also in those of the readers in the Weimar Republic.

Nobody defends middle-class rights and interests more emphatically than clerical workers, wrote the sociologist Ralph Dahrendorf and this sentiment appears to have held true also for 1920s and early 1930s Germany (99). Flämmchen is a true fictional example of *kleinbürgerlich* (petty bourgeois) individualism striving to secure for herself a social position that accords with her talents as she perceives them.[14] She exhibits no political consciousness nor does she perceive herself as being involved in a class struggle. Rather, she believes that she will have to negotiate the world on her own, and that her personal effort, combined with luck, will earn her a place in the sun. That is her constant dream—a very common one that she shares, not only with other fictional heroines of the day, but also with many women in real life.[15]

Flämmchen's age-old idea of using her body as the instrument for obtaining a better life for herself is one that both before and after the 1920s was looked upon with great moral indignation. As an aside, it is interesting to observe how sanitized Joan Crawford's Flämmchen is in the 1932 Oscar-winning American film version of *Grand Hotel*. Although Flämmchen essentially pursues the goals of a "gold digger," Crawford's character never exhibits the single-minded purposefulness of her literary twin nor the shimmering eroticism so characteristic of Louise Brooks, whose Lulu character had been brought to the screen just a few years earlier.[16] By the time *Grand Hotel* was filmed, the pendulum had already started its swing back toward a more sedate and traditional female ideal.

Having said this, one of the premises of this chapter is that acceptance of relaxed sexual behavior is contingent upon more than just time and place. Again class plays a role. The author's choice of a stenographer—a white-collar worker—to symbolize the free-floating eros both mediates and constitutes Weimar reality. The typist or stenographer was the most visible emblem of the independent woman in the Weimar years.[17] During the years, 1925 to 1933, the number of female white-collar workers increased by 250,000 whereas women's work in other—often blue-collar—areas such as food and beverage establishments (taverns, inns, and cafés) and the clothing industry, dwindled by almost 300,000.[18] In Weimar, lower middle-class women served a new purpose and thus Flämmchen and her sisters did not just represent a new phenomenon. They had become a marketing dream: a group of young women, almost exclusively unmarried, who could be persuaded to spend some of their hard-earned wages on modern commodities. As Flämmchen says: "You just cannot imagine how happy a new dress makes me" (393) and even Fräulein Brückner from Brück's grimly realistic novel of 1930, *Schicksale*, dreams: "Oh, to be able to go shopping, not in the throng of the last-seconds crowds but savoringly, choosing, searching, rejecting." (196-97)

It is not in novels but in the pictorial arts that the working class woman is imagined repeatedly, although seldom to her advantage. In fact, Weimar artists were often brutally misogynist in their depictions of working-class women and female eroticism. Prostitutes were a common artistic subject, represented as the public or urban body. Such a notion certainly had a foundation in reality since the streets of Berlin toward the end of the nineteenth century were populated by an estimated 20,000 prostitutes.[19] Otto Dix portrays the prototypical working woman in his 1922 work *Dirnen* (*Prostitutes*). Their faces have broad, flat features, and they express a commodified, tired insatiability, a mask put on partly for the benefit of a presumably interested male and partly due to hard economic circumstances. Here is no glamor. Instead, the viewer picks up on the anxiety surrounding a stereotypical portrayal of sexuality that the male (bourgeois) artist imagines inhabits the face and body of the working-class woman.

In the case of popular literature, the reader discerns the cultural disregard for low-income characters that oftentimes is manifested through the voice of the narrator. Baum's novel, *And Life Goes On*, employs an omniscient narrator, who, as befits such narrators, has privileged access to the "insides" of the fictional characters. At one point in the novel, the people from the town of Lohwinckel assemble for a rare showing of a film of a so-called daring nature. The middle-class protagonists individually receive the attention of the narrator, who describes them as arriving singly or with a friend or partner. In contrast, true to the image of "the masses," factory workers are described as "slouching along" in groups. The nearest that the narrator comes to individual treatment is to mention the foreman's name, "old Hockling." (216) Such a class-specific treatment thwarts attempts to portray the cinema as a meeting place that all classes and generations, even both genders, frequent, a modern public sphere, as it were. The notion of modern technology in general, and film in particular, as the great leveler of historically set differences is not so much the problem as is the re-presentation of the event. By accentuating some individual characters and depriving others of their individuality along class lines, the representation of the event counteracts the possible liberating features of both the cinema and the film-showing.

Literary depictions of working class sexuality often mirror commonly held stereotypes such as the ones discussed above. In *And Life Goes On*, one lone worker singled out by name is made to stand in synechdochical fashion for the other members of his group, even for the whole of his class. That becomes particularly bothersome when the reader finds Hockling staring at some still photographs of the leading actress, smiling "lasciviously, as he looked at the various poses in which she had been photographed." (216) There is more than a hint of lewdness in that textual moment when the male gaze is connected with the photographic poses of a scantily-clad female subject. This effect is magnified through the lascivious smile. No other male character is described in such a fashion but the working-class man appears here to act without the restraints demanded by polite society. By ogling and smirking, Hockling does what good manners prevent middle-class men from doing overtly. In a few lines the narrative has revealed a classed and gendered interpretation of working men's attitudes toward female eroticism.

With the single exception of Frank's *Karl und Anna*, whose female character displays much sexual modesty, most of the texts used here exhibit no new ways to consider the combination of sexuality and working-class people. On the contrary, they perpetuate stereotypes about class, particularly the proletarian "masses" who already were the site of much political and cultural anxiety in Weimar. Historical dread of the under-classes goes a long way toward answering the question that inevitably arises as to why the working classes are portrayed in such a negative light. Novels sometimes reverse the fear of proletarianization and project it onto the working class as a remark from a radical nationalist in Georgy's *Der Konfektionsbaron* indicates: "They [the workers] cannot take our culture away from us. Hence their furor." (64-5) Other explanations come to mind, among them one that on the surface of things appears to carry much weight, namely the issue of reproduction.

As we have seen, the lower one moves in the social order, the less differentiated the concept of sexuality becomes. The sexuality of working-class women was frequently conflated with the biological ability to bear children. Consequently they were perceived as "breeders" of large families. Since the wealth and means of production in Weimar Germany were concentrated in few hands, as was the case in most Western, industrialized countries, and since the higher income groups had typically limited their families to two or three children, fears of an even more unbalanced proportion of the "haves" and the "have-nots" were always present. Some conservative factions of the republic gave high priority to controlling the seemingly rapid growth of the lower-income classes. After all, they were the revolutionary classes. But the fact that population growth had declined steadily since the end of the previous century was also of grave concern in Weimar Germany. Central to the dream of a greater Germany was a growing, healthy and fecund population, able and willing both to increase the country's industrial output and to expand and defend its territorial borders. As has already been discussed in a previous chapter, the horns of this dilemma—whether to control or encourage (proletarian) fecundity—appear regularly in popular texts. We now understand how that translates into being a constitutive element of the discussion on gender and class in Weimar Germany.

When we maintain that the perception of women differed according to their class affiliation, it is with full awareness that there are many factors involved in shaping that perception. The identity of poor or working-class women was primarily fused with reproduction, that is, with their biology. In stark contrast, well-to-do women appear as metaphors for consumption as in Baum's *Grand Hotel:* "Women with naked arms, in sparkling clothes, with jewelry, in furs, extraordinarily beautiful and ornate women." (22) Modernity had brought about a difference in who footed some bills but few women could afford to pay for luxuries; although women's earning power and their concomitant independence seemed to increase, the level of their consumption was more often than not dictated by their husbands' incomes rather than their own. Yet, many fictional heroines neither glitter with jewels nor sparkle as erotic objects. Frau Elizabeth Zienkann, from Baum's "Der Weg," is a lower middle-class protagonist whose whole life defines the agony of respectability and lack of desire. Rather than being an active, modern consumer, she is consumed by the lifestyle afforded her and her family by her husband, Herr Zienkann. Neither does Frau Zienkann symbolize reproduction. She cuts the figure of the lower middle-class paradigm of respectable and often de-sexualized womanhood, and it is only too easy to imagine her tired and resigned reception of Herr Zienkann's amorous advances. Her body bears no inscription of the male sexual fantasies that either delight, like Flämmchen's, or frighten, like that of the loose (working-class) woman. Her body is devoid of sexual markers, although her gender is marked by her name, title, and two children. But that is all.

Some speculation as to why women from the same class—Baum's Flämmchen, Keun's Doris from *Das kunstseidene Mädchen*, and Frau Zienkann—are imagined to possess diametrically opposed sexualities may prove fruitful. Although there may be ten or fifteen years between Frau Zienkann and Flämmchen or Doris, it is not so much the women's ages as the era they represent that is one aspect of this issue. For one thing, the contrast between Wilhelminian and Weimar Germany is inscribed as the contrast between the fictional women. The foregrounding of traditional duties and the cage of inevitability in Frau Zienkann's case pits her against the constructions of Flämmchen and Doris through sexuality and eroticism. The former's entrapment can also be seen stemming from the institution of marriage. While the young, single women have only themselves to live for, marriage too often transfers a wife and mother's *raison d'être* from herself to her family. In this manner, all three women are paradigmatic not only of material Weimar women and the debate about Weimar womanhood; they also respond directly to the conflicting emotions about duty and desire that women readers harbored about their brave new world.

* * *

If we talk about popular fiction being a sphere where women can experience and participate in their national culture, we have to be class specific. Proletarian women would find their world represented in but few of these texts and what they would meet there would be stereotyped. Historically, the working class has been faceless and as such its members could not come alive in novels and stories. It is much in evidence that the notion, namely that popular fiction constitutes a locus where women could participate in their national culture, evidently does not include working-class women as full agents. Unless they were willing to participate in a culture that frequently was openly hostile to their existence or only validated *aspirations* to traverse class lines, there was little in the run-of-the-mill popular novels that they could recognize as pertaining to their own lives. For purposes of identification, the working classes had to turn to cultural efforts specific to party-affiliated agencies. The class barrier was very real, in fiction as in fact.

That, in turn, begs the question of the classlessness of the "new" woman. Was it possible that the Weimar notion of classlessness was asserting itself in the "new" woman? As often as not, her fictional representation was constructed as a white-collar worker. The petty bourgeoisie's customary sorry lack of powerful social agents or role models in fiction was changed by the ascent of the "new" woman. Her modernity and demonstrative independence proffer a site of identification—even across class lines—if for nothing else than for utopian female desires. While the old, masculine world with its rules and hierarchies appeared to be fading, women reconstructed themselves out of the ashes of World War One. The stories they read and the characters they identified with were crucial elements of this process.[20]

As the discussions in this chapter have progressed, it has become increasingly clear that the "new" woman is the—not unproblematic—ideal of the creators of popular culture. Representations of her contain visions of modernity and dreams of economic and sexual emancipation. These representations, similar bodily constructs in popular women's magazines, and fashions for a "new" woman all suggest possibilities of transgressing class lines or even signifying classlessness. Yet, the ambiguities embodied in this construct, such as a reluctant longing for marriage and the compulsion of youth, were only too real to women readers of the time. Those conflicts resonated with many of the cultural dilemmas experienced by material women. In this light, the lack of representations of working-class women as narrative agents takes on an additional significance: they could not represent role models for upwardly-mobile dreams and aspirations. The "new" woman is the model who, in spite of her conflicting characteristics, can represent womanhood; who, although she is not "top-drawer," can signify classlessness; and who, despite her threatening promiscuity, can be brought back into the fold through marriage. The "new" woman thus takes on a utopian status, that, rather than revolutionizing German society, offers a liberal solution. In contrast, working-class women and their representations offer no such possibilities for reconciliation and thus the bitter class conflict so endemic in Weimar is blithely glossed over. For a short time, the concept of the "new" woman ushered in a new notion of feminine and sexual utterance that straddled perceived class differences. The dream was short lived. The Third Reich turned on modern womanhood, constructing instead its own vision of feminine nurturing of the family—and, by extension, of the state—that in turn contained its own contradictions.

Notes

1. Bernd, *Vergessene Schuld,* 55.
2. Hagemann, *Frauenalltag und Männerpolitik,* 168. Hagemann does, however, suggest that working-class sexual morals were approaching those of the bourgeoisie as the Weimar years wore on.
3. Ernst Georgy (Margarete Michaelson), *Der Konfektionsbaron* (Stuttgart: Union Deutsche Verlagsgesellschaft, 1922), 282. All translations are mine.
4. See also Anne Phillips, *Divided Loyalties: Dilemmas of Sex and Class* (London, 1987), especially Chapter Four.
5. Ibid., 38.
6. Jost Hermand and Frank Trommler, *Die Kultur der Weimarer Republik* (Munich, 1978), 124.
7. Bärbel Schrader and Jürgen Schebera, *The Golden Twenties: Art and Literature in the Weimar Republic* (New Haven, 1988), 124.
8. Abrams, "From Control to Commercialization," 279, 292.
9. King, *Best-sellers,* 79.
10. See also Dollimore, "Shakespeare, Cultural Materialism ..." *New Literary History* 21, no. 3 (Spring 1990) and Marjorie Garber's *Vested Interests* (New York, 1991) for treatment of these issues.
11. I am grateful to Susan Chase for pointing this out in a discussion.
12. Jacob Wassermann, *The Goose Man* (Harcourt, 1922), 100. Other research also points to the possible male fetishization of female proletarian sexuality from the late 19th century through Weimar. I think here in particular of an article by Barbara Kosta, "Employed Bodies: Female Servants in Works by Marieluise Fleisser" in *German Studies Review* XI. 1 (February 1992) and an unpublished paper entitled "Representatives of Sexuality in Marieluise Fleißer's Pioniere in

Ingolstadt" given by Belinda Carstens at the German Studies Association annual conference in Minneapolis, 1992.

13. Petro, *Joyless Streets*, 127.
14. Anthony Giddens, *The Class Structure of the Advanced Societies* (London, 1975), 185.
15. Someone who does not fall neatly into that category is Lämmchen in Fallada's *Kleiner Mann—was nun?* She is a working-class woman who marries a petty-bourgeois man. She scorns the reputed working class solidarity while at the same time showing a keen sense of the existing power discourses.
16. G.W. Pabst, *Pandora's Box* (UFA, Germany, 1928).
17. Among the many novels with typist as major characters are *Orga Privat, Schicksale hinter Schreibmaschinen, Gilgi, Die Angestellten,* and *Menschen im Hotel.*
18. Bridenthal," Something Old, Something New," 486.
19. George Mosse, *The Culture of Western Europe* (Boulder, 1988), 286.
20. I am grateful for Stephen Brockmann's commentary at a 1992 German Studies Association panel where part of this chapter was first presented as a paper.

Chapter Five

BEYOND THE PALE—OTHERS, SELVES, AND NATIONHOOD

Crucial to the formation of subjectivity are issues of racial and sexual diversity, those other sites of difference so often hidden by the aspect of gender and class. What follows is an investigation into some of the instances of sexuality and race that were considered undesirable by many in Weimar. In view of the horrors of the Third Reich and the Holocaust, it is safe to assert that the systematic, negative inscription of difference between self and other in the early part of the twentieth century was more strongly manifested in German culture than anywhere else in the West. The years from 1918 to 1933, in particular, that period which leads up to the dictatorship of the National Socialist German Workers Party (NSDAP), constitute *the* historical and cultural period whose cultural stereotyping would turn an entire people and other smaller groups into an "Other" to be exterminated by the Nazis. While Weimar culture during those years on the one hand was characterized by a candor and openness with regard to new and unconventional cultural phenomena, it, on the other hand, also exhibited a wide variety of stereotypical portrayals about many of those very phenomena that constituted Otherness: the proletarian mother, the prostitute, the "new" woman, the "Negro," the homosexual, and "the Jew," all of whom were ubiquitous in the cultural *textum* of the German 1920s.[1]

What links the communities whose representations are discussed in this chapter are not surface similarities. By conferring upon homosexuals, Jews, and, for lack of a better term, non-Nordic/Germanic people the stigma of Otherness, these particular Weimar discourses in turn consigned those groups to the margin. The char-

Notes for this section begin on page 131.

acteristics ascribed to and inscribed upon members of those communities offer us a view of pivotal cultural themes and anxieties engaging and fueling the energies of Weimar citizens.

My task here is not to prove links between Jews, lesbians, and "non-Aryans," although the perceived connections between them will serve as one explanation for their collective treatment in one chapter. As in previous chapters, my discussion will focus on how the literary representations resonate with the surrounding culture and the producers of this culture, among them, readers of popular fiction. How might these representations have been understood? What opportunities did they afford a reader's understanding of her own identity and the process of self-fashioning? In the complex processes of Othering, is there any latitude for doubt and resistance to stereotypes? My readings will help us speculate in different ways about women's experience as readers, as producers of culture, and, concomitantly, of themselves.

Excessively Lesbian

Censorship, the conflagration of the Nazi years, and the Second World War have been among the reasons given for the fact that lesbian Weimar novels are hard to come by today. Few, if any, pre-Second World War lists of German lesbian texts exist, although scholarship has begun its archaeological labor. There is no doubt that the mere thematization of lesbian existence in women's literature was and is an act of resistance which refutes suppression, silence, and the taboo of lesbianism and lesbians.[2] In view of this, it should come as no surprise that one can read through any number of Weimar texts without coming across any overt signs of lesbian existence. However, there is a body of works, incoherent as it may be, that conveys multiple representations of lesbianism(s). In the following pages, I shall attempt to unpack some of the cultural texts to reveal and examine such representations. Throughout this process, certain aesthetic and ideological strategies surface that in and of themselves refute definite, and thus constraining, answers. It is those strategies and their position in the larger literary and cultural conversation that I discuss.

According to Lillian Faderman, more than 1,000 articles and books on homosexuality were published in Germany between 1898 and 1908, a time when sexual discourses were still largely motivated by Richard von Krafft-Ebing's Wilhelminian, scientific mapping of sexuality entitled, *Psychopathia Sexualis,* published in 1876.[3] An integral part of that work's significance was its diagnosis of lesbianism as a functional sign of "degeneration and a taint."[4] During the Weimar Republic, the patriarchal obsession with order and categories existed dialectically with what appeared to be a dissolution of morals and subjectivities. It was during the 1920s and early 1930s that legal measures were periodically instituted which forbade certain lesbian texts, thus, inadvertently and paradoxically, lending veracity to the very reality of lesbian sexuality. Yet, despite legal, medical, and artistic attempts in Weimar to define and corral homosexuality, the inability to pin down any one identity, particularly a lesbian identity, becomes increasingly apparent. The oppositional struggle to stake out homosexuality as a site occupied by a multitude of identities rather than one single identity intensified during the Weimar years. As one reads through narratives written by lesbians, a profusion of lesbianisms emerges in texts that starkly contrast with and resist the rigid clichés of homosexuality that occupy heterosexual fiction of the period. Attempts to reclaim and represent lesbians outside the heteronormative paradigm were not without a price. The intense emotionalism that characterizes many such texts acts almost as a foil or armor, protecting the lesbian's vulnerable body from penetration by patriarchal gazes and colonizing graspings. In spite of the lesbian protagonists' desire for a world with a purpose and an understanding of themselves from this same world, their authors are unable—or unwilling—to define and fix the subjectivities.

Part of the price for moving off the heterosexual territory was the very real risk of censorship. It would wax and wane during the republic's existence but would never be absent, and censorship would always figure largely in the foreground of gay and lesbian writers' consciousness. In Paragraph 118, the Weimar Constitution promised that "there shall be no censorship," but 1920 already saw the reintroduction of film censorship in the Film Act. During the years 1926–1928, the "Schmutz und Schund" Act (Harmful Publications Act) prohibited the public exhibition in shop windows or on magazine racks of a number of gay and lesbian magazines and journals. In 1932, the police chief of Berlin outlawed public gay and lesbian dances and gatherings. Finally, on February 23, 1933, pornography—the definition of which included homosexual magazines—became illegal. While the battle over censorship obviously was a sign of the tug of war between liberal and conservative forces in the republic, its various manifestations seriously circumscribed the creative efforts of homosexual artists. For example, in 1926, Anna Elisabeth Weirauch's novel, *The Scorpion*, could be found on the index of Paragraph 184, a list of texts "suspected of indecency."[5] The German scholar, Claudia Schoppman, suggests that the reason *The Scorpion* has been excluded from the patriarchal body of literature may lie with its taboo theme, i.e., lesbianism, and "not exclusively with its aesthetic conventionality or triviality." (198) This remark brings aesthetic issues to the fore, describing Weirauch's style as "conventional," or even "trivial." If the formal aspect of some lesbian novels is indeed trivial, the question needs to be asked why this is so. The following investigation attempts to bring into the open possible reasons why the prose in many lesbian novels is so impenetrable, so excessive. Excess was a significant feature of the Weimar cultural and political arena in that dislike, even fear, of excesses was a crucial part of modernist aesthetic and philosophical discourses. This is confirmed by Freud's cultural position that without management of excesses, there could be no civilization. In the literary world, a similar rejection of excess—or "narrative surplus," as Judith Roof calls it—also served to set apart and to devalue so-called emotional narratives, often written by and for women (50). It may thus be argued that marginality and excess stood in a direct relationship to each other and that one aspect of the argument would be that the more marginal the discourse, the more excessive the style would be.

Whereas Erich Kästner's and other authors' huge popularity with Weimar readers may have been linked to their exposition of increasingly sober and "objective" writing styles, that would later be consolidated into a fashionable aesthetic known as "New Objectivity," Patrice Petro has recently pointed to the excesses of style and content in the very popular Weimar films we label melodramas. Those films represent class and gender. It is one of my contentions that when the topic of representation—here lesbianism/s—is on the edge of the writeable, melodrama appears to have won out over all other available styles. The struggle to move homosexual lifestyle and choices away from the realm of (heterosexually) perceived sexual excess and into the respectable sphere of thinkable and doable behavior appeared on the page as emotional and philosophical superabundance.

While engaging the restrictive and negative formulations of lesbian subjectivity floating in the larger cultural conversation, lesbian writers had the rigorous task, as always, of debunking current myths and providing new constructions. The formation and attempted stabilization of lesbian identity in Anna Elisabeth Weirauch's three-volume novel *Der Skorpion* (*The Scorpion*) is a complicated task.[6] Following young Myra's coming of age, Weirauch's *The Scorpion* traces her delinquent childhood, her rebellion against a restrictive guardian aunt, and her covert love affair with an older intellectual woman, Olga Rado. After Olga's public denial of her affair with Myra, the latter ventures into the city on her own, heartbroken but independently wealthy as a result of her father's death. After a series of encounters, she leaves the city in loathing and retires to the countryside. Even there, infatuation and love catch up with Myra, but she finally resolves to abstain from erotic love and attempt to live in peace with herself and nature.

Entwined in Weirauch's process of articulating alternative sexual identities are responses to her contemporaries' theories on the origin and character of lesbian sexuality. Consequently, the novel offers a typology of sexual practices sorted and classified both according to, but also against, the lines common to the medical, psychoanalytical, and scientific discourses of the day. It is from this all-too-familiar range of sexual characters—from a closeted, suicidal upper-class lesbian to shameless, urbanite cross-dressers, and neurotic, immoral homosexual prostitutes—that Myra must distinguish herself. In one pivotal moment, Myra separates her own desires from the perceived perverted ones of lusty sexual deviants, foreshadowing her later violent rejection of her urban lesbian community. In this scene, young Myra finds on her father's desk dozens of texts on one of the themes that were so *au current* in Weimar cultural debates: psycho-sexual abnormalities.

> There were strange and weird stories of countesses who dressed in men's attire and frequented various dives until they were lured into a trap and brutally murdered .... There were statistics showing all the unfortunates who fell victim to softening of the brain, lunacy, tuberculosis of the spine and other diseases as a result of unnatural practices. Or descriptions of the soul life of sexual inverts which led one to suppose that these thousands of human beings constituted a vast community, a community bound together by no ties of common interest, no similarity of education, origin, taste or attitude toward life, and never by love, but by a common lust for a common form of excess. (112-13)

The contrast between the rather good-hearted, proper Myra and the litany of sexual perverts who supposedly serve as accurate representations of homosexuals, posits Weirauch as a vigorous critic of such popular depictions. Yet her fictional heroine is no clear-cut embodiment of this critique. Rather, *The Scorpion* is, to recall Elaine Showalter's pronouncement about women's writing, "double-voiced ... embodying both the muted and the dominant ...." discourses.

(191) Constructed by and reacting to the culture surrounding her, Myra ritually cleanses herself of exactly those symptoms ascribed to homosexuals in heteronormative medical and popular discourses: sexual excess. When Myra discovers the texts on her father's desk she becomes physically ill. This marks the distinction between her own love (for Olga Rado) and the "filth" of sexual perverts not only in her mind but on her body. Rather than allowing the common markings of lesbianism to stand—pathologization, degeneracy, criminalization, immature sexuality—the text seems interested in severing the connection between those properties and a hygienic love between women. In so doing, *The Scorpion* realigns the ills normally attributed to lesbians with other locations identified with cultural affliction, particularly to urban areas and modernity, while it attempts to clean up and raise woman-to-woman desire into a respectable moral and perfectly natural category. In this manner, a particular (but always unarticulated) kind of lesbian love in the novel is separated and saved from the unnatural, performative, deranged, and excessive sexual practices of the urban world. Once she has withdrawn from the city, Myra's type of lesbian sexuality, thoroughly disentangled from its unfortunate associations, fits more neatly into the safe zone of acceptable behavior. Free of the excessive sexuality of her friends, Myra completes her cleansing rite-of-passage and thus recovers the adulthood denied lesbians by Freud and the moral decency denied them by Kraft-Ebbing. Indeed, her move away from the urban, homosexual community may be seen as an attempt to establish her as an independent, even isolated, being. The maneuver to remove love between women from perversity is a clear parallel to Magnus Hirschfeld's efforts in the arena of German sexual politics in the early twentieth century. His declaration that personal fulfillment and love were more important in modernity than reproduction or marriage cleared a path to his theory of a natural, third, homosexual sex. By naturalizing a third sex, Hirschfeld's theory attempted to sever homosexuality's traditional link with pathology and crime and remove it from medical and psychological discourses of cure.[7]

In the process of debunking popular myths about lesbianism, *The Scorpion* creates a lesbian who quells her desire. Out of Myra's repeated failure to keep her sexual appetite under control grows the lesbian protagonist who learns to locate her sexual desires in the controlled and controllable realm of the intellect. Myra's happiness is a chosen isolation, free from the threat and temptation of physicality. Consequently, the novel seems to advocate a lesbian identity that, in fact, must eschew sexuality if it cannot be controlled. Myra's move to the countryside presumes to alleviate the tension between two notions of nature: (urban) nature as dirty and animalistic—to be conquered—and (country) nature as romanticized, noble, and harmonious.[8] This strategy is not without consequences because it amounts to an alignment with anti-urban and anti-modern values and throws a light on questionable tactics frequently forced upon marginalized groups in their struggle for acceptance. In the novel, the effect is that the image of lesbianism is reconstituted as clean, natural, and restrained. Thus, lesbians may be members of a community whose members would be linked in all the ways other members of humanity are linked, rather than through sexual excess.

Clarity in Excess?

In his declaration: "The man who speaks does not cry and moan but clarifies and defines—thus becoming clear and definitive himself," (519), Kurt Pinthus exalts the primacy of clarity as patriarchy attempts to grasp, name, categorize, and evaluate identities. It is against this exaltation of clarity that we must read what Sedgwick calls "new and incoherent mappings of homo/sexual definitions."[9] Many lesbian-authored novels from the mid-1920s onward fit under Sedgwick's rubric: they are written in an intensely emotional, excessive language that appears as an obstacle for the reader since it prevents her from grasping any clearly defined paradigms of identity. Among these is 1927 novel, *Der wilde Garten* (*The Wild Garden*).[10] Chronicling the coming-of-age of young schoolgirls as it is perceived by their teacher and the novel's main character, Hanna von Südekum, the work is a prime example of an aesthetic of excess that constantly acts as an impediment to a coherent sense of meaning. The text employs the most torrid prose when writing about the young girls' sexual coming of age, as, for example, in von Südekum's lament over the perceived changes in her pupils.

> Frankly: All of these differences [among the schoolgirls] existed only until the one point in time that changed them all. On the outside it would place dark, melancholic shadows under bright children's eyes, lend the first signs of languishing tenderness to their gestures and a deep pallor around young foreheads. Imperceptibly and soundlessly, the power was invading her class like a bad spell on a herd, like a searing wind among white, fleeting summer clouds. It propelled the girls toward each other in a common, mysterious fate, while it slowly and in a frightening fashion erased previously existing differences. It robbed each child, who just weeks before had each been a world unto herself, of her individuality,

> tilled them hard like coarse soil into uniform pieces of land, one done like the other (29).

Similar excessive gestures recur throughout the novel. The desire to say it all without giving anything away is just as obvious in the following quote. An artist, Alexandra, is reflecting on her just-consummated love affair with a young woman; the following citation is another example of the emotionalism that frequently disrupts any discursive order or clarity: "You see, there was always a slight knowledge, rising up from the primeval depths, that loaded her with hot fear. It came from the ur-depths and out of this night it grew towards her, from the borderless loneliness with a loved one under this big sky. And Alexandra fought against this knowledge about herself." (252) Such prose makes the criminalization and pathologization of lesbians a difficult task: if you cannot pin down lesbian identity, how can you criminalize and pathologize it? After reading such prose, the possibility of a witting strategy arises, namely that those lesbian writers or writers supportive of love between women examined here, while desiring to make visible and justify lesbianism/s, refused to circulate the vilified representations so constitutive of Weimar discourses on homosexuality.

In novels like von Urbanitzsky's, it is particularly evident that hymns to love and, in turn, love's legitimization of (homo)sexual behavior are frequently much longer and more intricate than the narrative foreplays to heterosexual relationships. In the latter texts, many representations—presumably heterosexual—of the "new" woman emphasize the sexual and the erotic at what often seems to be the expense of the emotional. Faderman's research confirms this tendency on the part of heterosexual writers to overstress the erotic in narratives involving women when she observes that "love between women has been primarily a sexual phenomenon only in male fantasy literature." (17) For sexual titillation, it seems, one had to read heterosexual narratives about homosexual desire. Lesbian narratives appear to aim for a different telos.

Excess is as deeply anti-modernist as is the female protagonists' search for meaning in their universe. The profoundly moral intent of the lesbian-authored texts examined here constitutes a strong antidote to the popular detached cynicism—often tinged with varying shades of despair—that characterizes many works of fiction in Weimar. The aesthetics of the 1920s literary texts, and particularly those of the New Objectivity, contained little if any hope for a moral universe. The melodramatic style, with its "significantly different version of reality" is perfectly suited for this purpose.[11] Such a reading supports the hypothesis mentioned earlier that the choice of melodrama was deliberate. Could it be that lesbian writers chose not to avail themselves of the objective literary style in vogue halfway through the Weimar years?

Judith Roof asks how lesbian desire can be portrayed "without necessarily being translated into the phallocentric terms by which sexuality in general tends to be depicted ... as a systematic expression of the feminine as merely a version of the masculine ...." (74-74) This query provides us with an alternative to the general assumption that the lesbian authors in question simply were unable to write anything but conventional or trivial prose. Instead it becomes possible to speculate that the cool, realistic, and detached style, popular from the mid-1920s to 1933, was perceived as turf staked out by patriarchal, heterosexual privilege. After all, that mode of expression was a manifestation of a belief in a universal norm circumscribed by scientific positivism, technology, and objectivity, all expressed through a phallomorphic language. In contrast, the texts under consideration in this chapter abound with what Peter Brooks calls "indulgence of strong emotionalism ... extreme states of being ... inflated and extravagant expression ...." (11-12) In short, they display the stylistic elements that we associate with melodrama. It can therefore be argued that the aesthetics of those novels appear to be in such utter opposition to contemporary Weimar styles of expression that they make it virtually impossible to dismiss their witting existence.

The attempt to eschew overt constellations of lesbian desire and sexuality and the choice of a stylistic paradigm that might indeed offer new ways to do just that, appear, at first, somewhat contradictory. The arguments do, however, make room for more than just a binary opposition. The excessively emotional narratives perhaps represent that which at first glance seem to be missing in the texts: expressions of lesbian desire and sexuality. In speaking of the feminine sublime, Barbara Claire Freeman defines it as "a crisis in relation to language and representation that a certain subject undergoes." (2) This particular definition is also valid for the melodramatic excess we find in the novels: it signifies precisely a crisis in the representation of that which defies patriarchal categories, which does not yet have any paradigms, and thus cannot (yet) be articulated.

Eve Sedgwick's point that it is extremely difficult for any text to provoke serious response if it has a lesbian plot "carrying value and sustaining narrative" would normally ensure that such a plot only emerges in a secondary fashion.[12] *The Wild Garden* not only makes girls and women visible as bearers of action, it also exposes heteronormativity as an integral part of social morals that have entangled and imprisoned girls and women and caused female agency to wither on the vine. This is evidenced by the following citation: "'[Girls] come into bloom,' as poets so often put it. They are seduced or get married, they have crushes, dream, and wait for the man who will determine their lives." (65) In addition, and even more important for the present purpose, von Urbanitzky's text posits women in a double fashion: as viable alternative subjects and as objects of each other's love and desire.

One of the striking features of the lesbian narratives under examination is the strategic avoidance of all things prurient. Lesbian authors presented here appear far too intent on representing serious emotional attachments and/or qualms about their existences to engage on paper in frivolous or lightheaded prose or activities. Instead, Magnus Hirschfeld's scientific attempts to normalize the third sex as simply one of nature's variations and consequently to occupy a space inside respectability for its concomitant practices find their literary analog in this as well as other lesbian-authored texts. In a crucial interchange in *The Wild Garden,* Dr. Südekum asks "but love between a woman and a woman is disgusting, surely?" (128) The fact that the question is asked by a sympathetically portrayed, old-fashioned, older woman pre-empts the reader from jumping to that very conclusion without an intervention. No longer can the reader nod in unarticulated acquiescence with unveiled homophobic utterances similar to those often found in other popular Weimar novels. As an example, we find Baum's Helene, from the novel of the same name, pondering upon the nature of her roommate and "something suddenly leaped from her—tenderness, terror—a secret, devious, masked, dissembled, abnormal love." (112) Similarly, in von Lengerke's 1928 *Gloria, The Amazon,* Gloria's "innocent" confrontation with Blanche's amorous intentions constitutes another example of homophobia: "How miserable, how ugly was the animal in human beings .... [Gloria] didn't believe it, forced herself not to think about it. This frightful truth threatened to destroy her life's work." (166-67) In *The Wild Garden,* the strategic value of Hanna von Südekum's frank question is that it "outs" the issue of lesbian love and sexuality and pleads for it to become a topic of discussion. This is, of course, precisely what happens in the text, now the palimpsest for the reader's own internal or external dialogue. The textual interlocutor and defender of women's love for women,

Alexandra, an artist, replies: "What sick thoughts you have. In some cases you may be right, of course. It is depravity when tired desire is looking for new titillation, when the brain becomes subservient to lust, always finding new, refined variations. That could be disgusting ...." (129) Here Alexandra is arguing for a "natural" desire, one which, according to the title of the novel, is perhaps wild and untamed, but genuine. According to her, desire is not circumscribed by gender. Consequently, depravity is not connected to the object of the sexual desire but rather to the source and articulation of the desire. When sexual desire is the call of nature, she says, how can it be ugly?

In the socio-historical context of Weimar Germany, notions of good and unmediated versus depraved and premeditated desires fly in the face of increasingly scientific attitudes toward sexuality from official structures. The Weimar period was, after all, the first time that marriage-cum-sexual counseling was taking place on a large scale. One consequence of this was that men could be taught sexual techniques that aimed at satisfying their wives; it was hoped that these techniques, in turn, might reduce the divorce rate and confine free-floating female sexual desires to the marriage bed. Those and other scientific measures notwithstanding, Alexandra's outspoken condemnation of calculated and calculating desires might very easily have found resonance with those who were in disagreement with the official attempts to demystify sexuality. In addition, consequences of the notion of natural or depraved desire are not articulated in the examined texts. The issue is in true tandem with current theories: homosexual existence was not a matter of a lifestyle or choice; it occurred naturally. Magnus Hirschfeld and others' theses of the third sex as a natural phenomenon echo here.

Pathological Love

When violence and women combine, says Lynda Hart, the lesbian functions "in a structural dialectic of appearance/disappearance where the violent woman is visible ....She is, in a sense, the silent escort of the violent woman" (x). Hart's contention seems to offer a particularly fitting paradigm for an examination of Alfred Döblin's 1924 documentary short story Döblin ("Two Women Friends and How They Murdered with Poison").[13]

Döblin's story is about a young marriage that goes sour, presumably—we are lead to speculate—due to the woman, Elli's, disgust with sex. Her husband, Link, responds to her aversion with repeated violent abuse and rape. Elli appears to be caught half wittingly and willingly in the cycle of violence. She makes the acquaintance of Grete, whose marriage is also on the rocks, and after a while their liaison becomes sexual. Together, with the quiet consent of Grete's mother, they plot the murder of Link with rat poison. The story leads the reader, by means of a relentlessly "objective" and journalistic prose, through the cumulative physical and psychological consequences on both victim and perpetrators of repeated applications of the poison. The documentary nature and consequent verisimilitude of "Women Friends" are finally anchored in Döblin's representation of Elli and Grete's trial, complete with statements from expert witnesses. The story appeared as the premier volume in a series entitled "Outsiders of Society: The Crimes of Today" (*Außenseiter der Gesellschaft—Die Verbrechen der Gegenwart*). In this manner, the story is thoroughly annexed by the series' nomenclature as well as the title. Both serve to criminalize the text's leading characters and consequently incarcerate them inside a category of pathology.

It is the genital contact between the two women that appears to provide the point of transgression in the text. Elli is transformed from being childlike and repulsed by marital sex to depend on the new friendship with Grete and ultimately into the following incarnation: "[Elli's] vigorousness, her masculine decisiveness gained a sexual foothold which in turn intensified it in a dangerous manner." (35) The description posits several claims, all mutually interdependent: first, since the friendship has moved into a sexual phase, it is now considered lesbian, that is, we discover here a definition of lesbianism that pinpoints it as women's physical, sexual love for other women. Next, a description of Elli's "masculine" decisiveness in a woman-to-woman relationship contradicts the masochism her character displays in a violent heterosexual relationship. Finally, danger is located in a same-sex relationship which, according to the above definition, is lesbian and masculine.

As to the first claim, such a restrictive notion of lesbianism is a cliché and certainly contradicts centuries of women's romantic friendships. Next, the textual tension between Elli's inferred masochistic participation in her own violent abuse in a heterosexual relationship and her putative masculinity in the same-sex relationship are indicative of the tone found in a deluge of discourses on women and homosexuality in Weimar. In Döblin's textual version of the "true crime," there are no indications of Elli's murderous inclinations until after her involvement with Grete has moved onto a sexual plateau. Indeed, during the heterosexual relationship with Link, her character appears to be a study in masochism. Döblin writes of the violence between Link and Elli: "[Elli] soon developed an inclination to participate in much [of the physical violence] as a self-punishment for her sexual failure." (14) This speculation into a woman's reputedly willing participation in violence against her finds an interesting resonance in Krafft-Ebing's ever-popular pronouncement that masochism was not an aberration in women, only in men; women were naturally inclined to subordination due to their passive role in procreation.[14] However, after the friendship with Grete has become sexualized, Elli "only thought of being active, masculine, so as to demonstrate her love to her friend" and it is the love and passion for her friend that "drove Elli and impelled her toward masculinity and heroism." (54) This brings us back to Döblin's view that a very real danger obviously arises from lesbian usurpation of the male prerogative to women's sexuality. It appears that Elli's masculinization and subsequent penchant for heroism are what transform her masochistic bent and Elli is now, in a manner of speaking, a man in a woman's body. This is a phenomenon that historically incorporates both criminality and degeneracy. Whether it is in fact what "really" happened is of no interest to this examination. What matters here is how heterosexual texts grasp and represent lesbian identities. In this case, the sexual invert and the "ultimate violation of the social instinct" are inexorably linked.[15] "Women Friends" resonates with Krafft-Ebing's diagnosis of lesbianism as pathology and/or degeneracy.

If we consider the infantilizing paradigms operating in the text: "Elli ... was a cheerful child, merry as a canary," (7) "[n]ow, here was Elli, this small playful person with her merry, roguish ways," (25) and its criminalizing bent, an acknowledgment of a woman-loving woman as an adult acting in full possession of her faculties is no longer possible. The intense search for the reason for female violence against males is found in a sexuality which is deviant, pathological, threatening, and infantile, all at once. Women acting out in rage against patriarchal systemic violence *must be*—and are—pathologized. The authorial comment that "a group of educated men had examined the physical and psychological states of the women and attempted to paint a picture based on wide experience" (99) reverberates widely, spanning both the past and the future as a caption for an all too well-known patriarchal definition, categorization, and management of female violence. Not least due to its documentary verisimilitude, Döblin's text, unwittingly or not, becomes a pernicious arena for violent and heterosexual discursive attempts to control the gestalt of lesbianism.

Degenerate Eros

Like Döblin's story, Kästner's novel, *Fabian. Die Geschichte eines Moralisten* from 1931, follows in the trend of New Objectivity closely, offering, in reporter-style prose, the story of a single, cynical protagonist wading through the cold, murky waters of urban living. Characterized on the jacket of its English translation as an "unparalleled personalization of the collapse of the Weimar Republic," *Fabian* devotes many of its pages to unfavorable descriptions of sexual practices, many of which are lesbian interactions.[16] Like other heterosexual representations of lesbians, Kästner's portrayals center around degeneracy, unnatural desires, and a general social condition of immorality. While nearly all the women in *Fabian* are unrestrainably sexual, the sexual excesses of the lesbians pose the greatest threat to—and also most clearly indicate the decline of—the health of the city and its citizens. This commonplace attribution of the collapse of Weimar to a sexual immorality propagated largely by women both masks and marks the relationship between reactionary masculinity and the rise of fascist totalitarianism and its ostensibly strict morality. *Fabian's* subtext, similar to that of Goebbels' 1929 novel, *Michael*, is an attempt to reclaim a clearly delineated and powerful masculinity through the definition and management of its binary: femininity and female sexuality. In light of this, the oversexed hetero- and homosexual women might be read as representations of a disease afflicting men, a dis-ease that must be either eliminated or minimized to cure the city and the republic.

In a piece on contemporary women that appeared in 1929, Lola Landau writes: "Women no longer wait for marriage, frequently not even desiring such a tie for themselves, which they fear might hinder their free development" (702). Landau's remark bridges the anxiety circulating so forcefully in Kästner's text, appearing as it does amidst demographics that just after World War One showed a population with three million more women than men, where the marriage rate held steady but where the divorce rate grew at a phenomenal pace.[17]

In the following passage from *Fabian*, female sexuality is brought home to the fold even though it is still exhibited in an aggressive and non-patriarchal manner. A beautiful model, Selow, who is finally disgusted by the sexual attentions of her sculptor girlfriend, interrupts the pleasure of the crowd: "'No!" screamed Selow again. "'I've had enough. I'm fed up to the back teeth! I want a man! A man, do you hear me? Get away from me, you randy goat!' She hauled Labude from his stool, gave him a kiss, slammed her hat on her head, and dragged the young man to the door, scarcely giving him time to snatch up his coat. 'Vive la difference!' she cried." (71) Curiously, it is in this bar full of crossed-dressed women, where lesbians dangerously appropriate the male space, role, and activity, that Kästner recovers the possibility, at least, of heterosexuality and some form of male identity. Still, the visible markings of traditional masculinity are rendered ineffectual by the women in waistcoats and high collars who are acting out roles reserved for heterosexual men. Since he is unable to control the visible representation of gender differences, Kästner must appeal to a more substantive indicator, namely heterosexual desire. Selow, the model, embodies this appeal. Sickened by the perversity and excess of the masculine women, she turns to the male friend and leaves with him. In this fashion, she realigns herself with "natural" sexuality and consequently marks his masculine, heterosexual authenticity, although not authority. Selow's switch reduces the blurred categories of gender and sexuality in the bar to a tableau where the cross-dressers are impostors and performers rather than being anchored in reasonable reality or genuine resistant practice.

Both Weirauch's and von Urbanitzky's texts seem ultimately to have relinquished control over the signifier "lesbian" and we are reminded of Judith Butler's remark about "the uncontrollability of discourse [and] its penchant for superseding and reversing the purposes for which it is instrumentally deployed." (119) This apparent lack of control is a common thread in lesbian-authored texts and, in a sense, this measure works, again in Butler's words, to "undermine politically the 'category of homosexuality.'" (120) Thus, due to their common trait of indeterminacy, lesbian characters in the examined texts engage in conversation with one another through their participation in and/or contradiction of the prescribed categories of deviance and pathology. Even though heterosexual representations of lesbianism are not monolithic but rather depict lesbianisms, there is a clear line of demarcation between lesbian-created characters and those caught and marked in the heteronormative attitudinal prose. To readers, the latter appear to have supported all extant cultural suspicions of deviant or inverted sexuality. Lesbian-created texts presented women who questioned their heterosexuality or who experimented with their sexuality with an array of identificatory models. Such models may have facilitated a deliberation among readers of their (sexual) identity or a confirmation of personal and behavioral attributes. Moreover, for some of their readers they constituted positive symbolic sites on which to celebrate and enjoy a community of "like-minded" as much as did the actual clubs and public dances that were so popular in Berlin at the time.

Beyond the Pale

In 1886, when the Berlin Museum für Völkerkunde opened, its collection contained more than 10,000 African objects, indicating that the population of the Second German Empire already had enjoyed some exposure to people of color.[18] By 1914, on the eve of World War One, Imperial Germany had colonized such geographically dispersed areas of the African continent as Togo, Cameroon, and those that had become known as German Southwest Africa (now Namibia) and German East Africa (now Tanzania). The first physical presence on a grand scale of Africans in the German homeland came about through the 1920 occupation of the Ruhr by French troops who, in 1923, aided by Belgian troops, moved into the Rhineland. During the years of occupation, between thirty and forty thousand African troops from Algeria, Tunisia, Madagascar, and Morocco were stationed throughout the Ruhr and the Rhineland.[19]

The presence in Germany of this double insult—a French occupational force constituted mainly by Arab-African soldiers whom German soldiers had already met in combat during the war—caused an intense national resentment. Given the belief in a strong German link between landscape and national character, the occupation of the Rhineland fed into German nationalism during the years of occupation and zealously proprietary and national sentiments were the order of the day.[20] The following statements from male characters in Herzog's *Die Buben* are thus self explanatory: "The Rhine, Germany's river, not her border (108)" and "the Rhine, the desecrated river of the fatherland." (319) In addition Max Schneckenburger's poem from 1840, "Die Wacht am Rhein," was receiving renewed popularity and is quoted in its entirety in the novel.[21] Racist statements about the African soldiers were made on the floor of the German National Assembly; but the most extreme manifestation of racial nationalism is no doubt the medal struck by the Bavarian mint in 1920 depicting, on one side, a naked woman shackled to an oversized helmeted penis purportedly representing a black French soldier.[22]

Considering that such uninhibited, public discourses on race and nation were circulating at the time, the percolation and articulation of the issues into popular fiction make these texts important sites for private and intimate negotiations of selfhood, community, and nationhood. All the same, as Abdul R. JanMohamed rightly points out, since most readers seldom had contact with the objects of racial representations, the truth value of those representations was not an overwhelming concern in such fictions.[23] Be that as it may, it is precisely representations that allow us to gain insights into some of the many negotiations Weimar Germans undertook to understand and structure the world they inhabited. Otherness thus becomes a signifier for cultural subject positions, ab/normality, and power.

Turning to the texts, we find that a racial discourse pitting black against white is almost exclusively a phenomenon found in urban novels. After all, cities attracted immigrants and it was here that the "Americanization" of German culture was most apparent, among other places in the many jazz clubs. But color is not the only constituent in Weimar racial discourses. Images of non-German nationalities are also sites of identificatory differentiation. Most certainly, the glorification in *Heimat* fiction (frequently rural fiction about the native German home/land) of the "true German" man and woman similarly shores up racial purity in a racially charged atmosphere against a deep-rooted fear of miscegenation. In this section I attempt to plumb conventions about race and color as they appeared in popular fiction during the particular historical period of Weimar Germany. This investigation of popular texts and their contexts strives to expose the numerous ways in which difference is categorized and codified and to uncover the complex and often contradictory discourses through and in which women shaped their (racialized) notions of self and national identity.

The Black Mark

The unspoken is often as tendentious as the spoken and Gustav Frenssen's *Heimat* novel, *The Pastor of Poggsee* from 1922, illustrates this.[24] The quote, "[t]hey could see ... between twenty and thirty men, one of them looked like a negro, and five or six ... like criminals," (335) contains one of the many pernicious threads making up the multi-patterned fabric of racial and racist discourse that was such an integral part of Weimar culture. Frenssen's rhetoric or, to use a Dickensian expression, "dress of thought," in this passage is transparent in its allegation of a similarity between "negroes" and criminals. The ease with which such a notion was pronounced and the high currency it possessed should, of course, be measured against Germany's colonial past and the presence of foreign, black soldiers on the desecrated Rhine. This particular combination was not Frenssen's invention inasmuch as black men were indeed perceived to be the embodiment of criminal behavior. The notion was largely based on the dualistic symbolism of white and black, a dyad that traditionally has been allegorized to mean "good and evil, salvation and damnation, civilization and savagery, superiority and inferiority, intelligence and emotion ...."[25] Linking Otherness to criminality during the Weimar Republic does not stand out by its singularity. But, at this particular time, the bifurcation of black/white, good/evil effectively enabled The Society for Racial Hygiene (founded in 1905 for eugenic reasons) to deprive German citizens of color of some of their most fundamental rights, in effect treating them like criminals: in 1919 the society began conducting sterilizations, ostensibly to protect Germany against and eliminate what were perceived as racial diseases. Four hundred mandatory procedures had been recorded by 1937, none of them on a legal basis.[26]

A reductive binary schema of opposites marks most literary representations of race in popular novels. In the following context, it is useful to remember that the pair "subject/object" or "self/other" occupies an important place in such a binary. This becomes clear when considering Frenssen's line from *The Pastor*: "[T]he negro-like creature had said he was the best dancer in San Paolo and [he] wanted to demonstrate his art in the open space before the altar." (336) Discussions of (other) race(s) indicate discussions of self and the above quote is no exception. Troubling properties are once more projected onto an imaginary character, here the "negro-like creature." His symbolic function as the Other is to shoulder the negative, in this case ugliness, bestiality, racial inferiority, and sacrilege. In so doing, one's self is separated from such troubling characteristics. The separation process is greatly facilitated through the textual presence of a religious space, the open space before the altar. That creates a shared cultural text among the readers upon whose outrage the writer can count when the profane transgression—dancing—is suggested, not to say performed.

The nature of the above act of dancing directs our attention to the stereotyped rhythmic abilities of Africans: "She sings like a child and a negro;""Down at Petermann's you could hear two saxophones sob in their heartbreaking nigger [sic] sadness."[27] These lines from a Baum novel demonstrate that liberal (Baum) as well as conservative writers (Frenssen) participated and were therefore implicated in confirming stereotypical discourses about race. This fear of contamination by, but at the same time also fascination with, foreign (and erotic) cultural influences finds a resonance in some of the responses to the influx of new and scandalous dances into Germany, many of them from America. The new dances, among them the Charleston, with their emphasis on corporeality and eroticism, were thought to have come from American blacks. Accordingly, they bore witness to the growing American influence and the strong seductive attraction "negro decadence" supposedly held for the masses. Earlier, another popular dance, the Tango, that likewise originated from a far-away and purportedly wild and swarthy continent, was considered so indecent that Wilhelm II, in 1913, had prohibited all men in uniform from dancing it.[28]

Dancing also marks interracial proximity in Vicki Baum's *Helene*. In one scene from this work, a group of academics is enjoying a summer evening with some wine and music. Among them, an American guest, Harry Samson, "a black man of superb figure, faultlessly attired" (85) asks a woman for the next dance. A "sweaty, languorous tango was beginning to stir their pulses." (89) As they dance, someone describes the couple as "chocolate puff with whipped cream." (89) In the text, the black/white color scheme, although in plain sight, is not visible, that is, not suspect, as long as Samson is intermingling with men. It is his proximity to the white woman that impels the recognition of the racial other. Such a pairing, black man/white woman, confers the unspoken realm of sexuality, here invigorated by the fiery, alien rhythms of the tango, upon both the black, American man *and* the white, German woman. Consequently, this particular composition imputes serious infringement upon and threats to white patriarchal property rights, both over women in general and purity of the race in particular.

Amerikanisierung, or Americanization, was a phenomenon perceived to be linked to the process of rapid, modern urbanization taking place in Weimar. Associated with, among other things, technology, movies, and jazz, the last connection had introduced black Americans as agents of exotic sounds and rhythms that in many conservative quarters were considered decadent. To others, jazz was "the very incarnation of American vitalism."[29] It was a cross-cultural phenomenon in the true sense. In a 1929 survey of the German working class conducted by Erich Fromm, question 338 "Do you like Jazz?" was answered in the positive by forty percent of those surveyed and in the negative by fifty percent (148-50). Surprisingly, despite official rejection by the Nazi party, as many Nazi as Communist party members approved of jazz according to Fromm's survey. Among the criticisms lodged against it were its lack of soul and discipline; apparently, German musicians had difficulty moving from the traditional march-time with emphasis on the first beat to the equi-weighted beats of jazz.[30] In addition, the "no" votes in the survey characterized jazz as decadent, un-German, negro music, and immoral. The immorality objection stemmed from its perceived erotic stimulus which became a major reason for its rejection by those who were demanding stricter (sexual) morals.[31] Finally, the sensuous nature of jazz apparently separated it from the indigenous high culture and inspired Alfred Rosenberg to claim that "this cretinized American art form symbolized everything that was insidiously evil in a Jewish-Negro plot to undermine German culture."[32]

Many of these sentiments found their way into other manifestations of popular culture, such as fiction. Baum's references do not overtly carry any of Rosenberg's sinister connotations. She and many fellow liberals tended to romanticize the exoticism and Otherness of black culture that were viewed so negatively by people on the right.[33] But, in their own way, many of the well-meaning or intrigued sentiments from popular culture buttressed stereotypical understandings and characterizations of black culture and its agents. Moreover, linking sad, childlike, spontaneous musical and rhythmic expressions to race trivializes and excludes the historical reasons for the so often sentimentalized black sorrow. Once again, the texts make no authentic pronouncement about black culture; rather, among the things those utterances do is to display ways in which contemporary racial issues were generally discussed. One effect of such discourses was the infantilization of black creativity and performativity, which in turn rendered the cultural products, in some quarters, ahistorical, harmless, and ready for unhazardous consumption. Simultaneously, devaluing an "alien" cultural expression becomes a self-validating gesture. In the binary schema of the non/self and of cultural definitional criteria, such a gesture confirms the solipsistic view that there is only one right culture, namely one's own. Historically, the 1920s was the period when the need for confirmation of the superiority of Germanic culture was the greatest. Blamed and scorned by the rest of the western world for World War One, maimed and torn apart within its borders by defeat, political violence, and the unrelenting march of modernity, German selfhood needed all the boosts it could get, even if they came about by degrading the culture of others.

Returning to Frenssen's quote—"and [he] wanted to demonstrate his art in the open space before the altar"—we discern authorial anxieties about cultural shortcomings inside his own racial community. On one level, the scene and its setting—an altar in the woods—

nostalgically connote a celebration of a mythical ritual in the Germanic ur-*Wald*, and it indicates the complex and often contradictory struggles for spaces and characteristics that German nationalists could lay claim to through an imagined past. In this instance, the mere fact that the black-like character proposes to dance in front of the open-air altar emphasizes his disruption of what by extension is German Christian cultural space. It makes him no better than a savage, upon whom undesirable properties are easily transferred. By way of the familiar strategy of displacement, the outsider in this passage is shouldering some of the contemporary sins: questioning, or worse, rejecting a Germanic past, thereby dismissing mythical national role models, such as Siegfried and Wotan and thus profaning the destiny of the Nordic race.[34] The cleansing action of such an act of transference is one of its most powerful consequences. Once outsiders disappear from the narrative, as such characters invariably do, they take their characteristics along with them, cleansing the German community in the process and removing from the notion of German-ness any danger of contamination. Weimar culture repeatedly designates race as the marker of contemporary anxieties over (national) subjectivity, linked as it was—and is—with moral propriety and Western comprehension.

There are, of course, also works of popular fiction that, due to their pronounced lack of ethnic others, advocate a stable, simple, i.e., pure, national subject position. One such work, Herzog's *Die Buben* from 1920, achieves national rootedness by means of the German woman portrayed as a strong, intelligent individual, fiercely proud of her geographical location, and clear about her goals. This, interestingly enough, is the position vacated by the male subjectivity with the defeat of World War One and so we see emerge a new adjustment: in attempts to create a convincing national identity, the woman takes on male properties that have been maligned when linked with women in other settings, as in the case of working class women, women of color, and the "new" woman. Nonetheless, in these *Heimat* novels, traditional masculine characteristics such as agency, rootedness, and intellectual strength are feminized by means of their overt and single-minded telos: in the absence of a powerful male presence, to raise the next generation in tandem with protecting, blessing, and tending the sacred soil of the fatherland. Herzog's novel relates how two young boys grow into staunch and stellar German men. The guiding principle in their young lives is the "bright and shiny integrity of the feminine spirit" of Christiane

Opterberg, their mother. This immensely popular novel glorifies a "strongly rooted," maternal femininity that unselfishly, like Christiane, "in silent happiness gave and gave [and] only then felt the abundance of her wealth."[35] The Christiane Opterbergs of this utopian world would perhaps be able to oust and replace the modern—and thus un-German—woman as a role model for German womanhood, but only as long as their power, vigor, and competence were directed away from their own individual, narcissistic pleasures and instead aimed toward an imagined national community. As Christiane advises her future daughter-in-law, such qualities are needed to make women their husbands' true companions as long as women know their place and "don't want to be know-it-alls, because that would, of course, deprive men of their enjoyment of being the stronger sex." (344) The caveat lies in the definition of women. Only good, German women could and should be emblematic of Germanness and responsible for its continuation; and, yet, such a woman was defined by possessing proper German-ness and maternal instincts. By insisting that those properties were genetic and consequently inherent in "true Germans," all obstacles of such circular logic are overcome in the text.

Nationalist and racial discourses address men and women differently, and German national struggles after World War One are no exception. By assigning to women dual roles, as both symbols of the nation and biological producers of the ethnically correct group, properties ordinarily dreaded in women are redeemed. Moreover, such a nationalist discourse impresses upon women a moral and national responsibility not to waste their ethnic reproducibility. This made *Heimat* fiction very powerful in traditional circles. Through this genre, women, whose experience of the war on the home front had led to greater recognition of their own survival skills, community qualities, and independence, were provided with respectable avenues for their newly found strengths. After the loss of World War One, fictional women could once again build up the German nation with unwavering German nationalist men: "We must go back to the family, to the bosom of simplicity, health, and vigor ... [and there], with the help of our ancestral gods, we will struggle back to our faith [in ourselves]."[36]

Raced Sexualities

The claim by Foucault that nineteen-century technologies of science, medicine, psychiatry, and demographics shaped sexuality as the matrix of subjectivity, is amply born out in Weimar racial popular fiction. The form which sexuality supposedly took among people of non-Western origin was considered primitive, denoting a "stage that is past, condemned, and even feared ...."[37] By inferring a causality between "primitive" and "sexually intensive," a non-white, raced sexuality came to be seen as boundless, uninhibited, and worse, unconstrainable.[38] Of course, this perception, containing within it the colonial psychology of superiority and inferiority, was restricted neither in time nor space to the Weimar Republic but was shared by the other Western colonial powers. Yet the notion that German culture was being raped by the occupation of the Rhineland casts its symbolic net widely, counting among its catch the fear of venereal disease—purportedly spread by the racially "other" body—and of miscegenation.[39]

In the construction of German, white, bourgeois womanhood, sexuality was a crucial element, not least in the way in which aspects of identity politics intersected with each other. What appeared to pervert the formation of a constant national fe/male identity at this time, was the fact that the boundaries between gender, race, sexuality, and criminality were shifting as prejudicial fears and fantasies were transferred arbitrarily among racialized and/or marginalized groups. As Marjorie Garber has shown, such transferences are "self-evidently a sign of what we have been calling 'category crisis.'" (270) Cultural enterprises such as stereotypical portrayals of raced sexuality were therefore all the more important to help strengthen an image of German-ness, including German womanhood, purged of all negative connotations. Wolfgang von Lengerke's *Gloria* presents the viewer with an array of undigested racial stereotypes. Anti-Semitism, homophobia, and sexism notwithstanding, the text offers up representations of a series of undesirable sexualities, ranging from exotic/erotic Asian women and inscrutable/criminal Chinese men to black servants and black, poor criminals, and a singular mention of "negro women" with no stated occupations. The latters' membership in a women's state, that the novel's female protagonist, Gloria, plans to create on her land somewhere in Texas, is turned down, for Gloria "refused to admit differently colored [*Andersfarbige*] people into her community." (91)

After a disingenuous nod to the fact that white, too, belongs on the color spectrum, the text offers no explanation as to why "differently colored" women should not be admitted to a utopian community. Female sexuality in one of its many manifestations provides part of the answer. Sander Gilman points out that, by the eighteenth century, black sexuality has become the icon for deviant sexuality in general.[40] The black woman was the embodiment of the sexualized female, a notion clearly reinforced by the many live shows during the Weimar years by black women performers, the Chocolate Kiddies and Josephine Baker being the most famous of these. Baker's body, festooned with bananas or exhibited with leopards, marked her performances as clear exhibitions of the erotic Other while they naughtily, even scandalously, titillated her audience. Moreover, it was precisely through racism's construction of her as Other that she afforded her audience a sexualized space where they could at once enjoy but also condemn such "savage" sexuality. Obviously, self-respecting white women wanted to avoid the link to sexuality, moral corruption, and disease which marked the body of the black woman.[41] Although apparently a male-authored send-up about feminism and feminist separatism, *Gloria* presumably would have legitimized itself even more in the eyes of respectable readers by including black women in a women's state, thereby vilifying it. But perhaps such an inter-racial alignment would have been too far beyond the pale to be considered, even in jest.

Black women are not the only markers of the sexualized female body; Asian women bear a similar burden in popular fiction. Since the turn of the century, European fascination with things Asian had been growing and with the height of colonial rule came both the moral disavowal of colonized cultures and their very appropriation, the latter mainly through the collection of objects d'art and artifacts and a burgeoning tourism. Simultaneously, the Orient became a fantasy realm for, among other things, forbidden, dangerous, indeed "inscrutable" eroticism and sexuality. Into this realm were projected sexual longings and fantasies illegitimized by the increasing sterility of modern Western official morality and yet encouraged by the commodification impulse of consumer capitalism. The following passage from *Gloria* speaks to stereotypes about Asian female sexuality: "But suddenly ... appears a doll's face, a sweet, small, childlike figure with large lids covering her eyes and a mouth like a flower, mysteriously smiling .... Such are the girls from Chinatown ... who in their Asian faces carry the still lust that in this strange Asia drives the feverish European crazy." (153) This passage demonstrates how, in the case of female sexuality, racialized and sexualized bodies are similarly interchangeable and how one racialized body may double as another. It bears out JanMohamed's statement that European writers commodify "natives" by robbing them of individuality and subjectivity, rendering them generic.[42] By changing a few stereotypical adjectival qualifiers, Asian becomes Indian, Native American, African, Gypsy, Jewish or any other ethnic group deemed inferior or marginalized as Other.

Further indications that racialized sexuality is not limited to Africans may be found in Kästner's *Fabian*. The novel contains a short, curious passage that corrals a motley crew of Others into a stylistic and demographic holding pen: "Over there ... is a cafe where Chinese sit with Berliner hookers, only Chinese. There, in the front, is a bar where perfumed guys dance with elegant actors and chic English folks ....To the right, on the corner, lies a hotel where only Japanese live and next door there is a restaurant where Russian and Hungarian Jews cheat and touch each other for money." (101) The list of aliens is squeezed into a short paragraph and because the items on the list, despite exhibiting many nationalities, are not always separated by punctuation, the aesthetics of the representation effectively lump them together as interchangeable constituents of the Other. It is the stereotypical pairing of Otherness with assumed suitable properties and the link to female sexuality that is the focus of the following investigation.

When we consider the physical segregation of nationalities indicated in the passage, it breaks down in the case of the Jews. In their case, ethnicity conquers nationality, and Eastern European Jews seek each others' company, apparently driven by base monetary desires.[43] But a closer look at the passage reveals another space where nationality appears to be of no importance (but for the text itself): in the bar, sexuality, narcissism, and artistic talent make bodily contact; apparently these kinds of characteristics and dispositions cut right across national boundaries. The Chinese (as opposed to the Japanese who evidently live without any cultural or racial appendages) are closely linked to sexuality, and an illicit sexuality at that. The emphasis on "only Chinese" signifies a segregation according to nationality but it also ties Chinese closer to a commercial eroticism in which none of the other groups mentioned takes part. At first glance, German-ness is not an issue here. The reader is busy negotiating the various national and other collective coherences and identities imposed by the text which simultaneously exclude the right to self-definition on the part of the groups. Yet, despite linking sex with aliens in the case of the Chinese and the English, the sexual agents in both cases do in fact appear to be German. Not the respectable, containable and contained bourgeois sexuality, of course, but rather its negation: prostitutes and other persons of questionable sexuality. By linking non-German elements—that also make the sexuality visible—to the (German) sexual illicitness, the passage makes such sexuality alien to *respectable* German-ness. Once more, the notions of national affiliation and sexuality emerge as inextricable aspects of the constitution of the subject. The (fictive) ethnicities produce an arena around which nationalism organizes itself and German national identity comes into view at once buttressed and circumscribed by its excluded properties.

There seems to be no end to writing Otherness on the human body. From Winckelmann likening Moors' mouths to those of monkeys, to Jews with predator-like glances, and to lesbians' lithe bodies ready to strike like birds of prey, the list goes on.[44] The obvious mechanism at work is the degradation of difference and such a recourse bears particularly upon the turbulent Weimar years. This period experienced a blurring of those binary distinctions between categories that ordinarily constituted the dominant order: man/woman, heterosexual/invert, self/other, right/wrong. And yet, it is the fear of losing those very distinct and discriminating categories that results in border-crossing comparisons. Weimar (popular) fiction abounds with fictional constructions that transgress orderly categories and that, in turn, act as sites for fears of dissolution of national and "private" identity. Invoking such discursive representations creates a symbolic body whose culpability is certain. Further, the distance from certain culpability to inexorable sacrifice is not far. One only needs to think of the witch hunts, slavery, and the Holocaust to realize that such fears have been acted upon historically with horrific consequences.

There are no liberating moments in racist representations. White readers in Weimar Germany read and reproduced raced stereotypes as much as white readers in other Western countries. More often than not, it was an uncritical, but never innocent, mental activity that presumably confirmed one's membership in the desirable group. Where women were concerned, the frequent linking of Otherness to a dangerous female sexuality made such a group membership tenuous. The racialized sexualities inherently castigated other ethnicities as well as modern female sexuality, points of view that seemed comfortable in many quarters. At the same time, the destabilization of boundaries in effect may have had conflicting effects. If we look at the material reality of the Weimar Republic and its eager affair with modernity, it appears that many women were finding personal—albeit often ambiguous—empowerment precisely in their sexual freedom. Consequently, stereotypes that confirmed their racial superiority while at the same time condemning their sexual experimentation may have been less heartily embraced by women, at least for a few years.

German?/Jewish?

Popular novels from the Weimar period strike the reader as revealing a somewhat remarkable lack of sensitivity towards their fictional Jewish characters. Jewish and non-Jewish alike, the writers seem to have created stereotypes of the worst kind—the greedy Jew, the power-hungry Jew, the separatist Jew, for instance.

Upon further reflection, however, it becomes clear that such a sentiment places me historically *after* the Holocaust and that the urgent need I feel to warn the writers to abstain from their frivolous stereotyping is based on the horrified hindsight of someone who has been reading these texts after 1945. The texts examined were not privy to our post-Holocaust knowledge and thus this section, in particular, should be understood as an expression of my spatial and historical locality. All texts, but these in particular, should be historicized for they are part and parcel of a discourse on Jewishness and German-ness. As such, they engage historical and ideological contexts that cannot be ignored. Consequently, my examination will move between the realms of before and after while constantly taking stock of its historical whereabouts. The two strands of reading may throw some light on emerging paradigms of Jewishness and assimilation. It is my hope that this and the other investigations in this chapter will advance our understanding of the location of popular fiction in the fateful discourses of German, Self, and Other that circulated in the Weimar Republic.

Henry Giroux's statement, that "the struggle over identity can no longer be seriously considered outside the politics of representation ..." (22) applies precisely to the Weimar Republic and the proliferation of representational media of the time, among them popular fiction, film, and illustrated weeklies. How were these typological perceptions mediated through contemporary popular fiction, and did they modify the way in which some of those Weimar citizens imagined themselves and/or were imagined? While we can trace textual stereotypes with relative ease, proof of direct causality is less available to us, if it exists at all, and we can thus only speculate on their effect in materiality. Instead, because this section and, indeed, chapter, inevitably are embedded in a "privileged" knowledge of the Holocaust, I must consider, as does Sander Gilman, the "catastrophic potential" of those stereotypes as a basis for communal understanding and action.[45]

Since much has already been said and written about Jewish intellectuals in Weimar,[46] I shall turn my attention to representations of "the Jew" in those cultural manifestations that reached the widest reading audience, namely popular fiction. Moreover, in all of the texts examined here, assimilation issues are thematized through a male narrative, possibly—even probably—expressing traditional notions of the universality of the male subject or a closely connected idea that these notions of agency would be a male prerogative. This particular investigation does not mean to ignore the different issues pertaining to gender and antisemitism. Indeed, such is the subject matter of the literary representation of Jewish women that it deserves a separate examination which, in this case, is not part of my focus.

Popular texts of the period resonate with discrepant interpretations of orthodox and reformed Judaism, each responding to, as well as constituting, cultural discourses in circulation at that time. It is crucial to emphasize the heterogeneity of the Jewish population in Weimar Germany or we come dangerously close to essentializing Jewishness. Due to the enormity of the subject, I shall examine only a few of the many positions concerning Jewishness, cultural behavior, and representation, which doubtlessly leaves a great deal unsaid. What I undertake, then, is a two-fold examination of the then current inscriptions of Jewishness: first that of the Jews as Other; second, the problematic assimilation attempts of Jewish characters as portrayed in popular fiction. Since this fictional, and increasingly nervous, discourse, with one exception, arises out of cultural and political circumstances that are specific to Weimar, what follows is a short review of the material conditions of actual Jewish communities in the German Republic.

An emancipatory and assimilatory rhetoric on behalf of the German Jewish community had existed since the Enlightenment. By 1850 there was, at least on paper, no legal distinction drawn between Jews and gentiles in Prussia; this extended to the Second Reich as a whole upon its creation in 1871.[47] While such political emancipation met with much resistance from many Christian communities, it was also not without problems for the Jewish communities.[48] As Bluma Goldstein points out, German, or most European Jews for that matter, now faced the predicament of assimilating into societies which had always considered themselves superior, while at the same time maintaining their Jewish identity (4). I want to argue that versions of that dilemma and (again in Goldstein's words) "this very difficult, often destructive transition and unresolved assimilation," (45) aggravated by growing antisemitism and the politics of a national German identity, are played out repeatedly in cultural texts circulating in Weimar.

During the early years of the Second Reich, Jewish participation in economic and professional activities grew at a rate considered alarming by conservative and/or antisemitic segments of the population. During the years 1919 to 1933, the German Jewish population was calculated at approximately 600,000, amounting to one percent of the population in Germany. Also during this period, the figures concerning the integration of Jews into the German economy were high: for example, 3.5 percent of all trade positions, and forty percent of all German textile firms had Jewish owners. Of retail and wholesale clothing businesses, sixty percent were in Jewish hands, and in 1932, seventy-nine percent of German department stores had Jewish owners. Among the professionals in Germany, eleven percent of doctors and sixteen percent of lawyers were Jewish. It is also worth mentioning that two of the largest publishing houses, Ullstein and Mosse, were owned by Jews.[49] Jews were also numerous as members of the intelligentsia and the artistic community. But there was another, growing segment of the Jewish population which did not feature in the widely heralded success story of Weimar Jews. Claims that the inflation had hardly affected Jews were blatantly fallacious. During World War One and after, in the subsequent years of growing inflation from 1912 to 1924, the number of Jews with a taxable income of 5,000 marks or more fell from 10.6 percent to 5.8 percent.[50] Concomitantly, the number of Jewish people with a taxable income of less than 1,200 marks rose by 10 percent from 73.3 percent to 83.6 percent.[51] This is to say that around 1923–1924 approximately 500,000 Jews, five-sixths of the entire German-Jewish community, were among the working/poor. By 1923, the Jewish community in Berlin had found it necessary to establish nineteen soup kitchens, seven shelters, one employment bureau, and one placement office for members of its community. Such numbers translated into some even darker statistics: in 1922, sixty-one Jews committed suicide; and by 1925 that number had risen to 117, amounting to twelve percent of all suicides in Berlin. The ratio of suicides in 1925 for Catholics was thirty-two per 100,000, among the Protestants it was forty-five per 100,000, but it was as high as sixty-five per 100,000 Jews.[52] So divergent were the realities of German Jews in the Weimar Republic.

Such disparate (and often desperate) conditions should for all intents and purposes have brought into conversation a set of diverse perceptions and representations of Jewishness, of German-ness, and of class constitution during the Weimar years. Yet there was little, if any, improvement in the quality of the discourse. Quantitatively speaking, the intensity of the debate grew and with it, the question of national identity and belonging. The long-formed habits of antisemitism were, not unexpectedly, stronger than any incipient new paradigm. Defeat in the First World War—in which many Jewish soldiers had fought and given their lives for their German fatherland—and the ensuing economic chaos inflicted psychic as well as material wounds that had their horrible and only too visible manifestations in the maimed and torn-apart bodies of a large section of the male population.[53] Such daily reminders of defiled German honor was an excellent medium for the sustained growth of a particularly virulent strain of German nationalism, which recalled the war as, among other things, a conflict in which Germany had fought united as a nation.

In the years just after the war, quite a few small—often secret—right-wing groups sprang up, existing side by side with large groups of Jewish artists, intellectuals, and influential business people. In addition to hating Jews in particular, these groups also tapped into and added their voice to other dislikes flourishing in the German Republic at the time, for example, hatred of the Weimar constitution, of liberalism, of the Versailles Treaty, of Berlin (the urban phenomenon), and of modernity in general. It was common to find one or more of these realms of concern or fear embodied in the fictional Jewish figure. An article in *Morgenrot*, a monthly magazine for "cultural and social reform," collapses Jews, Socialists, and Freemasons under the rubrics of "Rotjuda" and "Weltjuda" (185-86). These rather undifferentiated categories were meant to cover a broad range of adversaries to petty bourgeois, conservative, or antisemitic political positions. The "red" Jew and the "world" Jew were part and parcel of the stereotypical views of Weimar Jewry as Communists or liberals, big-time capitalists, and/or members of secret, world-wide organizations sworn to bring Christianity and Western culture to an end. The terms clearly divulge how the psychological undercurrents, mobilized by the fears of general disempowerment, converged upon the Jew, in particular, as the common scapegoat for all that was perceived to be wrong. Thus, Hitler's question in *Mein Kampf*: "Is this a Jew? ... Is this a German?" once more lends a weighty voice to the split between Jewishness and German-ness that was, in fact, an agenda of long standing among many Germans. Embedded in the same question is also a search for the marks of a national character or identity. Not only would such marks identify those who deserved to be members of the *Volk* but it would, of course, also isolate those who did not. In a perverse way, Hitler, on the one hand, articulates one of the cruxes of assimilation as perceived by the Jews, while, on the other, he exacerbates the dislodging of those national and cultural positionalities that Jewish communities had painfully gained since their emancipation.

The Power of Assimilation

In 1911, a novella entitled "Raffael Butmann," appeared in *Ost und West*, the first Jewish magazine. It was written by Vicki Baum who was of Jewish descent and the story is, among other things, a scathing critique of East European Jewry.[54] According to Brenner, some of the magazine's producers thought writings like Baum's story "went too far in their anti-Eastern sentiment" (112). Curiously enough, it appeared again in 1922, serialized in three parts, in the *Leipziger Illustrirte*. Despite its Wilhelminian conception, it then became part of the Weimar discussion about high/low culture, East/West Jewry, and assimilation. Hence its inclusion in this investigation. "Raffael Gutmann" puts forward the predicament of assimilation in the shape of a struggle for greater cultural freedom from the Jewish Orthodox tradition, here considered antiquated and unadaptable.[55] Through the hopeless struggle of its protagonist, "Raffael Gutmann" also becomes a story about the unacceptability of cultural migration in Germany, the outmoded hostility of Orthodoxy toward modernity, the closing of ranks by the bearers of those elusive marks that constitute German-ness, and the cost of departing from one's own cultural position, even if it does bear the stigma of Otherness.

Raffael, a Jewish adolescent of orthodox origin, ardently wants to participate in the gentile world: "There was a city out there, streets ... without womenfolk yelling from the steps or kids in Caftans." (307) But Raffael's culture has, within its own confines, de-centered the dominant culture—the unorthodox realm—by excluding that world and denying it any validity. There is no bridge between the orthodox Judaic and Christian cultural terrains but the one Raffael is trying to force. He shares the fate of those who, in Kafka's words, "with their little hind legs ... were still glued to the Jewishness of their fathers and with their little front legs ... found no new ground." (337) Indeed, in this text, Raffael cannot occupy both positions anymore than he can cross over; he is "at the barred window, so unsalvably enmeshed and caught ...." (354) Any option for change dies with him when he lies down on the railway tracks just as (unbeknownst to him? The text leaves this question pending) an oncoming express train approaches in the distance.

The *Leipziger Illustrierte* reprinted "Raffael Gutmann" three and a half months after the murder of Walter Rathenau, the Jewish foreign minister of the Weimar Republic. Vilified as the Jew responsible for the depths of shame of a defeated Germany, Rathenau was attacked and murdered in Berlin-Grunewald on June 24, 1922, by assailants who used a submachine gun and a hand grenade.[56] In a period of right-wing terror that culminated in the Beer-Hall Putsch of 1923, Baum's text, in its own modest way, becomes part of the nervous activities linked to defensive or assimilatory discourses. In this debate, the body of antisemitic literature was expanding, as was the number of antisemitic organizations. The thought that Jewish culture had contributed positively to the Western (i.e., Christian) world was extremely provocative. Partly in response to that notion, so well articulated in Heine's comment a century earlier that the Bible was "the great family chronicle of the Jews ... [that] became the national book in the Germanic North ..." (186), Houston Stewart Chamberlain's work separating the Jewish and Aryan elements in European culture and the Christian faith had become one of the basic arguments in racist and antisemitic discourse.[57] This conceptualization was heartily embraced and furthered by the Freikorps and other German nationalist organizations such as the *Deutsche Schutz- und Trutzbund* (Hamburg), the *Deutschvölkische Bund* (Hamburg), the *Reichshammerbund* (Hamburg), and the *Deutschbund* (Gotha), which had sprung up since the turn of the century, espousing and promoting essentially antisemitic principles.[58]

In Weimar Germany, race was as important a property for the Germanic Christian or Aryan community as for the Jews, Slavs, or Africans, for that matter. A racial discourse was very much part of everyday life: "The German public is possessed by the Jewish Question," complains the 1929 introduction to a re-issued work on the nature of antisemitism.[59] In this context it is important to keep in mind that the Jew as the emblem of alienness is a cultural construction effected by socio-economic and politico-historical power-relations; it was not chosen by members of the Jewish population themselves. Elaine Grosz has pointed out that in marginal and outsider positions are embedded oppressions as well as strategies of resistance to those very oppressions (77). Isaac Landauer, a character from Lion Feuchtwanger's 1925 *Jud Süss* (*Power*), embodies such a resistance in that "[h]e wore his caftan as he wore his skin .... In it he entered the closets of princess and of the Emperor .... He was indispensable, and this was his triumph, even in his caftan and his ritual curls." (13) Feuchtwanger, too, was Jewish, and his character, Süss, openly turns his back on Christianity during the final days before his execution. His celebration of Judaism thwarts any possibility of a commuted sentence, but it redeems him in the eyes of the (novel's) Jewish community. While Süss's gesture and its consequences signify the ultimate resistance to oppression, also embedded therein lie the difficulties and complexities of Jewish identity and assimilation, even the notion of the improbability of assimilation.

In comparison, many segments of the German-Jewish community thought it necessary to demonstrate their German-ness, their adherence to modernity, and its concomitant faith in science and enlightenment. In the Weimar polarization of culture, George Mosse claims, Jews were at least perceived as playing "a visible and crucial role in encouraging the modern rather than the traditional."[60] "Raffael Gutmann" serves as a perverse example of this. Perverse, not only because Raffael's support of modernity has less to do with a belief in science and reason than with his participation in the Christian high arts in general—Wagner's music in particular—but also because the protagonist fails to realize his desire. Compared with Feuchtwanger's treatment of his characters, Baum portrays the desire for modernity, that is, assimilation, as a separation of self and Other that, due to Raffael's suicide, compels an inscription of a quasi-demonic, death-wishing rigidity onto the traditional. This inscription occurs through the story's apparent corroboration and support of existing stereotypes that in and of themselves constitute elements of the isolation experienced by German Jews during the early twentieth century. In this sharpening conflict, many discursive formulations of the Right insisted on severing all purported links between Christianity and Judaism—a compelling move considering the success of many non/fictional texts bearing antisemitic messages at this time.[61]

Taking the actual and growing isolation of Jews into consideration, it becomes clear just to what extent Baum's tale becomes part of the intensifying debate about Germanic/Christian culture versus Judaism. Tradition in "Raffael" is more than an encumbrance, it is the prison that holds the protagonist captive and the leech that in the long run bleeds him of all hope of future happiness: "Parts of him, the light, the longing, that which was his true self, gave way and broke apart, piece by piece." (354) The overpoweringly negative qualities attributed to the Mosaic tradition in this text have the curious effect of sounding like a voice from the antisemitic camp. In fact, the story's "catastrophic potential" lies in this narrative's paradoxical positioning of voice. Mindful of Baum's Jewish heritage, one can wonder about her granting of permission for the reprint and its timing. After all, the more persuasive a member of the oppressed group is in speaking on behalf of the oppressors, the more this persuasion facilitates the reproduction of the oppression. Vicki Baum, however, prided herself in being apolitical and assimilated and did not possess the hindsight that characterizes this investigation.

Another Jewish writer, Joseph Roth, satirizes the assimilation trope in his novel from 1923, entitled *Das Spinnennetz*, by way of the Jew, Goldscheider, and his exaggerated efforts to assimilate. Goldscheider's figure is a locus of the perceived identities of the enemy. Through him Roth characterizes the stereotypical collapse of the twin ideological properties of the alien, namely socialism and Judaism, to create the "Rotjuda." Moreover, Goldscheider invades essential territories of German-ness by plagiarizing Luther through his opportunistic quotations of the New Testament. From the reader's side, there is a sense of witnessing a (perhaps not so exaggerated) Jewish perception of gentile cultural criteria for assimilation. Simultaneously, the character incorporates and emphasizes the intrusion into a perceived sacred cultural terrain and, by extension, the outrageousness of assimilatory desires.

The culmination of such outrageousness—a successful (and hateful) assimilation—is found in *Das Spinnennetz* in the figure of Efrusi, a wealthy Jewish jeweler and as such the prototypical "Weltjuda." The protagonist, Lohse, is a poor, gentile lieutenant who has returned unscathed from World War One. Roth conveys true German patriotism through Lohse's mother and sisters who cannot forgive Lohse for not having done his duty as a German and an officer by dying for his country. To add insult to injury, Lohse, who "nurtures a burning hatred against Socialists and Jews," must earn his living upon his return as a tutor in the Jew Efrusi's house. There, every day, he is served "coffee with so much cream that it formed a skin ... and a ham sandwich" and, what is more, in these financially troubled times, he also receives a salary every month.[62] Roth's bitterly ironic comments on assimilation are inescapable but so are the anguish and schizophrenia of the assimilated Jew. The agony and the ecstacy of trespassing Mosaic law and occupying a strategic position of power in the hegemonic terrain are embedded in that daily ritual of ham and cream. Furthermore, it exemplifies widely-held Christian beliefs concerning the luxury of Jewish life when, in fact, Efrusi's character belongs to the small percentage of Jews who were members of the upper class. Nevertheless, Efrusi's power and wealth are enviable and there was plainly a material basis for his character in the affluent Jewish community. Nonetheless, according to cultural prerogatives, such power and wealth must be had without the taint of Jewish alienness. Lohse, for his part, fantasizes about telling his employer: "Mr. Efrusi, I am a poor German and you, a wealthy Jew. It is treason to eat from a Jew's table." (23) He wants wealth like Efrusi's but concurs with the criminalization of Efrusi's wealth. The principle is clear: power is desirable in any shape, but it belongs rightfully only to the gentile German.

Lion Feuchtwanger discusses assimilation by means of his historical figure, Josef Süß Oppenheimer, in *Jud Süss*. The fictional, as well as the historical, Süss's father was Christian. Still Süss's zealous climb to power inside the Christian ruling classes takes place with sole emphasis on his Jewish heritage. His character seems to concur with Mosse's previously mentioned observation that Jews were often perceived to play a crucial role in promoting modernity. Süss's modernity frequently operates on the visual level as it manifests itself in an up-to-date, almost foppish, fashionableness: "Slender, elegant, formal, Süss confronted the clumsy, heavily breathing, inarticulate ... [Jewish] men." (222) In this passage, the writer sets Süss off against orthodox Jewry and makes him fit into a Western cultural landscape. This becomes much more interesting when we recall that Jews had long been subject to sumptuary laws, even to the point where the earring was a shared marker between prostitutes and Jews. Dress, in other words, marks identity, and in presenting Süss in different and distinctly modern garb, the text is not only distinguishing him from his fellow Jews, but it is also destabilizing the viewers' (and readers') notion of identity and social hierarchies so tightly bound up with appearance.[63]

Throughout the texts examined here, intertwined with the stories of assimilation and identity, is a narrative of power and powerlessness, a dynamic that is and has been central to the arena of antisemitism and the image of the Jew. "Raffael Gutmann" is one of the texts that exposes the complex nature of power. When the text denies Raffael his desires to participate in the cultural terrain outside the *Judengasse*, it exposes those who have not the power to leave the tradition. By extension, it confers tremendous power on the traditional, the Orthodox culture. It would be erroneous to deny that orthodox Judaism is powerful; adherence to the Mosaic Law and its cultural legacies has sustained Jewish communities throughout centuries and thus endorses the premise of its cultural vigour and authority. In "Raffael Gutmann," however, it is overwhelmingly the darker side of this power that is exhibited: while the text acknowledges Orthodox authority, it has assigned to it the authority to prohibit, to forbid, even to kill. It is in the tension between the authority and its execution that this text mediates the heavy quandaries of Jewish-German assimilation.

It is the partaking of German "high" culture that Raffael craves as *the* experience of his "Outside." This is made clear in the passages referring to Raffael's thorough and proud knowledge of Beethoven's *Fidelio* and Wagner's "Gesamtkunstwerk," *Die Meistersinger*. What such passages communicate is that true proof of German-ness lies in the adherence to the sacred Germanic culture of Beethoven and Wagner rather than in religion. The young man becomes an exemplar of the striving towards a Germanic utopia, a sort of renaissance man, who struggles—in this case, in vain—to transcend or even to free himself of the circumscriptions of his local culture. It is almost as if Raffael tries to achieve what Baum thought she herself had become: a person who through her own strength of character had risen above political, ethnic, and gender issues and who operated in a modern world as an unmarked member of an enlightened universe of culture. To exercise his human and artistic potential, Raffael must leave the *Judengasse*, for here, Baum writes, even the houses look Jewish with "hollow chests, bent shoulders, and small, greedily twinkling eyes." (404) It is difficult not to be taken aback by what now reads as egregious, stereotypical images of Jewishness. It is, nevertheless, crucial to recall the often excruciating decision Jews were forced to make regarding their political loyalties and the politics of identity in Germany. If, indeed, Baum intimates the measure of strength necessary to leave Orthodoxy behind, it is hardly surprising that its cultural location is painted in paradigms nobody would want to own. And yet, today, with the benefit of hindsight, one can assume that it is precisely here that the "catastrophic potential" of these images is generated.

Body Image

Images of Jews, allegorically described as their ghetto abodes, effectively evoke that which Jews purportedly do not have, namely muscular, lithe, tall, and upright bodies with forthright blue eyes. In late eighteenth-century Germany, Winckelmann's works on Greek art had brought to his contemporaries an idealized Greece. By the end of the nineteenth century, such a figure with its "passionless beauty" became the ideal Germanic body and a symbol of the nation.[64] The on-going *Körperkultur* (body culture) throughout the Weimar years attests to an unabating interest in not only a healthy body but more significantly yet, the beautiful body and a particular beauty, at that.

The spectacle of the Nordic/Germanic body, and simultaneously of the un-Nordic, is highly visible in Gustav Frenssen's novel, *The Pastor of Poggsee* (1922). The rhetorical measures differ but the effects are similar for here, too, the body of the Other is called forth. In *The Pastor*, the inhabitants of Poggsee demonstrate their Germanness through the yearly patriotic village athletic festival games. In the Poggsee games, "[n]o one was to present himself whose face was in anyway ignoble, whose limbs weren't straight, and whose body wasn't upright" (383–84). The words serve not merely as another tribute to the cult of the body as expressed in *Körperkultur*, they are also constituents of the growing narrative concerning the body politics of antisemitism. The popularized visualization of this discourse can be found in all its artistic glory in Leni Riefenstahl's 1938 hymn to pure Germanic beauty, her film, *Olympia*.

The phrenological notion of a direct correspondence between body typology and personal characteristics has long been commonplace in racist discourse. In the strictest sense, phrenology applies specifically to the skull but, as is most often the case, public use of "science" tends to blur the lines. In "Raffael," the physical environs described in the text come to stand for Jewish communities *in toto*. In quasi-phrenological fashion, the physical environment becomes a stand-in for an emblem of the psychological/physiological state of the dwellers of the ghetto (although that word is never employed). The pale light that appears to trickle down sickly from the sky, the heavy air that makes it difficult to breathe, the gray, stagnant water in the puddles, Jews dressed in caftans, and the refuse in the alleys, all occupy positions in the material, psychological, and spiritual spheres. It becomes clear to the readers, that the ghetto, and by extension, Orthodox Judaism, is something to abhor, to fear.[65]

Other descriptions of the ghetto contain some positive sentiments. *Das Spinnennetz* dwells briefly on the Lodz Ghetto and its gaze encompasses more than the negative aspects. Roth's novel does indeed describe the dirt and poverty present in the ghetto, but the physical deprivations are not transferred onto the mental health of Judaism. The description of the squalor is mediated by an immediate reference to the dignity and wisdom, even the humor and laughter of some of the inhabitants of that community. There is a sense, here, of what Goldstein has described as "the power of Jewish religion/tradition to maintain cohesion of generations and to sustain life itself." (46) A century earlier, Heinrich Heine had characterized the ghetto as a place where the great treasure and vitality of Judaism is preserved.[66]

At the same time, a perception of and an often malevolent fascination with (orthodox) Judaism as a realm of "fanatic strangeness,"[67] alien to Christian Western civilization and incomprehensible in its habits, pursuits, and interests pervade many popular Weimar texts.[68] Baum's *And Life Goes On* exotizises the local grocer by way of his desire for knowledge. Books "made him highflown, odd, and clever in this curious Jewish way." (49) Less benevolent is the use of gentile images of and myths about Jews, such as the vampire, and the question must be asked: who could or would benefit from such a paradigm? Both Joseph Roth and Lion Feuchtwanger make overt use of the vampiric discourse in which orthodoxy or even merely "the Jew" takes on the bestial form of a vampire drawing the vital juices out of its prey. In Roth's novel, the blood of decrepit Europe is greedily sucked away by the lurking eyes of Lenz, a Jewish counterspy: "his watchful eyes drank Europe's blood" (97)—a mixed metaphor, the oddity of which intensifies the unholy and frightening action. Moreover, it moves over into another paradigm, that of the "evil eye," a common superstition and something Jews have historically been accused of possessing and casting at innocent Gentiles and/or their possessions. In *Power*, Joseph Süss brags to Gabriel Landauer that "to-day [sic] he hung over the country, the Jew, and sucked of its blood and grew fat on its marrow." (230) And let us not forget *Nosferatu*, Murnau's 1922 expressionist rendition of the Stoker novel, in which the vampiric figure, Count Orloc, is a vehicle for the collective *Ängste* of the Weimar Republic, one of which was world domination by the Jews. Such use of metaphor easily forefronts the Jew as an "alien, evil, antisocial, and antihuman creature, essentially subhuman ...." Moreover, the images almost unavoidably lock into place myths held over from the medieval imagination, one of which held that the sole effective therapeutic remedy for the secret afflictions of Jews (loss of blood through male menstruation or hemorrhoids, for instance) was human (read "gentile") blood.[69]

The question I raised earlier about who would be served by this usage, is somewhat rhetorical, since history records precisely its benefits and injuries, who profited and who was injured. But it is perhaps through insisting on this question that my own post-Holocaust position becomes most obvious. To those who share my temporal location, there is little doubt about the catastrophic potentials of such cultural representations of the Jew in the Weimar Republic. However, if we consider Feuchtwanger and the literary context in which his Jew-as-vampire image appears, other possibilities open up. In the case of Joseph Süss, his leech-like and bloodletting behaviors manifest themselves the more he is caught in the web of the power struggles of the Christian prince whom he serves. It is Süss's errant ways, his loss of Judaism, that misdirect him and cause his wickedness; thus it would appear that it is the dangers of assimilation and the loss of Judaism that is one of the novel's major concerns.

* * *

The ways in which women were asked to identify themselves were, as we have discovered, not all positive, but, then again, their need to find a "niche" was perhaps less urgent. Having just freed themselves from the straight jacket of the Wilhelminian era, many women were in no hurry to curtail their modern way of life. Moreover, it appeared that female sexuality was still a pivotal issue connoting vice and wickedness, thus rendering some of the nationalist paradigms very uninviting to women. Still, no reader escapes a text unscathed, and gender presents no barrier to stereotypes. The themes and issues examined here do not readily afford women liberating practices or readings against the grain. Alternatives available to women readers in Manichean paradigms were that they become one of the historically vilified Others. It seems reasonable to assume, therefore, that in most cases, they were caught, as were male readers, in the psychic trap of affirming themselves through the castigation of others.

I neither can nor want to second guess authorial intentions. The mechanisms at work in texts and readers on the terrain of Jews, blacks, and lesbians are too complex to reduce to a tidy bundle. It is, nonetheless, possible to unpack ideological and cultural assumptions available in a particular historical moment. The effort has been directed toward exposing and examining the discursive politics operating in these texts. What has become visible, not surprisingly, is the process of structuring the Outsider and by extension, the process of shoring up one's own belonging-ness through the denunciation of this Other.

The discourses of assimilation and Self/Other are inextricably bound to each other in the texts I have discussed. In the case of

Weimar Jews, assimilation, adaptation, and adoption of the characteristics of an-Other group, implies choice and rejection. It should not be forgotten that the process takes place by way of extremely hierarchical frameworks, fraught with often deadly power struggles, as was the case for Jews living at that time. The choices and rejections made, when seen in their historical contexts, are seldom free, but rather are contingent upon the future viability of the minority group as understood and constructed at the time. Moreover, as we have seen, literary stratagems in use are not innocent. They are constituents, not only of the literary texts, but of the larger contexts in which popular fiction plays a part.

The systematic line of demarcation between Self and Other is an essential characteristic of national cultures. The need to confirm categories of that which is desirable and fix boundaries to keep out the polluting non-desirable are all mechanisms that serve to separate "them" from "us." By projecting attributes of undesirability onto the Other, we confirm and stabilize our sense of identity. The creation of stereotypes in the Weimar Republic functioned as a protective zone against fears beyond individual control. The numerous references to an undesirable Jewish, black, or lesbian (body-)type serve as a reminder that the body is a visible symbolic field "for the reproduction of dominant values and conceptions."[70] It is on the body that we inscribe our messages of difference. Elaine Scarry's observation articulates the main, but at times covert, dynamic at work in Weimar fictional texts discussed above when she states that "when there is within a society a crisis of belief ... the sheer materialness of the human body will be borrowed to lend that cultural construct [the belief] the aura of 'realness' and 'certainty.'" (14) In Weimar, the body that was Other, particularly if it was Jewish, signified and constituted one of the most *unheimlich* aspects of this crisis in German national identity.

Notes

1. I want to thank Rick McCormick for bringing out these complexities in his comments about the chapter.
2. Madeleine Marti, *Hinterlegte Botschaften. Die Darstellung lesbischer Frauen in der deutschsprachigen Literatur seit 1945* (Stuttgart, 1992), 7. The following section concerning excess and lesbian writing was conceived as an (unpublished) article co-written by Tanya Beer and myself. Without her insights and articulations, this part could not have been written and conventions of style rather than the importance of her work guide this marginal mention of it.
3. Lillian Faderman, *Surpassing the Love of Men: Romantic Friendship and Love Between Women From the Renaissance To the Present* (New York, 1981), 248. Although Freud's theories were the latest rage in the US and most of Europe from 1920, many psychiatrists still used Krafft-Ebing's concept of congenital defect.
4. Faderman, *Surpassing the Love of Men*, 241. Moreover, Judith Raiskin points out that such a diagnosis bears an uncanny resemblance, as we shall see, to colonial discourses on race and degeneration. Judith Raiskin, "Inverts and Hybrids: Lesbian Rewritings of Sexual and Racial Identities," in *The Lesbian Postmodern*, ed. Laura Doan (New York, 1994), 158.
5. Claudia Schoppmann, "Ein Lesbenroman aus der Weimarer Zeit: *Der Skorpion*," in *Eldorado: Homosexuelle Frauen und Männer in Berlin 1850-1950. Gecshichte Alltag und Kultur*, ed. Michael Bollé (Berlin, 1984), 198.
6. Anna Elisabet Weirauch, *Der Skorpion*. 3 vols. (1919-21), trans. Guy Endore (reprint edition New York, 1975). Arno Press published the sequel to *The Scorpion*. as *The Outcast.*, trans. Whittaker Chambers (reprint edition New York, 1975). The English translation is used here.
7. See also Michael Bollé, Ilse Kokula, and James Steakley for the importance of Magnus Hirschfeld for Weimar sexual politics.
8. I want to thank Dan Spencer for bringing the notion of two perceptions of nature to my attention. It is afforded greater discussion in his book *Gay and Gaia: Ethics, Ecology, and the Erotic* (Pilgrim Press, Cleveland, 1996).
9. Eve Kosofsky Sedgwick, *Tendencies* (Durham, 1993), 49.
10. Grete von Urbanitzky, *Der wilde Garten* (1927; reprint Wiesbaden, 1995). von Urbanitzky, like Vicki Baum, was an Austrian-born writer, but *Der wilde Garten* first appeared with a German publisher, Hessel & Becker Verlag, Leipzig and thus became part of the discourse in and about Weimar popular fiction. Further citations are noted in the text as *The Wild Garden*. All translations are mine.
11. Peter Brooks, *The Melodramatic Imagination: Balzac, Henry James, Melodrama and the Mode of Excess* (New York, 1985), 203.
12. Sedgwick, *Tendencies*, 175.
13. Alfred Döblin, "Die beiden Freundinnen und Ihr Giftmord." Außenseiter der Gesellschaft. Die Verbrechen der Gegenwart (Berlin, 1924). Further citations are noted in the text as "Women Friends." All translations are mine.
14. As quoted in Bram Dijkstra, *Idols of Perversity: Fantasies of Feminine Evil in Fin-de-Siècle Culture* (New York, 1986), 101.
15. Hart, *Fatal Women*, 30.
16. The page references in this chapter refers to the English translation. See note 14, Chapter 2.

17. In 1919, Germany's population numbered 29,011,216 men and 31,887,368 women. The marriage rate was at eight or nine per 1000 inhabitants whereas divorce rate in 1932 was at sixty-five per 1000 inhabitants. Stephenson, *Women in Nazi Germany*, 52.
18. Pieterse, *White on Black*, 186.
19. May Opitz, Katharina Oguntoye & Dagmar Schultz, eds. *Showing Our Colors: Afro-German Women Speak Out*, trans. Anne V. Adams (Amherst, 1992), 41.
20. J.M. Coetzee, *White Writing: On the Culture of Letters in South Africa* (New Haven, 1988), 61.
21. Es braust ein Rief wie Donnerhall
    Wie Schwertgeklirr und Wogenprall
    Zum Rhein, zum Rhein, zum deutschen Rhein
    Wer will des Stromes Hüter sein
    Lieb Vaterland magst ruhig sein
    Fest steht und treu die Wacht am Rhein.
22. Opitz et al., *Showing Our Colors*, 47.
23. Abdul R. JanMohamed, "The Economy of Manichean Allegory: The Function of Racial Difference in Colonialist Literature," in *"Race," Writing and Difference*, edited by Henry Louis Gates, Jr. (Chicago, 1985), 82.
24. Gustav Frenssen. *The Pastor of Poggsee*, trans. Katharine G. Potts (1921; London, 1981). By 1935, the novel had climbed to a position among the twenty top best-sellers through its sale of 97,000 copies. Further citations are noted in the text as *The Pastor*.
25. Abdul R. JanMohamed, *Manichean Aesthethics: The Politics of Literature in Colonial Africa*. (Amherst, 1983), 24.
26. Opitz et al., *Showing Our Colors*, 52. Anita Grossmann also discusses the growing attraction of sterilization among sex reform workers and leaders. She writes that the procedure was performed as a eugenic birth control measure, particularly on poor and "asocial" women. Grossmann points out, however, that even in the most extreme cases, doctors sought the agreement of the person in question. *Reforming Sex*, 71-75.
27. Vicki Baum, *Hell in Frauensee. Ein heiterer Roman von Liebe und Hunger* (Berlin, 1927), 48, 64. All translations are mine.
28. Pieterse, *White on Black*, 145.
29. Michael H. Kater, *Different Drummers: Jazz in the Culture of Nazi Germany* (New York, 1992), 17.
30. Kater, *Different Drummers*, 14.
31. Fromm, *The Working Class in Weimar Germany*, 148-50.
32. Alfred Rosenberg, *Der Sumpf: Querschnitte durch das "Geistes"-Leben der November-Demokratie* (Munich, 1930), 23–36 as quoted in Kater, *Different Drummers*, 24.
33. Again I would like to thank Rick McCormick for his generous comments.
34. See also von See, *Barbar—Germane—Arier* for an in-depth examination of German national identities.
35. *Die Buben*, 43, 87, 88. By 1940, the novel had sold 265,000 copies and rated an all-time second after Hans Grimm's 1928 novel, *Volk ohne Raum*, which in 1940 reached a sale of 480,000 copies. Cf. Donald Ray Richards, *The German Bestseller in the 20th Century: A Complete Bibliography and Analysis* (Bern, 1968).
36. Ibid., 380, 369.
37. Pieterse, *White on Black*, 172.

38. Sander L. Gilman, "Black Bodies, White Bodies: Toward an Iconography of Female Sexuality in Late Nineteenth-Century Art, Medicine, and Literature," in *"Race," Writing and Difference*, ed. Henry Louis Gates, Jr. (Chicago, 1985), 231.
39. Showalter, *Sexual Anarchy*, 189.
40. Gilman, "Black Bodies," 228.
41. Sander Gilman, *Difference and Pathology: Stereotypes of Sexuality, Race, and Madness* (Ithaca, 1985), 101.
42. JanMohamed, "The Economy," 83.
43. A later part of this chapter will examine the representation of Jews and Jewishness in popular fiction at this time and that discussion will therefore not be taken up here.
44. Cf. both *Gloria*, 106 and *The Scorpion*, 45.
45. Gilman, *Difference and Pathology*, 12.
46. Among the best known works are Dagmar Barnouw, *Weimar Intellectuals and the Threat of Modernity* (Bloomington, 1988); Peter Gay, *Weimar Culture: The Outsider as Insider* (New York, 1968); Anthony Phelan, *The Weimar Dilemma: Intellectuals in the Weimar Republic* (Manchester, UK, 1985); Anson Rabinach, *In the Shadow of Catastrophe: German Intellectuals Between Apocalypse and Enlightenment* (Berkeley and Los Angeles, 1997); Detlev. J.K. Peukert, *The Weimar Republic: The Crisis of Classical Modernity*, trans. Richard Deveson (New York: 1993); and John Willett, *Art and Politics in the Weimar Period: The New Sobriety 1917–1933* (New York, 1978).
47. Donald L. Niewyk, *The Jews in Weimar Germany* (Baton Rouge, 1980), 5.
48. According to David Sorkin, incomplete emancipation and partial integration of Jews into society were indeed crucial constituents of a new Jewish identity. *The Transformation of German Jewry, 1789–1840* (New York, 1987), 5.
49. Niewyk, *The Jews in Weimar Germany*, 12ff.
50. Figures from 1910 show that more than 21,000 Eastern Jews lived in Greater Berlin, most of them orthodox and in a low income bracket. Cf. Jack Wertheimer, *Unwelcome Strangers* (New York, 1987), 4, 187.
51. Niewyk, *The Jews in Weimar Germany*, 12ff. As a basis of comparison, a general typist would earn 1,400–1,700 marks/year.
52. Ibid., 6ff.
53. Although the numbers of dead and wounded German soldiers vary, well over two million men died while almost six million crippled male bodies survived the war. Robert Weldon Whalen has compiled these and many more frightful statistics in his fascinating and compassionate work *Bitter Wounds: German Victims of the Great War, 1914–1939* (Ithaca, 1984), 38ff.
54. In an earlier paper, I describe the novella as having been written in 1922. David Brenner points out, that "Raffael Gutmann" was indeed written in 1911. Cf. David A. Brenner, "Neglected "Women's" Texts and Contexts: Vicki Baum's Jewish Ghetto Stories," *Women in German Yearbook* 13 (1997): 101–21).
55. "Raffael Gutmann," parts 1–3, *Leipziger Illustrirte Zeitung* 159, (12 October 1922): 307–08; (19 October 1922): 353–54; (2 November 1922): 403–05. Further citations are noted in the text as "Raffael." The Orthodoxy at issue in Baum's and the following popular works are the writers' perceptions. All translations are mine.
56. Gunter W. Remmling, "Prologue: Weimar Society in Retrospect," in *Towards the Holocaust: The Social and Economic Collapse of the Weimar Republic*, ed. Michael Dobkowski and Isidor Wallimann, 8. See also Harry Kessler, *Walter Rathenau: Sein Leben und sein Werk* (Berlin, 1928).

57. Houston Stewart Chamberlain, *Die Grundlage des 19. Jahrhunderts* (Munich, 1899).
58. August Bea, "Antisemitismus, Rassentheorie und Altes Testament," *Stimmen der Zeit* 100 (1921): 177.
59. Graf Heinrich Coudenhove-Kalergi, *Das Wesen des Antisemitismus* (1906; Vienna, 1929), 12.
60. George Mosse, *German Jews Beyond Judaism* (Cincinatti, 1980), 22.
61. Artur Dinter's novel *Die Sünde wider das Blut* (Leipzig, 1917), a cautionary tale of intermarriage, is a case in point. By 1920, it had already reached its twelfth edition; also Theodor Fritsch's pamphlet *Mein Beweismaterial gegen Jahve* (1911) was reprinted in 1916 as *Der falsche Gott: Beweismaterial gegen Jahve* and appeared in its second edition in 1919; see also note 15 concerning Chamberlain.
62. Joseph Roth, *Das Spinnennetz* (1923; reprint Cologne, 1988), 6, 5. All translations are mine.
63. Garber, *Vested Interests*, 223–24.
64. George Mosse, *Nationalism and Sexuality: Middle Class Morality and Sexual Norms in Modern Europe* (Madison, 1985), 10ff.
65. In *Unwelcome Stranger*, Jack Wertheimer points to another association linked to East European and, by extension, Orthodox Jews, namely vermin and plague. Jews traveling from the East during the Second Reich underwent obligatory delousing procedures and their trains were steamed after use in the East, 24–25.
66. As quoted in Goldstein, *Reinscribing Moses*, 46.
67. "Raffael," 354.
68. Cf. Joshua Trachtenberg's explanation for this fascination in *The Devil and the Jews: The Medieval Conception of the Jew and its Relation to Modern Antisemitism* (1943; Cleveland, 1961).
69. Trachtenberg, *The Devil and the Jews*, 6, 50.
70. Robert Crawford, "A Cultural Account of 'Health'—Self-Control, Release and the Social Body," in *Issues in the Political Economy of Health Care*, ed. John McKinley (New York, 1985), 95.

Chapter Six

THE SHAPE OF THINGS

The work that has unfolded above is about the representation in Weimar popular fiction of women, their issues, their bodies, their rights, their identitities, and how German they are. Throughout the topics that we have examined—class, sexuality, marriage, reproduction, work, sports, and difference—the female body surfaces as the main motif. Just as her presence in Weimar material reality contained simultaneous reminders of the past and the future, cultural representations of the "new" woman and her embodiment may be read as metaphors for the confusion and chaos that we perceive as Weimar. This is further borne out by the fact that when the boundaries of gender categories shift, they not only indicate a dislocation in extant power relations; they also constitute integral features of the changing power constellations. Said differently, the unsteady, capricious gender borders and the frequent appearance of the androgyne during the years of the Weimar Republic are here read as simultaneous indications and ingredients of an unsettled and changing status quo.

Human gender formation and the coming into being of our gendered selves are instrumental in negotiating, shaping, and formulating the world around us. There is constant flux in shaping and re-shaping not only gender and sexuality but also the criteria that form and are themselves components of these concepts. The Weimar Republic faced specific, historically rooted tensions which greatly affected the formation of Weimar society. Indeed, when we look at Germany after World War One, we see a nation less than four decades old. The country's demography was in flux.[1] The last borders that the nineteenth-century middle classes had drawn so

Notes for this section begin on page 145.

tightly between private and public spheres (historically much more applicable to the urban middle and upper classes than to urban workers or the rural population) were crumbling. The continual class struggle to free the German nation from the last vestiges of Prussian feudalism and enter into modernity contained within it a distinct, but not separate struggle: the struggle against the overwhelming cultural hegemony of authoritarian structures stretching from the army right into the intimate sphere of family relations and power structures.[2] Perhaps it is not so remarkable that from those forces in play—sometimes collaborating, sometimes oppositional—came the experimental, societal process we refer to as the Weimar Republic.

Weimar Germany was a society that came up for air, gasping, soaked in late-capitalist, Wilhelminian values, but then went under again after a short time. The volatility on most cultural fronts—and certainly in the political arena—of the Weimar Republic was more than the last frivolity of a dying Western culture, as described in Spengler's *The Decline of the West*. It was the sign of a wounded patriarchy, a patriarchy in crisis, whose most terrifying convulsion was to be the Third Reich. Among the crucial manifestations and ingredients of this fatal crisis were the partial dissolutions of gender and sex categories along with the right-wing reactions to the same. These changes figured large in cultural representations from the Weimar period and this examination has shown how the fluidity of gender notions and experimentation with Weimar's cultural and social fabric as represented in popular fiction are interwoven, creating a repeated pattern in an exceedingly fragile *textum*.

An ubiquitous emblem of Weimar modernity in popular culture was the "new" woman. Manifestations of the material body in German popular culture of the 1920s tell us that the new shape is the *girl*, an ideally slender, long-limbed, flat-chested female figure with narrow hips. The elongated waistline of the 1920s was one that obviously left the natural waist and its circumference out of the picture. This meant that countless women could now throw their corsets away, a gesture that in itself intimated a reclamation of the female body. Our only entry into this world is through our bodies, but women's bodies serve an additional function. Theirs, more than men's, are icons of culture, its mores, its hopes, and its anxieties. We can therefore suspect that the new look represented more than liberated women's wish to surpass their reproductive function. The new body was as tyrannical as the corseted and bustled fashions that preceded it. No sooner were middle-class German women enjoying their newly gained freedoms—the right to vote, and to careers outside the home—than they were asked to conform to a new body image dictated by daring fashions. Diets and exercise were instruments with which the body was tamed, constructed, and managed. However, Weimar bodies, both male and female, were circumscribed by criteria other than linearity and androgyny. The bisexual look was one that would be "sexy" only as long as the wearer was young. As the fashions stood, materials such as batique and silk were so thin and revealing, and underwear so scanty, that bodies displaying the new fashions had to be modified in a very strict manner. Hence, beauty aids, diets, and recreational sports all became instruments in the fight against aging and its physical effects and figurations.[3]

Patterns and conflicts, even patterned conflicts, are revisited from text to text, heightening readers' attention to the issues of the period. Particularly prevalent are the discourses on sexuality and gender in all their manifestations. The blurred lines of demarcation between male and female, feminine and masculine, hetero- bi- and homosexuality echo in popular representations in the image of the "new" woman. This image is irrevocably situated along and across those unstable borders, and she represents one of the many, although not equally viable, sexual alternatives in the Weimar period. Weimar women had made inroads into the masculine arena of the workplace, but they had gone further by appropriating and redefining masculinity itself. One of the visible effects of this was a certain playful masculinization of the representation of women. Weeklies from the middle to the end of the 1920s carry numerous advertisements featuring women in pants, from fashionable riding breeches to leather bike-pants. Write-ups contained advice on women's tuxedos. One such article in the *Leipziger Illustrirte Zeitung* claims that there is hardly a tailor who has not fashioned this hottest item in the world of women's fashion.[4] Moreover, representations of the "new" woman as a vessel of restless, volatile gender doubt and eroticism were operating as a major factor. Icons such as Asta Nielsen, Pola Negri, and later Marlene Dietrich and Louise Brooks, exemplify the difficulty of containing the eroticism and androgynous sexuality that had become the representational *lingua franca* for an urban, liberated, and younger generation. Such images were components of a representational economy that derived part of its dynamics from the contradictions between the imagined and the real in women's situations.

Weimar morality, or the lack thereof, was carried by and inscribed upon specific bodies that were often perceived and conceived as overlapping or even interchangeable, namely the bodies of women, homosexuals, and Jews. In most popular texts, morality is an act performed by women. Christiane Opterberg in Herzog's 1920 *Die Buben der Frau Opterberg* is the uncorruptible force transmitting old and true values to the next generation of Germans while keeping un-German influences at bay. Rosalie Scheuflein from Lena Christ's *Madam Bäuerin* (1920) acts morally when she refuses her mother's "good" match for her, marries Franzl Schiermoser and settles down to a non-glamorous, hard-working, but honest rural life. Likewise, it is the female protagonist, Leonora Woltka, in Ernst Georgy's novel from 1922, *Der Konfektionsbaron, ein Zeitbild aus der Konfektion,* who, with a fierce moral integrity, negotiates loss of privileges, class differences, female emancipation, and independence when she leaves her aristocratic home and embarks on a career.

When we look at popular novels collectively, we see the particular conundrum contained in the paradigm of woman and morality. While the perceived breakdown of morals was linked closely to the "new" woman, "the German woman" was constantly under construction as the mother of the nation and the future German people. The anxieties produced by the new female behaviors are very much present in *Sittenromane,* or morality tales. Stories with titles such as "Forgotten Guilt," Wrong Morals," Frau Lola's Trouble," and "His Wife's Friend," employ stock figures such as the operetta singer, the dancer, and the actress who embrace a free-ranging, carnivorous sexuality that devours otherwise morally inclined men.[5] In this manner, they conform to Otto Weiniger's claim in *Sex and Character* that neither women nor Jews possess moral sense but only sexual passion (89). Moreover, what Mary Ann Doane says about the *femme fatale* in the late nineteenth century, namely that she "is a clear indication of … the fears and anxieties prompted by shifts in the understanding of sexual differences," (2) finds its expression in the next century in the many popular stories.

As in reality, the fictional body, its appearance, and language becomes a field of cultural signification. In the *Sittenromane,* it is the female body that signals the un-nature of women with overt sexual appetites: these women are tall, often as tall as the male hero, with bold eyes and a "mannish" appearance. Their physical presence and self-assurance are usually perceived as aggression, which in turn leads the reader to speculate on the character's femininity. Her unusual stature seems to outgrow the original physical aspect of her while it magnifies her sexuality. Although her eyes are set on the man, the spectre of "butch" and lesbianism flits through the texts. As a contrast to the seductress, the same texts abound with frail, blue-eyed, and very virtuous women whose love relationships with their husbands contain no female passion; that is the property of "the other woman." Instead they represent a redeeming possibility for women thus salvaging their role as the future mothers of the nation. In this manner, they serve a function similar to that served by the Christiane Opterbergs in *Heimat* literature.

As these texts refuse to stay inside Weiniger's moral strait jacket with regard to women and sexuality, we are faced with another version of the same conundrum. In order to negotiate its anxiety, patriarchy has to make its enemy visible. And so, for each happy ending with the acceptable kind of woman acquiescing to *Kinder, Küche und Kirche*, the plot must slay a dragon, most often in the shape of a strong, independent woman with a sexual appetite. In order to make the victory of morality illustrious, its opponent must be formidable and so the unvirtuous woman occupies center stage in large sections of the *Sittenromane*. Sexual extravagance always loses in these novels, and in that they differ little from most popular Weimar novels. Nevertheless, readers are exposed to alternative life praxes through the exciting, immoral woman who is independent, smokes cigarettes, wears sexually inviting clothes like the movie stars and who enjoys sex. In fictional representations from popular culture, it is the physical that reveals inner qualities and the body of the "new" woman has been invested with contemporary discussions about virtue and wantonness.

Naturally, vast numbers of women did not fit into that mold and chances are that they might have looked more like Frau Zienkann from Vicki Baum's novella "Der Weg" (1925): "not large and not small … not ugly but not pretty either. No longer young, but also not yet old." (4) If her body took part in the debate about morality, it was not as a site of conflict. At this point, we must train our focus on the distance between women's representation and their everyday existence. On the whole, we are looking at a generation of women who, like Gilgi, refused to understand their destiny solely in the light of reproduction and motherhood. Infecundity is scripted on their very bodies—small bosoms and narrow hips—signaling a turn away from the reproductive function. Women were now in the public sphere both as consumers—of commodities and education, for instance—and as workers, stenographers, teachers, and nurses, to name but a few professions. However, most women's realities were still located firmly in their traditional roles, with the added burden of work outside the home. The appearance of the "new" woman as the refiguration of a body image simultaneously with the reshaping of her social roles is no coincidence. It can be read as a result of the energy created at the confluence of women's wishes, their socio-material reality, and the patriarchal circumscriptions circulating during this period.

According to Lucka in "Verwandlung der Frau," the slender, boyish-looking woman approximated every man's dream of a younger brother. Indeed, he continues, gender relations in the 1920s are so marked by similarities and approximations that glaring gender contrasts are considered somewhat embarrassing (83, 82). In 1923, in the midst of these discussions about the androgynous and its very real manifestations, another cultural voice, Sigmund Freud, wrote *The Ego and the Id*. The "simple Oedipal complex is by no means its commonest form" he insists; "bisexuality takes a hand in the ... vicissitudes" of that very construction (641). His remarks situate him at a specific historical and cultural juncture, indeed, for Freud evidently considered sexuality to be as unstable and floating as its bodily representations made it out to be "in reality." The material stimuli for this direction in his discourse could easily have come from a casual glance at any metropolitan crowd where the signification of the sexual oscillation was nowhere more clearly visible than in the *Bubikopf* and her male counterpart.[6]

What political goals, if any, could the "genderless" body be mediating and interpreting? Asked differently, what kind of power did early twentieth-century bourgeois society bestow upon this androgynous form? In order to answer, we need to return to the conflicting metaphorical content of the female body and the plurality of sites occupied by it. As we have seen, female characters from the *Sittenromane* and *Heimat* novels also served as vehicles for debates about national identity, and during the Weimar years, tension was building between metaphors employed by relatively progressive texts and those used in reactionary novels. While women characters were treated relatively mildly in liberal texts, representations of the "new" woman amounted to an embodiment of negative power, delineating that which was not German.

In "Totem and Taboo," Freud writes about children who "uninhibited as they are in the avowal of their bodily needs ... no doubt feel themselves more akin to animals than to their elders." (491) The generation most often present in Weimar popular fiction came of age in the 1920s. It consisted of men and women who, in their intense and at times uninhibited relationship with their bodies and their bodies' desires, were indeed children of a body revolution. The cults of the (naked) body had been body-centered phenomena present throughout the early part of the century and spokespersons for such body cults went to a great deal of trouble to keep them clean of any association with sexuality and eroticism. Nevertheless, a certain amount of pollution from the arena of bodily urges into that of the healthy body/healthy mind dyad seemed unavoidable. Overall, this generation perceived their bodies and their bodies' functions and desires in a way that was easily distinguishable from that of their parents; the modern body was out in the light, while that of the older generation still lingered in the dark shadows of late-Wilhelminian repression. Chapter Three examined the disciplining discourses that circulated in Weimar with regard to the physical body at rest and at play. From women's revealing fashions to popular participation in sports like boxing, where half-naked men fought and sweated under lights in front of an excited audience, the human body was displayed and admired. Nonetheless, the kinds of physical energy called for were similar both in the work place and in the boxing ring which, in some perverse way, shines a different light on Adorno's (later) statement that leisure activities in modernity approximate work.

It is the confluence of often oppositional discourses that is so fascinating about Weimar reality and popular culture, or, expressed differently, the material reality and the *representational* play with and embodiment of contemporary ambiguities, anxieties and conflicts in popular culture unfold. In Weimar film we meet Louise Brooks, whose boyish figure exudes a mysterious eroticism; the melancholy Asta Nielsen's almost "mannish" manners; Conrad Veidt's heavily kohled eyes and lipsticked mouth; Max Schreck's very androgynous and devouring Count Nosferatu; women with their hair cut in the style of *Herrenschnitt;* the open lesbianism of Sagan's *Mädchen in Uniform*. This wide variety of images of sexual and gender transgressions are all scripted on the body. Although most of the live examples of this new way of life were confined to Berlin and other large cities, the *imagery* was popular throughout Weimar Germany. Shifts in the economic structures of a society have a discernible impact upon the way sexual difference is articulated. If we link this with our knowledge of the precarious political and economic Weimar reality, the combination goes a long way toward explaining how discourses about and representations of destabilized gender identities are indications of a destabilized patriarchy. However, it is necessary to add the following caveat, namely, that the approximation of male to female characteristics, or, if you will, the so-called effeminization of the male, had more to do with the loss of male power than with women's gain of the same. To clarify this statement, we need to sidestep for a moment and examine men's and women's material realities and the representations thereof.

What were women's gains and losses between 1919 and 1933? It would be incorrect to attempt to speak for all women at that time, but the *Frauenfrage* appears to be a variation on a given theme. The aftermath of World War One afforded women what appeared to be new privileges: the vote and the possibility of financial independence. This presumed empowerment was a constituent of the popular conception of women; they were perceived to have achieved, or at least to be well on their way to, equality, when for most of them this very equality consisted of a badly-paid job in addition to the duties connected with home and family. In effect, from the fictional examples used in this investigation, it appears as though the experience of middle-class women had moved a little closer to that of working-class women, for whom the double burden was nothing new. Neither Flämmchen, Doris, nor Fräulein Brückner, who are lowest in the pecking order in the office and teetering on the border between respectability and destitution/prostitution, feel liberated. Not that Flämmchen and Doris care much about equal rights; their concern is to climb out from under the rock of anonymity and become the kind of film stars that shone larger than life every night in the nearest *Kino*. The currency that they use to this end is their bodies, the emblem of the "new" woman.

In Weimar Germany, the diminishing power experienced by many men was expressed representationally in two ways: as a loss of absolute male body characteristics and as the assumption of female physical traits. Images of passive and often deferring men had a large circulation in popular culture. Among films alone *Nosferatu* (1919), *Metropolis* (1926), *Zuflucht* (1926), and *Pandora's Box* (1929) are cases in point. In *Grand Hotel*, of the four male protagonists, one is killed, another imprisoned, and the third, seriously crippled in the War, contemplates suicide. Only Kringelein, the little timid bookkeeper, is left, and he suffers from a mysterious terminal illness, presumably stomach cancer. In *Gloria*, women contemplate a world without men. Fabian, from Kästner's novel of the same name, proves perfectly incapable of negotiating life in Weimar and drowns. Von Flintschs from Georgy's *Der Konfektionsbaron* may have the most positive future of those mentioned here. The erstwhile baron's life is in shambles while he meagerly supports himself as uniformed doorman in a department store. At the very end of the novel, his childhood friend, Leonore, brings about an opportunity for him to tour America lecturing about the political complexities of post-war Germany. However, the reader is left uncertain whether that is enough to "save" von Flintschs. It is evident from the above examples, that on this one subject alone popular texts are an extraordinary medium in their appropriation of the current discourses on gender and its destabilization and, most importantly, the haunting decline of male potency.

In the embodied manifestation of Weimar culture, the female body often assumed male-identified markers. It is traditionally considered a stigma for a man to take on female characteristics. It was therefore imperative that he retain some feature that would set him apart from his "opposite" and, more important, one that would recuperate his claim to power. One reliable way of doing this entailed maintenance of the paradigm of self and other, drawing upon the binary system, have-have not, either-or. So when *she* is shown as the risky, presumptuous, aggressive, and, most probably, immoral, sexual being, whose eroticism endangers cultural norms as we know them, *his* body is not home to any of those frightening characteristics. He inherits the world precisely because she contains the danger. The oscillation between femininity and masculinity by no means de-eroticizes the male body, but the inscription of dark menace and devouring eroticism is on the female body. The representation of the male shows him as delicate, yes, endangered even, from the onslaught of war and women but, in Judeo-Christian fashion, through his purity the power is his. There appears to be little he has to do. The negativity connected with the "new" woman is what proves his positivity. Her modernity and annexation of territory previously forbidden to her unsettle cultural norms and destabilize the everyday way of life. By extension, men, then, are defenders of tradition, the old ways, a time when there was order in the world, stability. And yet, in the novels, it was on the female body, albeit a traditional one, that the German future was scripted. The hard-working female body that completed the daily drudgery with a smile denied the need for labor organizations, pledging a bridge to the (feudal) past. The sturdy and femininely curved body insisted on traditional genders and held great promise of reproducing the population. The same body's adherence to traditional gender-specific behavior demonstrated shared knowledge of and roots in the past thus protecting time-honored customs and a (German) national identity.

It is obvious that the female body is a vast field of cultural signification. This practice is in itself nothing new as it can trace its lineage to Genesis and through to modernity in the binary paradigm of Madonna/Whore; the classical, "high" culture tradition goes back to Sophocles and Aristophanes. What is new, however, is mass or popular culture's uses of women's bodies as signifiers and its wide distribution aided by modern technology and consumerism. The female body, moreover, constitutes a field of *conflicting* signification influenced by pressures stemming from repeated political volatility and fractious cultural discourses. Some of the resulting diverse positions have been demonstrated by the readings produced here. Discourses circulating in material life were invested in fictional spaces and characters and consequently contradictions that spoke out from those vehicles indicated a high degree of cultural fluidity.

We might ask how the destabilization of identity affected women's experiences in culture, as objects, subjects, and producers of the culture, and how it may have de/regulated their own subject formation. Where are women's perceived locations in this struggle and what may we surmise about their experience of their self-fashioning? If representations of women in fiction are anything to go by, female subjectivity is represented as a series of unstable positions, swinging from "masculine" to "feminine" while simultaneously acting on and unsettling those very indices in the process. As much as instability of identity appears to have been troublesome to some, particularly men, it also has another effect: through its very ambiguity, female subjectivity becomes a powerful agent for the destabilization and disruption of traditional social order and also the marker of a constantly shifting array of possibilities for the self.

This work was not meant as a theoretical investigation into the psychological reception of cultural signals and consequent sub/conscious actions. Instead it has shown that readers were exposed to a vast array of popular novels from which they chose among competing images and discourses. The texts offered an arena of divergent notions, each with a set of outcomes, that is, each story offered a set of scenarios showing how the issues were resolved. Through popular novels, the readers were exposed to a number of solutions—be they fictional examinations—of consequences of certain modes of behavior. The specific combination of actions and their consequences may have been different from those of the reader's choice, but it gave them a wider perspective on how life could be lived differently.

To conclude, it is my hope that the preceding chapters have demonstrated the significant role Weimar popular fiction played in the creation and maintenance of a female public sphere and cultural imaginary. The aim of this study has been to explore the range of female identities circulating in Weimar so that we can better understand "what cultural resources ... [woman] drew on in conceiving and living a social self."[7] A multiplicity of debates that were constituent parts of Weimar culture found their way into often trite plots, but the banality of the novels did not preclude the breadth of their collective cultural sweep. Only a fraction of the many popular works produced in Weimar Germany has been examined here, but it is clear that they constitute a valuable source for cultural insights. The textual manifestations of gender and sexuality that we have examined throughout this work may all be seen as functions of "the cultural reproduction of social and political values," a phenomenon which in turn also plays an important role in the formation of the cultural subject of the time.[8] The gendered investigation into Weimar popular fiction undertaken here first of all unearths the intensity with which women's issues were examined and interpreted and solutions prescribed. Second, it identifies some of the ways in which cultural practices normally identified with the Third Reich were anticipated in Weimar culture.[9] Finally, an examination from a gendered perspective has shown conclusively that although traditional history still has too little to say about it, gender issues played a crucial role in shaping the extant cultural paradigms and with them the subject formation of Weimar citizens.

Notes

1. By 1925, only 25 percent of the population was rural, a measure of the flight from the land in the first decades of the twentieth century in Germany. Before World War One, Berlin counted two million inhabitants; by 1925 the number had grown to 4.5 million. Janet Lungstrom, "*Metropolis* and the Technosexual Woman of German Modernity," in *Women in the Metropolis: Gender and Modernity in Weimar Culture*, ed. Katharina von Ankum (Berkeley, 1997), 129.
2. A very important player on the political and cultural scene was the SPD (the Social Democratic Party) that, until World War I, was the largest workers' party in Europe. That *per se* constitutes a phenomenon that could be viewed as both an integral part of and a reaction to the patriarchal and paternalistic discourses pervasive throughout prewar Germany.
3. *Informationsblätter zu der Ausstellung "Frauenalltag und Frauenbewegung in Frankfurt 1890-1980."* Historische Dokumentation 20. Jahrhundert (Frankfurt am Main, 1981), 9-12.

4. *Leipziger Illustrirte Zeitung*, no. 4234 (May 6, 1926): 607.
5. These stories, each of 79 pages in length, can be found in Heinz Bernd, *Vergessene Schuld und andere Sittenromane* (Dresden, 1921).
6. "Counterpart" is used here in the sense of a part that complements the other since it is clear from the preceding that, in many cases, contrast is not a valid concept. Indeed, according to Lucka, the ideal, even if it remains unformulated, is genderlessness. "Verwandlung der Frau," 82.
7. Marie Louise Roberts, *Civilization Without Sexes: Reconstructing Gender in Postwar France, 1917–1927*. (Chicago, 1994), 14.
8. Linda Mizejewski, *Divine Decadence: Fascism, Female Spectacle, and the Makings of Sally Bowles*. (Princeton, 1992), 6.
9. See also Kate Lacey, *Feminine Frequencies: Gender, German Radio, and the Public Sphere, 1923-1945* (Ann Arbor, 1996), 221-245.

Appendix

Baum, Vicki. And Life Goes On. (Zwischenfall in Lohwinckel, 1932). Garden City: Doubleday, 1932.

Elizabeth Persenthein lives in a rural backwater with her husband, an eccentric country doctor and amateur inventor, and their precocious child. She is questioning her married bliss as she performs her daily housewife's routine in a existence marred by money trouble. Her intellectual thirst is stilled by her "Hebraic" friend, Marcus, who owns a bookstore. One night, a car with city folks, among them a couple of filmstar lovers and a boxer, crashes in the crossroads, killing the driver. Dr. Persenthein treats the victims and they are farmed out to various homes in the area, among them the local manor owned by Herr von Raitzold and his sister, Fräulein von Raitzold, a closeted lesbian. The latter falls for the filmstar, Leore Lania, but is once more doomed to unrequited love. Peter, the boxer, and Elizabeth fall in love and she contemplates leaving husband and child. However, after more ruminations about marriage, compromises, and sacrifices, she stays. One of Nick Persenthein's inventions succeeds and the patent is sold for a goodly sum. The patients are discharged and go back to the city, leaving life to go on in Lohwinckel.

Baum here contrasts rural with city ways of life. Sexual mores, marriage and independence, female sexuality, popular culture in the shape of film, class issues, lesbianism, tradition, family life, and life options for women are among the issues discussed in depth in the novel.

Baum, Vicki. *Hell im Frauensee.* Berlin: Ullstein Verlag, 1927.

Hell is employed during the summer as a swimming instructor in Frauensee's biggest hotel where he gets free room and a percentage of the swimming lessons he provides. One day he swims across the lake and meets a young woman, Puck, with whom he develops a friendship. She is the precocious daughter of a philosopher and a famous actress and therefore suitably strange and exotic. Through his job, he strikes up an acquaintance with May, an English translator, who is visiting Frauensee. He falls in love and May leaves to go back to work. The weather is almost always bad and he earns hardly enough money to feed himself properly. Hell is young and good-looking and has to fight off many a temptation from the female staff and bathing guests alike. Puck disappears after he turns down her attention and is believed drowned. However, she turns up at Hell's hospital bedside when he is fighting for his life due to blood poisoning. While there, he receives a letter announcing that his invention has been patented and that he will receive a large sum of money. May joins Puck in watching Hell in the hospital and it looks as if Hell and May will live happily ever after.

Sports, sexuality, hunger, temporary poverty, Otherness.

Baum, Vicki. *Menschen im Hotel* (1929). Frankfurt am Main: Ullstein, 1986.

Baron von Gaigern is a penniless, but gallant hotel thief who aims to steal the valuable pearls of the erstwhile prima ballerina Grusinskaja. She surprises him in the act and he fakes fascination for her. However, he falls in love with her and in order to follow her to Paris, decides to rob another guest, the provincial Kringelein. Upon learning that he is fatally ill, the latter has withdrawn all his savings, left an unhappy marriage, and gone to Berlin to "live." Gaigern takes him under his wing and consequently trains his attention on another possible victim, the (just as provincial) businessman Preysing. During an intimate moment in Preysing's room between Flämmchen, an unscrupulous, beautiful secretarial temp, and Preysing, Gaigern breaks in. He is discovered and unwittingly killed by Preysing. While Preysing unsuccessfully talks to the police, Flämmchen is saved from questioning and embarrassment by Kringelein, who persuades her to accompany him to Paris. Among the many minor characters is Dr. Otternschlag who kills the pain of his WWI wounds with morphine, the doorman whose wife is having a baby, and a hierarchy of hotel staff.

The grand hotel is a microcosm of Weimar modernity. Vulnerable masculinity, voracious female sexuality, the "new" woman, class, modernity, technology, old world versus new, and the ravages of war are all topics treated here in a style that deftly weaves all the threads into a narrative about Weimar and Berlin in the 1920s.

Baum, Vicki. *Helene. (stud. chem. Helene Willfüer,* 1928). Garden City: Doubleday, 1933.

Helene Willfüer studies chemistry in Heidelberg under Professor Valentin Ambrosius who is married to the passionate but faithless Yvonne Pastouri. Fritz Rainer, a medical student, is an adoring friend of Helene's and after a summer party at the Ambrosius,' Helene and Fritz make love. Fritz really loves music and dislikes medicine but his dying father makes him promise to become a doctor and take care of his mother and female siblings. In the meantime, Helene discovers that she is pregnant. She tries to obtain a legal and safe abortion but is turned away. Desperately, she decides to go to a back-alley abortionist, but is saved in the eleventh hour due to a police raid on the place. Fritz and Helene are out of options and decide to commit suicide by lethal injection, but Helene opts out at the last moment and lets Fritz die on his own. For some months Helene is held for questioning but in the end she is free of suspicion. She leaves Heidelberg, gets her Ph.D., give birth to a son, Valentin, and Ambrosius helps her find a good job. Ultimately, she is successful in creating a rejuvenating agent, and takes a holiday on the French Riviera where she meets the long-divorced Ambrosius. She realizes that he is the only man in her life and she agrees to marry him.

The novel treat such issues as reproductive and abortion rights, women and education, female sexuality, the 'new woman,' women in the workforce, modernity, marriage and independence, Weimar decadence, and exotic Others.

Baum, Vicki. *Secrete Sentence* (1926). London: Geoffrey Bles, 1932.

The impetus of the novel is the shooting and killing of Foreign Minister Walter Rathenau in 1922. A fanatically nationalistic young man,

Joachim Burthe, gets involved in and carries out a plot to kill a government minister for his "crimes against the fatherland and the German people." He escapes and flees the city with the help of one of the accomplices and lives the rest of his life "on the run." The novel describes his flight, how he changes his name to Jan Brömmel and finds temporary work in a coal mine. The novel paints a picture of the volatile relationship between organized workers and employers which characterized the Weimar Republic. In this particular instance, violence breaks out, a worker is killed (inadvertently), and to avoid police inquiries, Joachim must flee again. He has an epiphany after listening to some music and returns to the city where his family has fallen on hard times. He decides not give himself up to the police but to atone for his crime by living his life in heavy guilt. Joachim flits through the country and gets work as a gardener in a mental hospital where he attracts the attention of the chief psychologist. He is recognized and must flee again but finds refuge in the psychologist's villa. Here Joachim is treated by his host and decides to talk about the minister's murder for the first time.

The last third of the novel finds an older, centered Joachim in a fishing village that "belongs" to an estate where he works as a fisherman under his own name. The aristocratic estate owner remembers his crime but leaves him alone. An erstwhile accomplice in the plot, now an important government official, and Joachim meet by happenstance, but Joachim declines all help declaring that he is happy in his new life. He drowns in a spring storm while saving another fisherman and his net, thus atoning for his earlier crime.

Baum highlights nationality, religion, German-ness, music, sexuality, women, rural versus urban, class.

Vicki Baum. "Der Weg," 1925. In *Der Weg*, ed. Erwin T. Moline. New York: F. S. Crofts & Co., 1931.

Frau Zienkann is a housewife and mother in a petit-bourgeois household. This short novella portrays a woman's housely chores and her life with her husband and son, who studies for his university entrance exam, and daughter who is in commercial college. On one particular day, Frau Zienkann sets out to find a linen-press and after hours of looking returns home soaked by a downpour. She develops pneumonia and in her feverish dreams she fantasizes about the love she once had but lost to World War One. She dies with a sense of having wasted her life and her daughter takes up where the mother left off.

Baum looks at domestic drudgery, family life, and gender division of labor.

Berend, Alice. *Der Kapitan von Bodensee*. Berlin: Fischer Verlag, 1932.

Balbine lives on a farm on Lake Constance with her father, Lorenz and the housekeeper, Josefa. Balbine's mother died when she was a baby and Josefa has brought her up. She goes to school in Constance and tends to her many duties on the farm. It is the unspoken expectation that she and the neighbor's son, Andreas, will one day get married. At a carnival she meets the young count Zeppelin, who presently is a student in Thuringia, and becomes fascinated by him. Andreas understands that Balbine won't be making up her mind to marry him in the near future and decides to set out to see the world and learn a trade. Balbine's father, Lorenz, pursues the favors of the local blacksmith (who is a woman) to Josefa's irritation; in the past, she had her sights set on Lorenz. Balbine and Zeppelin manage to meet "by accident" several times but in the end, reason prevails. Zeppelin becomes an officer in the army and leaves; Andreas returns and Balbine agrees to marry him and travel to America with him. In the bottom of her suitcase lies a Thuringia student's cap.

The social construction of gender, class, rural work, life choices for women.

Bernd, Heinz. *Vergessene Schuld und andere Sittenromane*. Mascotte Bücher. Dresden: Mignon Verlag, 1921.

A collection of moral tales in which virtue and desire are juxtaposed and modernity in most forms is proven to be immoral/izing and detremental to (married) life. Urban living, particularly Berliner life, gives rise to dishonesty, mass culture, alienation between children and their parents, 'new' women who invariably wear make-up, smoke, practice free love, and thus break up marriages. Male and female sexuality is opposed as is masculinity and femininity and traditional gender roles are upheld through the plots as the only sustainable way of life.

Braune, Rudolf. *Das Mädchen an der Orga Privat: Ein kleiner Roman aus Berlin* (1925). Frankfurt: Verlag neues Leben, 1930.

Erna Halbe, a young working-class woman from the provinces, arrives in Berlin where she gets a job as a typist (the brand of the typewriter is *Orga Privat*). One of her colleagues, Trude Leußner, determines to terminate an unwanted pregnancy but must go to a back-alley abortionist. The office boss, who was also Trude's 'lover,' fires her when she misses work due to complications from the abortion. Erna uses her working-class culture to her advantage and persuades her office colleagues to go on strike. Unfortunately, the union refuses to support the spontaneous strike and it fails. In the meantime, Trude dies from the botched abortion and the office boss agrees to allow the strikers back into their jobs—all but Erna, the instigator. At the end of the novel Erna has no job, but she nonetheless wanders undeterred into the Berlin cityscape knowing that she will prevail.

Braune's working-class novel figures a female protagonist who, unlike her bourgeois counterparts, does not aspire to climbing the class hierarchy, become a film star, or get married in a hurry. Rather, the story depicts the makings and workings of solidarity among white-collar workers, their daily lives in an urban youth culture, the sexual exploitation of female office workers, the consequences when safe and legal abortions are not available, and the hope that 'doing the right thing' will prevail. The novel sports numerous depictions of urban modernity and technology, women and work, *Bubiköpfe*, leisure time activities, and class.

Brück, Christa Anita. *Schicksale hinter Schreibmaschinen.* Berlin: Sieben Stäbe Verlag, 1930.

This is a novel about Fräulein Brückner and her career, or rather the lack of one. She is a typist and office clerk who goes through several jobs due to either sexual harassment or the preferential treatment of younger, prettier colleagues. The novel has very little plot but it gives a sharp impression of the kind of working conditions young women office workers had to deal with. *Schicksale* is a biting criticism of ageism and the high cost to women who resist the sexual predation of male superiors. It depicts the other side of women's economic independence and how miserable real life—as opposed to that presented in the movies or magazines—can be for the "new" woman. Fräulein Brückner hopes that somewhere there are jobs where a woman's erotic value will have no bearing on her promotion and admits that she too hopes to be "saved" through marriage.

Christ, Lena. *Madam Bäuerin* (1920) in *Dramen. Bauern und andere Erzählungen. Madam Bäuerin. Briefe*, hrsg. Walter Schmitz. München: Süddeutsche Verlag, 1990, 205-335.

The well-heeled Bavarian farmer, Schiermoser, takes in city summer boarders. The farmer's wife, "die Schiermoserin," and her aged mother despise everything and everybody urban. The city boarders consist of the impoverished, but noble widow, Rätin Scheuflein, her dead husband's sister, the middle-class and down-to-earth Tante Adele, and the Rätin's daughter, Rosalie. The Rätin's disgust concerning anything not noble or rural is as intense as is that of her counterpart, die Schiermoserin. Rosalie, a robust young woman, much more like her Aunt Adele than her mother, has just been forced into a engagement with a "suitable" match before they set off for a summer on the farm. Here, the powerful and well-respected farmer's son, "des Schiermosers Franzl," and Rosalie fall in love. Both mothers refuse to agree to the match and the Rätin leaves to go live with another of her daughters (who is already suitably married). Franz's mother moves out of the main house into an empty building on the farm, with her parents, waiting for her family to come running for help when the "city-girl" messes up. This, however, does not occur and the farmer's wife finally comes around at the birth of her first grandson.

Issues of middle-class versus nobility, rural and urban existences as well as tradition, modernity, entitlement, economics, and gender-specific roles and powers are discussed in the novel where most of the dialogue is conducted in Bavarian dialect.

Döblin, Alfred. *Die beiden Freundinnen und Ihr Giftmord* Reihe: Außenseiter der Gesellschaft. Die Verbrechen der Gegenwart. Berlin: Verlag die Schmiede, 1924.

Elli and Link are married but Elli soon stops being interested in sex. Link turns abusive and Elli turns to Grete. Grete's marriage is also on the rocks and after a while, Grete and Elli fall in love. With the quiet approval of Grete's mother, the two women start planning to kill Link with rat poison. They succeed but are caught, tried, and punished.

Döblin's docu/story probes female degeneracy as it is manifested in infantilism, masochism, lesbianism, and violence. It is a revealing study of the standard, male, "scientific" opinions of female deviance at the time of Weimar.

Fallada, Hans. *Kleiner Mann—was nun?* Berlin: Rowohlt, 1932.

All Johannes Pinneberg and his wife, Lämmchen (Bunny in the English translation), want is a decent life and a little happiness. But Pinneberg becomes a victim of the economic crisis when he loses his job as a bookkeeper. At the same time, they discover that Lämmchen is pregnant and they consider abortion for a while. They move in with Pinneberg's widowed mother, but when they discover that she is involved with some shadier elements of the criminal underground, they move out and into a garden house. In the meantime, he has gotten a job as sales clerk in a department store where the cut-throat competition for sales is dehumanizing, and he is let go there too. For Pinneberg nothing is left but receiving assistance and attempting to carry on through Lämmchen's and his love for each other and the baby.

The novel portrays in detail petty-bourgeois life on welfare, unemployment, petty criminals, *Freikörperkultur* (nudism), harassment on the job, the working class, and abortion.

Feuchtwanger, Lion. *Jud Süss* (1925). Frankfurt am Main: Fischer, 1985.

Based on the historical figure, Joseph Süß Oppenheimer, this historical novel looks at power, corruption, vanity, and antisemitism in eighteenth century Württemberg. Prince Karl Alexander of Württemberg employs the clever and elegant Süß as his secretary of the treasury. Both run their offices to their own advantages, although Süß is by far the more intelligent of the two. However, when Prince Karl sexually pursues and assaults Süß's beautiful daughter who consequently throws herself off a roof to her death, the father secretly vows to take revenge. He thwarts a Catholic plot to assume power by betraying it to its opponents at the eleventh hour; the

Prince dies of apoplexy. Süß now embraces his Jewishness and turns himself in to the plotters as a sacrificial lamb. Through a long, antisemitic trial he is condemned to death unless he converts to Christianity. This Süß rejects and he is executed.

Feuchtwanger exposes the workings of antisemitism, class, privilege, power, sexuality, faith, and innocence.

Franck, Hans. "Mamschka." In *Recht ist Unrecht. Neun Novellen um eine Wahrheit*. Berlin: Keil Verlag, 1928.

Marylla Urbinelakowsky arrives at the von Rathke estate as a migrant harvester. She becomes pregnant, the father dies (before they get married), and she stays on. Frau von Rathke gives birth in the same week as Marylla and persuades the servant to give her baby to foster parents in town. That way Marylla can wet nurse the new von Rathke. She agrees, loses her own baby due to the foster parents' neglect, and concentrates on being Eberhard von Rathke's "mamschka." They are inseparable until he is sent to school at the age of fourteen. Marylla goes back to serve in a low position in the kitchen. As the years go by, her position in the house deteriorates and Eberhard grows into a member of the landed gentry, who has little time for her. When she is no longer able to work for her keep, Eberhard offers her a room in an old-age home. Marylla is distressed over being removed from the countryside to the town and decides to seek out a good place to die. She chooses the river and drowns herself to no one's great sorrow.

Franck's story depicts rural work, servant life, class, motherhood, reproduction, loyalty, nationality, modernity and the image of the "new" woman.

Frank, Leonhard. *Carl and Anna* (1927). Translated by Cyrus Brooks. London: Peter Davies, 1929.

Carl and Richard have been prisoners of war in Siberia since the first weeks of World War One. In order to keep his wife, Anna, alive in his memory, Richard shares with Carl every thought about and conversation with her that he has ever had. Carl listens to everything many times over and comes to know and desire Anna through her husband's reminiscences. After four years, Carl and Richard are separated, and Carl escapes back to Germany. He shares a certain likeness with Richard and moves in with Anna under the pretext of being her long lost husband. She does not believe him but is fascinated by him, plays along, and falls in love with him. When the war ends, Richard returns, and Anna leaves him to be with Carl.

Working-class life, fatalistic love, loneliness.

Gustav Frenssen. *The Pastor of Poggsee,* 1922. Translated by Katharine G. Potts. London: George G. Harrap, 1981.

The novel is the simple life story of a Holstein pastor and his family during the period 1914–1920. Adam and Gude Barfood set up house in a northern part of Holstein where Adam is the young parish minister. His parishioners are simple folk with a fondness for tea-punch but Adam, too, is from poor circumstances and he is well-liked. Gude is an independent spirit and Adam doesn't always understand her ardor for life but feels the need to protect her from herself. In mid-career, the Barfoods, augmented by two daughters and two sons, move to a better paying position in the northern marshlands, the parish of Poggsee. His sexton there is a rogue and a lady's man, but Adam also reunites with a couple of his college friends. Life is not smooth sailing for Adam and Gude. They struggle financially, taking on the debts of Gude's spendthrift father who, in return, takes the liberty of speaking against the church. During his daughter's wedding to the son of one of Adam's old friends, there is news of the murder in Sarajevo and speculations about war. The Barfood sons are sent to the front in Flanders. Towards the end of the war, one of the daughters dies from influenza and the other is injured in a farm accident. In 1918, a few days before the Armistice, the Barfood sons are killed in the war. News of the end of the war and revolutionary activity reach Poggsee where some of the poorer parishioners are sympathetic to the Bolshevik cause. They steal church vessels and burn down the parsonage, and the rumor spreads that Adam did it himself. There is more unrest in the parish and the remaining daughter and the local (unhappily married) doctor become lovers. Adam and Gude are happy that the family will continue when they find out that their daughter has given birth to a boy. The novel ends with the village festival and games upon which occasion Adam Barfood gives a long optimistic sermon about Germany and Germans.

Coming from almost a *Heimat* perspective, the novel deals with simple faith, hard rural life, war, authority, nationality and Germanness, gender, sexuality, immediate post-war politics, and morality.

Georgy, Ernst (Margarete Michaelson). *Der Konfektionsbaron, ein Zeitbild aus der Konfektion*. Stuttgart: Union Deutsche Verlagsgesellschaft, 1922.

Herbert von Flintschs, his sisters, Maria and Martha—all three empoverished—and Leonora Woltka are members of the German nobility who, after Germany's defeat in World War One, must try to find their place in a new Germany. One strand of the plot revolves around Herbert's struggles as an erstwhile officer in the Emperor's cavalry to serve his country and himself in ways befitting a loyal but outmoded royalist in a modern republic. After jobs as a doorman and later accountant in Ressen's, an upscale department store, he accepts a German public-relations post for the press in the United States. A second plot concerns the twenty-four year old Lenore, who severs her ties with her wealthy noble family in order to find independence in a career as a window dresser, also at Ressen's. She insists on learning about Weimar reality and politics and we follow her development from a naive, privileged person to a politically and emotionally stable, modern woman. The Woltkas and von Flintschs were childhood friends and this female *Bildungsroman* demonstrates the sharpening conflicts in the Weimar Republic through the protagonists' differing philosophies of class, life, and *comme il faut*. Leonore, settling on the view of the *Mehrheitssozialisten*, mainstream Socialists, finds happiness in a relationship with a famous, left-leaning writer. Herbert, we are led to believe, will marry a young university student, the child of an "illegitimate" liaison between a nobleman and a commoner, despite serious objections from Herbert's sisters and his own sense of class.

The issues are a fatally wounded Germany (with Herbert, whose pride is wounded, as its metaphor), class struggle (the death of the aristocracy and struggles of the common working folks), modern life and mores, and Weimar political discourses.

Gluth, Oskar. *Bayerische Himmelfahrt. Ein fröhlicher Sommerroman*. Leipzig: L. Staackmann Verlag, Leipzig, 1933.

The conductor/composer Wolfgang Sebald's tendency to like women too much has estranged his wife, the beautiful singer Ulrike, who has bought a farm in Seerid, southern Bavaria. Here she hopes to live in seclusion while farming in a modern, "rationalized manner." The local doctor, Edwin Brühl, becomes infatuated with her and, with the help of Gertrud, the teacher's nineteen-year old daughter, gets to know Ulrike. Ulrike and Gertrud in turn visit a painter, Christopher, who has settled in the woods to get away from the city, and the gentle giant, falls in love with Gertrud. In the meantime, the local *femme fatale*, Kordula, the twenty-seven-year-old widow of the innkeeper, has both the father and son from the lucrative sawmill in hot pursuit of her favors. To top it all off, Wolfgang finds and visits Seerid, and creates havoc with Ulrike and Gertrud's emotions. However, all is well that ends well. On midsummer's night, Ulrike forgives Wolfgang, Christopher and Gertrud pair off, and Kordula promises the younger sawmiller her hand in marriage.

The novel plays with parochial notions, age, and bourgeois sensibilities in a gently ironic manner. The new woman, Ulrike, is portrayed as intelligent but somewhat nervous, fickle, and headstrong. The local young heroines, Gertrud and Kordula, are strong, independent, and reliable. In spite its date of publication—or perhaps because of it—there is no overt mention of the political situation. One of the characters in Seerid is called "der Nazi" but he is not portrayed differently from any of the other locals. Still, his presence has been made clear. A subtext is about art and artists and the inspiration they find away from an urban life in an "unspoiled" nature.

Herzog, Rudolf. *Die Buben der Frau Opterberg*. Berlin: Vier Falken Verlag, 1920.

Martin and Christoph are brought up by their mother, Christiane Opterberg on a farm in southern Germany. Arnold Opterberg, the father, is an artist (painter) but is fonder of drinking than painting. Christiane is tall, strong, open-faced, and blond and instills a patriotic love of the woods in the boys. They both study at the university of Freiburg where, as fraternity members, they fuel their love of the fatherland. They make the acquaintance of Therese Baumgart and Hilde Falkenroth, medical students at the university. Both Martin and Christoph fall in love with Therese, and she returns Martin's feelings. Their advanced studies separate the women from the brothers geographically and they drift apart, Martin to Holland via Berlin to learn shipbuilding and Christoph to the Rhineland for architecture studies. Therese keeps in contact with Christiane. When Martin returns to Germany, he marries the dark-haired, beautiful Sabine but her unfaithfulness mars his happiness. However,

Christoph and Therese are happily married and the brothers decide to join efforts in starting and running a shipyard. Martin surprises his wife in flagrante delicto and whips both of the lovers. The shipyard is working when World War One breaks out and the brothers go off to fight. The women manage the business until after the war when both men return. The social and political unrest that characterizes the post-war period finds its way to the shipyard, but the brothers' appeal to the German-ness of the workers inspires the latter to withstand the revolutionary cause. Martin recognizes his love for Therese's younger, blond sister, Linde, and the Opterberg family looks into building up their (German) lives again.

This novel is prototypically *deutsch*-national and deals with race, modernity, tradition, the proper function of women, national identity, artists as outsiders/enemy, work ethic, nature, and patriotism.

Kästner, Erich. *Fabian: Die Geschichte eines Moralisten.* Zürich: Atrium Verlag, 1931.

Jakob Fabian is the protagonist through whose eyes the reader sees Berlin—and by extension, Germany—in the late 1920s. As a moralist, Fabian is a sharp observer whose own bourgeois morality, nevertheless, creates no obstacle to acquainting himself with all walks of life: lesbian bars, female procurers, the mass media (newspapers and film, primarily), among others. With his friend, Labude, he comments on the lack of moral fiber in the late Weimar years, falls in love, loses his job, his love, and his friend. He returns to his childhood town, a backwater, where he is bored beyond belief. One day he witnesses a boy fall into the river and without thinking, he jumps in after him. The boy swims, crying, to shore and Fabian, who cannot swim, drowns.

Were one to see only the movie *Cabaret* and read *Fabian* one would get an overwhelming sense of the decadence of Berlin. Kästner casts a cynical eye on female sexuality, vulnerable masculinity, the consequences of war, media manipulation, the effects of modernity, industrial capitalism, and, finally, the non-viability of any kind of human decency in such a life.

Keun, Irmgard. *Das kunstseidene Mädchen* (1932). Bergisch Gladbach: Gustav Lübbe Verlag, 1987.

Doris is eighteen years old and longs for a life of glamour. To that end, she moves to Berlin where she works for a while as a typist earning 120 marks per month. Here she participates in the enjoyment of popular culture, watching movies, sitting in cafés, going dancing while she searches for love and glamour. She has relations with several men but doesn't take them too seriously. She moves in with a married man whose wife has left him but for reasons that are not entirely clear to Doris herself, she facilitates their reconciliation. Consequently, she moves out onto the street, aware that her search for glamour is over and that her future is very precarious indeed.

Keun examines the lives of young female white-collar workers, their dreams, their participation in the popular culture and their seduction by the same, the particular modernity of urban culture, female sexuality, "the good life," marriage and singlehood, employment, fashion, and youth.

Keun, Irmgard. *Gilgi—eine von uns* (1931). München: dtv, 1990.

Gilgi is a twenty-one-year-old office clerk who resists being bored by an ordinary life and marriage. Her biggest wish is to see the world, and her friend Olga advises her to stay employed, even if she falls in love: love is nice and fun but not serious and with an income you can stay financially independent. Keun lets us in on the constant—and baroque—sexual harassment that young women had to endure for fear of being fired, and Gilgi does indeed give up her job to live with Martin, with whom she has fallen in love. She falls pregnant and tries to persuade her doctor to perform a legal abortion. She is refused. Gilgi decides that dependence on a man cannot be the way she wants to live her life, and she leaves Martin. The novel ends with her saying goodbye to her previous life and friends as she boards a train to Berlin.

Gilgi is from a rebellious new generation, a "new" woman. The novel discusses popular culture and mass media, life options for Weimar women, marriage and independence, abortion rights, sexual exploitation, sexual morality, "sisterhood," modernity, and women in the workforce.

Kracauer, Siegfried. *Die Angestellten: Aus dem neuesten Deutschland*. Frankfurt am Main: Frankfurter Societäts-Drückerei, 1930.

A work about the "eroticism of everyday life" (14) of white-collar workers that "speaks about those who can only speak about themselves with the utmost difficulty" (9). Written on the eve of the depression, Kracauer examines the growth of the number of white-collar workers, their work in an era of automation and rationalization where workers are alienated from each other and their work, their search for an identity and struggle to belong to the bourgeoisie, and consequently also their class consciousness and solidarity—they are like bikers: they bend above and trample below (50). His observations are made in Berlin since "Berlin is *the* city with a white-collar culture, i.e., a culture made by and for white-collar workers which is considered culture by the majority of the white-collar workers" (20). Kracauer exposes their often miserable existence, the stigma of looking old, their leisure activities in popular culture via movies, bestsellers, *Schlager* (popular tunes), and dance clubs. He considers sports to be a crucial instrument for the conquest of the collective soul of white-collar workers. The work is a critique of industrial capitalism, the concomitant alienation of labor, the stupefication by popular culture of a class of workers who, due to all of the above, are also alienated from the proletarian class struggle.

Remarque, Erich Maria. *All Quiet on the Western Front* (1929). Greenwich, Conn.: Fawcett World Library, 1958.

Paul Bäumer volunteers, enthusiastically, with four of his high school friends, all nineteen years of age, to fight in World War One. Their romantic notion of the glory of soldiering is thoroughly destroyed in boot camp, where they receive a brutal training that does not have much bearing on surviving in real circumstances. Remarque describes in almost reporter-like style the gruesomeness of the trenches, poison gas attacks, nightly patrols through forests, and the materiality of death. This is done through the eyes of the "lost generation," that is, the generation that, having matured in the trenches, did not have the skills to fit into a society no longer at war. The novel ends with the death of the last of the quartet and the laconic statement that the army reports all quiet on the Western front.

The overwhelming issue is the brutality of war with the ensuing corollaries of nationality, masculinity, heroism, class, alienation, and generational conflict.

Roth, Joseph. *Das Spinnennetz.*(1923). Köln: Kiepenheuer & Witsch, 1988.

Second Lieutenant Theodor Lohse returns from World War One to a lower middle-class existence that seems bent on disempowering him. His resentment toward life outside the army and his hate for Jews and socialists fuels his view of the world and guides his life. He has no 'luck' with women and after a casual homosexual affair with a prince, Lohse joins a secret society where he acts as spy and informer, thus being well on his way to fulfilling his notions of his own right to power. After having killed two men who remind him of his powerless existence and stand in his way, Lohse rejoins the army and marries Fräulein von Schlieffen, who only wants to use him for her own socially ambitious goals. Enter double agent Benjamin Lenz, "a Jew from Lodz," who has nothing but contempt for the cultural decadence of the West and who—over Lohse's head—plays the powers against each other. The novel ends with Lohse plotting Lenz's murder and Lenz's leaving the country, presumably for the United States.

Roth's novel takes a sharp look at notions of power and powerlessness, antisemitism (particularly in early Weimar), early German fascist ideologies, women, and female sexuality.

Roth, Joseph. *Zipper und sein Vater. Roman* (1928). Cologne: Kiepenheuer & Witsch, 1985.

On his return from World War One, Arnold Zipper struggles in his attempt to negotiate most aspects of modern life in a democratic Germany. Roth illustrates how deeply the experiences of war shaped the perspective of a whole generation. The novel relates Arnold Zipper's relationship to modernity, to his father, Zipper Senior, and to his delinquent, one-legged, rebellious brother, Cäsar. It also explores his love/hate for his beautiful young actress wife, Erna. He must make his way without any help from his rather impoverished father, whose character Roth draws as a metaphor for a traditional, but sick, powerless, and useless Central European way of life. At the end of the novel, Arnold, as a token of his war-induced indifference to middle-class expectations, earns his living playing the violin in a clown's act.

The novel deals extensively with war, marriage, the "new" woman, sexuality, misogyny, high/low culture, cinema, and various other aspects of modern life.

von Lengerke, Wolfgang. *Die Amazone Gloria*. Berlin/ Friedenau: Weltbücher Verlag, 1928.

The locale is the United States. Gloria, after a brutal beating by her millionaire husband, leaves him and initiates plans for an independent women's colony. At the same time, the Jewish Samuel Josefsohn, her husband's one-time partner but now rival and deadly enemy, plots to take revenge on the Christian world. Blanche Ferguson, a chorus girl, joins Gloria's effort and together they establish the colony on land Gloria has bought in Texas. They populate it from a long list of vetted volunteers, "Amazons." Jack Seymour loves Gloria and is working his way into power and money in order to be worthy of her after having been imprisoned (he was innocent) and rid himself of an opium addiction. Josefsohn succeeds in taking revenge by crashing the stock market, kidnapping Gloria, who is in New York on some business, and raping her, whereupon he throws himself off the roof of a skyscraper. Back on the ranch, Blanche has been amassing power and upon Gloria's return, makes a pass at her. In the ensuing struggle, the colony goes up in flames and Gloria is saved by Jack Seymour after days in the wilderness.

The novel is derisive of women's utopian societies, particularly as formulated by the early American women's movement. It highlights connecting issues such as the image and perception of women, emancipation, marriage, reproduction, women's work, female sexuality, violence against women, eroticism, and lesbianism. Moreover, antisemitism, class, race, modernity, and urban living are also dealt with throughout the novel.

von Urbanitzky, Grete. *Der wilde Garten* (1927). Wiesbaden: Feministische Buchverlag, 1995.

Hanna von Südekum is a teacher whose mothering "instinct" makes her watch very closely over her female students. They are making their way through adolescence and von Südekum wants to save them from all the "smut" and dangers connected with adult sexuality. She deplores their transition into adulthood, which leads directly into marriage. That she interprets as the end of freedom. She befriends an exotic (and erotic) woman artist, Alexandra, whose sexual life is active and not restricted to the opposite sex. Frau von Südekum is the novel's conduit for somewhat safe and traditional thoughts about gender formation and sexuality, while Alexandra pushes at the limits of what can be thought and done in reality. In fact, she has a sexual affair with one of von Südekum's more radical students.

The novel is an intense discussion of gender, sexuality, love between women, the future for women, marriage, women's bodies, desire, emancipation and morality.

Wassermann, Jacob. *The Goose Man*. Harcourt, Brace & Co, 1922.

Daniel Nothafft lives for music. He is brought up by his uncle and endures years of utter misery and poverty to obtain his musical education. He gets a job as a conductor and marries Gertrud, thereby thwarting the family and its intended bride for him, his ugly cousin, Philippine. It is, however, Gertrud's sister, Leonore, he really loves and Nuremberg's citizens take delight in likening him to the statue of the goose man, a young boy herding geese with one under each arm. Gertrud commits suicide so that she no longer is in the way of Leonore and Daniel's happiness and after a while they marry because Leonore is expecting Daniel's child. Leonore dies during childbirth. A desperate Daniel once more leaves Nuremberg for a long journey and when, years later, he returns, he marries the beautiful but unfaithful Dorothea. He throws her out of the house and ends the marriage but more is coming. His vengeful cousin, Philippine, sets fire to his house and, as it goes up in flames, so does his *magnum opus*, the manuscript of his "Promethean Symphony." Broken and delirious, he sees the goose man at his bedside where the latter tells him to become a compassionate member of the human community rather than an artist in an ivory tower. Daniel recovers and spends the rest of his life as a noted music teacher.

The novel contains examples of perceptions of women, female sexuality, "art and life," antisemitism, bourgeois life, class, modernity, colonialism, reproductive issues, and women's roles in society.

Weirauch, Anna Elisabet. *The Scorpion* (1919, 1932, and 1933). Reprint. New York: Arno Press, 1975.

Myra is a young women from a "good" family who is madly in love with an older "mannish" woman, Olga. Myra's family finds out about Olga, separates them and sends Myra to live in virtual house-arrest with an uncle. Eventually, Myra is convinced that Olga doesn't love her anymore and she gets engaged to a prominent man. She cannot go through with the wedding but calls it off too late. She then receives the news that Olga has killed herself over her lost love. The first volume ends here and, in the second, Myra has moved to Berlin where she "studies life." She gets acquainted with a group of bohemians who experiment with sexuality as well as with the drug of choice in Weimar, cocaine. She is involved with both Sophie, a sculptor, and the singer Gisela but after some bad experiences she moves to Hamburg to recuperate. Her visit ends when she is set up for a love tryst in a menage á trois. The last volume finds Myra in a mountain town where no one knows her. On a trip to the city she meets Coronna, Olga's erstwhile lover; she stays in the city to be with Coronna. At the end of the novel, Myra is back in her mountain home where a visit from Coronna ends in disappointment. Coronna does not want to live with Myra and departs, leaving Myra to live alone and make peace with herself.

Weirauch investigates homosexuality and its theories, Berlin lesbian life, "Lila Nächte," the cabaret and bar scene, the "new" woman, and bohemians and artists in 1920s Berlin.

Selected Bibliography

Novels

Baum, Vicki. *And Life Goes On*. Translated by Margaret Goldsmith. Garden City, 1932.
______. *Es war alles ganz anders: Erinnerungen*. Berlin, 1962.
______. *Helene*. Translated by Ida Zeitlin. Garden City, 1933.
______. *Hell in Frauensee. Ein heiterer Roman von Liebe und Hunger*. Berlin, 1927.
______. *Leben ohne Geheimnis*. Berlin, 1932.
______. *Menschen im Hotel*. 1929. Reprint, Frankfurt am Main, 1986.
______. "Raffael Gutmann." Parts 1-3. *Leipziger Illustrirte Zeitung* 159, (12 October 1922): 307–08; (19 October 1922): 353–54; (2 November 1922): 403–05.
______. *Secret Sentence*. Translated by Eric Sutton. New York, 1932.
______. *Der Weg*. Edited by Erwin T. Molime. New York, 1931.
Berend, Alice. *Der Kapitan von Bodensee*. Berlin, 1932.
Bernd, Heinz. *Vergessene Schuld und andere Sittenromane*. Mascotte/Bücher. Dresden, 1921.
Boy-Ed, Ida. *Brosamen*. Dresden, 1922.
Braune, Rudolf. *Das Mädchen an der Orga Privat. Ein kleiner Roman aus Berlin*. Frankfurt am Main, 1930.
Breme, M.I., ed. *Vom Leben getötet: Bekentnisse eines Kindes*. Freiburg, 1927.
Brück, Christa Anita. *Schicksale hinter Schreibmaschinen*. Berlin, 1930.
Courths-Mahler, Hedwig. *Brittas Weg ins Glück.*. Bergish Gladbach, 1984.
Christ, Lena. *Madam Bäuerin*. 1920. In *Dramen, Bauern und andere Erzählungen. Madam Bäuerin, Briefe*. Edited by Walter Schmitz, 205–335. Munich, 1990.
Döblin, Alfred. *Die beiden Freundinnen und Ihr Giftmord*. Außenseiter der Gesellschaft. Die Verbrechen der Gegenwart. Berlin, 1924.
Fallada, Hans. *Kleiner Mann—was nun?* Berlin, 1932.
Feuchtwanger, Lion. *Die hässliche Herzogin Margarete Maultasch*. Potsdam, 1926.
______. *Power*. Translated by Willa & Edwin Muir. New York, 1928.

Frank, Leonhard. *Carl and Anna* (1927). Translated By Curys Brooks. London, 1929.

Franck, Hans. "Ernte." In *Recht ist Unrecht: Neun Novellen um eine Wahrheit*, 65–88. Leipzig, 1928.

______. "Mamschka." In *Recht ist Unrecht: Neun Novellen um eine Wahrheit*, 9–64. Leipzig, 1928.

Frenssen, Gustav. *The Pastor of Poggsee*. Translated by Katharine G. Potts. London, 1981.

Georgy, Ernst. *Der Konfektionsbaron, ein Zeitbild aus der Konfektion*. Stuttgart, 1922.

Gluth, Oskar. *Bayerische Himmelfahrt. Ein fröhlicher Sommerroman*. Leipzig, 1933.

Herzog, Rudolf. *Die Buben der Frau Opterberg*. Berlin, 1920.

Kästner, Erich. *Fabian. Die Geschichte eines Moralisten*. Zurich, 1931. English translation: Cyrus Brooks. Evanston, 1990.

Keun, Irmgard. *Das kunstseidene Mädchen*. 1932. Bergisch Gladbach, 1987.

______. *Gilgi - eine von uns*. 1931. 3d ed. Munich, 1994.

Kracauer, Siegfried. *Die Angestellten: Aus dem neuesten Deutschland*. Frankfurt am Main, 1930.

Remarque, Erich Maria. *All Quiet on the Western Front*. Translated by Arthur Wesley Wheen. New York, 1958.

______. *Der Weg zurück*. Berlin, 1931.

Roth, Joseph *Das Spinnennetz. Roman*. 1923. Reprint, Cologne: 1988.

______. *Hotel Savoy*. Berlin, 1924.

______. *Zipper und sein Vater*. Cologne, 1986.

Tucholsky, Kurt. *Castle Gripsholm: A Summer Story*. Translated by Michael Hofmann. London, 1985.

Seghers, Anna. *Aufstand der Fischer von Santa Barbara*. Neuwied, 1981.

______. *Das siebte Kreuz*. Neuwied, 1979.

von Lengerke, Wolfgang. *Die Amazone Gloria*. Berlin, 1928.

von Simpson, Margot. *Fürst Woronzeff*. Berlin, 1929.

von Urbanitzky, Grete. *Der wilde Garten*. 1927. Reprint, Wiesbaden, 1995.

Wassermann, Jakob. *The Goose Man*. Translated by Allen W. Posterfield. Harcourt, 1922.

Weirauch, Anna Elisabet. *The Outcast*. 1919–1921. Translated by Guy Endore. Reprint, New York, 1975.

______. *The Scorpion*. 1919-21. Translated by Whittaker Chambers. Reprint, New York, 1975.

Other Literature and Theory

Abrams, Lynn. "From Control to Commercialization: the Triumph of Mass Entertainment in Germany 1900–1920?" *German History. The Journal of the German History Society* 8, no. 3 (1990): 278–93.

Abrams, Lynn and Elizabeth Harvey, eds. *Gender Relations in German History*. Durham, 1997.

Adelson, Leslie A. *Making Bodies. Making History: Feminism & German Identity*. Modern German Culture and Literature. Lincoln, Neb., 1993.

Adorno, Theodor W. *Minima Moralia*. Frankfurt am Main, 1969.

Balibar, Etienne and Immanuel Wallerstein. *Rasse—Klasse—Nation: Ambivalente Identitäten*. Hamburg, 1990.

Barnouw, Dagmar. *Weimar Intellectuals and the Threat of Modernity*. Bloomington, 1988.

Bea, August. "Antisemitismus, Rassentheorie und Altes Testament." *Stimmen der Zeit* 100 (1921): 171–83.

Beier, Rosmarie. "Zur Geschichte weiblicher Lebenschancen—Alltagsleben, gewerkschaftliche Organisation und Streik Berliner Bekleidungsarbeiterinnen 1870-1914." In *Frauen in der Geschichte* II, eds. Annette Kuhn & Jörg Rüsen, 211–44. Düsseldorf, 1982.

Bothe, Rolf. "Einleitung." In *Eldorado: Homosexuelle Frauen und Männer in Berlin 1900-1950. Geschichte, Alltag und Kultur*, ed. Michael Bollé, 5–7. Berlin, 1984.

Boxer, Marilyn, J. and Jean H. Quataert, eds. *Connecting Spheres: Women in the Western World, 1500 to the Present*. New York, 1987.

Brantlinger, Patrick. *Bread & Circuses: Theories of Mass Culture as Social Decay*. Ithaca, NY, 1983.

Brecht, Bertolt. "Die Krise des Sportes." In *Der Sport am Scheidewege*, ed. Willy Meisl, 144–46. Heidelberg, 1928.

Bridenthal, Renate." Something Old, Something New: Women Between the Two World Wars." In *Becoming Visible: Women in European History*, eds. Renate Bridenthal, Claudia Koonz, and Susan Stuard, 472–97. Boston, 1987.

______. "Class Struggle Around the Hearth: Women and Domestic Service in the Weimar Republic." In *Toward the Holocaust: The Social and Economic Collapse of the Weimar Republic*, eds. Michael Dobkowski & Isidor Walleman, 243–265. Westport, Conn., 1983.

Brinker-Gabler, Gisela, Karola Ludwig and Angela Wöffen, eds. *Lexikon deutschsprachiger Schriftstellerinnen 1800–1945*. Munich, 1986.

Brockmann, Stephen. "Weimar Sexual Cynicism." In *Dancing on the Volcano: Essays on the Culture of the Weimar Republic*, eds. Thomas W. Kniesche and Stephen Brockmann, 165–80. Columbia, SC, 1994.

Brod, Max. "Women and the New Objectivity." In *The Weimar Republic Sourcebook*, eds. Anton Kaes, Martin Jay, and Edward Dimenberg, 205–06. Berkeley and Los Angeles, 1994.

Brooks, Peter. *The Melodramatic Imagination: Balzac, Henry James, Melodrama and the Mode of Excess*. New York, 1985.

Buck, Theo. "Zur Literatur der Weimarer Republik." In *Tendenzen der deutschen Literatur zwischen 1918 und 1945*, eds. Theo Buck and Dietrich Steinbach, 7–47. Stuttgart, 1985.

Butler, Judith. *Gender Trouble: Feminism and the Subversion of Identity*. New York, 1990.

Carstens, Belinda. "Representations of Sexuality in Marie Luise Fleißer's *Pioniere in Ingolstadt*." Paper presented at the annual conference of the German Studies Association, Minneapolis, Minnesota, October 1992.

Chamberlain, Houston Stewart. *Die Grundlage des 19. Jahrhunderts*. Munich, 1899.

Chickering, Roger. "'Casting Their Gaze More Broadly': Women's Patriotic Activism in Imperial Germany." *Past & Present* 118 (February 1988): 156–85.

Coetzee, J.M. *White Writing: On the Culture of Letters in South Africa*. New Haven, 1988.

Coudenhove-Kalergi, Heinrich Graf. *Das Wesen des Antisemitismus*. 1906. Vienna, 1929.

Crawford, Robert. "A Cultural Account of 'Health'—Self-Control, Release and the Social Body." In *Issues in the Political Economy of Health Care*, ed. John McKinley, 60–103. New York, 1985.

Dahrendorf, Ralph. *Society and Democracy in Germany*. New York, 1967.

Denning, Michael. "The End of Mass Culture." In *Modernity and Mass Culture*, eds. James Naremore and Patrick Brantlinger, 253–68. Bloomington, Ind., 1991.

Die Dame. (December 1932).

Dijkstra, Bram. *Idols of Perversity: Fantasies of Feminine Evil in Fin-de-Siècle Culture*. New York, 1986.

Doan, Laura, ed. *The Lesbian Postmodern*. New York, 1994.

Doane, Mary Ann. *Femmes Fatales: Feminism, Film Theory, Psychoanalysis*. New York, 1991.

Dollimore, Jonathan. "Shakespeare, Cultural Materialism, Feminism and Marxist Humanism." *New Literary History* 21, no. 3 (Spring 1990): 471–93.

Dudovitz, Resa L. *The Myth of Superwoman: Women's Bestsellers in France and the United States*. London, 1990.

Dyer, Richard. *Now You See It: Studies on Lesbian and Gay Film*. London, 1990.

Eagleton, Terry. *The Function of Criticism: From the Spectator to Post-Structuralism*. London, 1984.

______. "The Subject of Literature." *Cultural Critique* 2 (Winter 1985–1986): 95–104.

Edwards, Harry. *Sociology of Sports*. Homewood, Ill., 1973.

Enzensberger, Hans Magnus. *Einzelheiten I. Bewußtseins-Industrie*. Frankfurt am Main, 1964.

Faderman, Lillian. *Surpassing the Love of Men: Romantic Friendship and Love Between Women From the Renaissance To the Present.* New York, 1981.
Fallada, Hans. *Lille Mand, hvad nu?* Translated by Sonja Heise. Copenhagen, 1932.
Felski, Rita. *The Gender of Modernity*. Cambridge, Mass, 1995.
Fiske, John. "Popular Discrimination." In *Modernity and Mass Culture*, eds. James Naremore and Patrick Brantlinger, 103–115. Bloomington, Ind., 1991.
Foster, Jeannette H. *Sex Variant Women in Literature*. Talahassee, Fla., 1985.
Foucault, Michel. *Language, Counter-Memory, Practice: Selected Essays and Interviews*. Edited by Donald F. Bouchard. Ithaca, N.Y., 1977.
______. *The History of Sexuality*. Vol. 1. Translated by Robert Hurley. New York, 1980.
Fowler, Bridget. *Women and Romantic Literature in the Twentieth Century.* Hemel Hempstead, UK, 1991.
Freeman, Barbara Claire. *The Feminine Sublime: Gender and Excess in Women's Fiction*. Berkeley and Los Angeles, 1995.
Freud, Sigmund. "The Ego and the Id." In *The Freud Reader*, 628–58. Edited by Peter Gay. New York, 1989.
______. "Totem and Taboo." In *The Freud Reader*, 481–513. Edited by Peter Gay. New York, 1989.
Frevert, Ute. *Frauengeschichte zwischen bürgerlicher Verbesserung und neuer Weiblichkeit*. Frankfurt am Main, 1986.
______. "Vom Klavier zur Schreibmaschine—Weiblicher Arbeitsmarkt und Rollenzuweisungen am Beispiel der weiblichen Angestellten in der Weimarer Republik." In *Frauen in der Geschichte* I, eds. Annette Kuhn and Gerhard Schneider, 82–112. Düsseldorf, 1979.
Fromm, Erich. *The Working Class in Weimar Germany: A Psychological and Sociological Study*. 1929. Translated by Barbara Weinberger. Cambridge, Mass., 1984.
Garber, Marjorie. *Vested Interests*. New York, 1991.
Gay, Peter. *Weimar Culture: The Outsider as Insider*. New York, 1968.
Geyer, Michael. "The Stigma of Violence, Nationalism, and War in Twentieth Century Germany." *German Studies Review*, Special Issue: German Identity (Winter 1992): 75–110
Giddens, Anthony. *The Class Structure of the Advanced Societies*. London, 1975.
Gilbert, Sandra and Susan Gubar. *No Man's Land: The Place of the Woman Writer in the Twentieth Century*. Vol. 1 of *The War of the Words*. New Haven, 1988.
Gilman, Sander L. "Black Bodies, White Bodies: Toward an Iconography of Female Sexuality in Late Nineteenth-Century Art, Medicine, and Literature." In *"Race," Writing and Difference*, ed. Henry Louis Gates, Jr., 223–261. Chicago, 1985.
______. *Difference and Pathology: Stereotypes of Sexuality, Race, and Madness.* Ithaca, N.Y., 1985.

______. *Inscribing the Other*. Lincoln, Neb., 1991.
Giroux, Henry. *Disturbing Pleasures: Learning Popular Culture*. New York, 1994.
Goebbels, Joseph. *Michael: ein deutsches Schicksal in Tagebuchblättern*. Munich, 1934.
Goldstein, Bluma. *Reinscribing Moses: Heine, Kafka, Freud, and Schoenberg in a European Wilderness*. Cambridge, Mass., 1992.
Grimm, Reinhold and Jost Hermand, eds. *Popularität und Trivialität*. Fourth Winsconsin Workshop. Frankfurt am Main, 1974.
Grossman, Atina. "Abortion and Economic Crisis: The 1931 Campaign Against §218 in Germany." *New German Critique* 5 (Spring 1978): 119–37.
______. *Reforming Sex: The German Movement for Birth Control and Abortion Reform, 1920–1950*. New York, 1995.
______. "The New Woman and the Rationalization of Sexuality in Weimar Germany." In *Powers of Desire: The Politics of Sexuality*, eds. Ann Snitow, Christine Stansel, and Sharon Thompson, 153–71. New York, 1983.
Grosz, Elaine. "Judaism and Exile: The Ethics of Otherness." *New Formations* 12 (Winter 1990): 77–88.
Gunew, Sneja, ed. *Feminist Knowledge: Critique and Construct*. London, 1990.
Gutmann, Curt. "Boxen als Geschäft und als Sport." *Der Querschnitt* 8, no. 8 (1928): 560–63.
Haber, Samuel. *Efficiency and Uplift: Scientific Management in the Progressive Era 1890–1920*. Chicago, 1964.
Hagemann, Karen. *Frauenalltag und Männerpolitik: Alltagsleben und gesellschaftliches Handeln von Arbeiterfrauen in der Weimarer Republik*. Darmstadt, 1990.
Hake, Sabine. "Urban Paranoia in Alfred Döblins *Berlin Alexanderplatz*." *The German Quarterly* 67, no. 3 (Summer 1994): 347–68.
Hansen, Miriam. "Early Silent Cinema: Whose Public Sphere?" *New German Critique* 29 (Spring/Summer 1983): 147–84.
Harrigan, Renny." Die emanzipierte Frau im deutschen Roman der Weimarer Republik." In *Stereotyp und Vorurteil in der Literatur*, edited by James Elliot, Jürgen Pelzer, and Carol Poore, 65–83. Göttingen, 1978.
Hart, Lynda. *Fatal Women: Lesbian Sexuality and the Mark of Aggression*. Princeton, 1994.
Harvey, Elizabeth. "Private Fantasy and Public Interventions: Girls' Reading in Weimar Germany." In *Determined Women*, edited by Jennifer Birkett and E. Harvey. Lanham: Barnes & Noble, 1991.
Haxthausen, Charles W. and Heidrun Suhr, eds. *Berlin: Culture and Metropolis*. Minneapolis, 1990.
Heath, Stephen. "While Millicent bucked and writhed ..." In *Popular Fiction: Technology, Ideology, Production, Reading*, ed. Tony Bennet, 46–58. London & New York, 1990.
Heine, Heinrich. "Ludwig Marcus Denkworte." In *Sämtliche Schriften*, edited by Klaud Brieglb et al., vol. 5, 175–91. Munich, 1975.

Hermand, Jost and Frank Trommler. *Die Kultur der Weimarer Republik.* Munich, 1978.

Hermann, Anne. Review of *New Women, New Novels: Feminism and Early Modernism,* by Ann Ardis. *Signs* 18, no. 3 (Spring 1993): 728.

Herzklotz, Ellen. *Literatur als Mittel der Bildung und Beeinflussung: Die Frauenbeilage der Weser Zeitung 1919–1923.* Pfaffenweiler, 1991.

Hiller, Kurt. "Wo bleibt der homoerotische Roman?" *Jahrbuch für sexuelle Zwischenstufen* 14 (1914): 338–41.

Holzner, Johann. "Literarische Verfahrensweisen und Botschaften der Vicki Baum." In *Erzählgattungen der Trivialliteratur,* edited by Zdenko Skreb and Uwe Baur, 233–50. Vol. 18. Innsbrucker Beiträge zur Kulturwissenschaft, Germanistische Reihe. Innsbruck, 1984.

Huyssen, Andreas. *After the Great Divide: Modernism, Mass Culture, Postmodernism.* Bloomington, Ind., 1986.

Informationsblätter zu der Ausstellung "Frauenalltag und Frauenbewegung in Frankfurt 1890–1980." Historische Dokumentation 20. Jahrhundert. Frankfurt am Main, 1981.

Jäger, Georg. "Der Kampf gegen Schmutz und Schund: Die Reaktion der Gebildeten auf die Unterhaltungsindustrie." *Archiv für Geschichte des Buchwesens.* 31. (1988): 163–91.

Jameson, Fredric. "Reification and Utopia in Mass Culture." *Social Text: Theory/Culture/Ideology* 1, no. 1 (1979): 130–48.

JanMohamed, Abdul R. "The Economy of Manichean Allegory: The Function of Racial Difference in Colonialist Literature." In *"Race," Writing and Difference,* ed. Henry Louis Gates, Jr., 78–106. Chicago, 1985.

______. *Manichean Aesthetics: The Politics of Literature in Colonial Africa.* Amherst, Mass., 1983.

Jay, Martin. *Adorno.* Cambridge, Mass., 1984.

Jordanova, Ludmilla. *Sexual Visions.* Madison, Wisc., 1989.

Kaes, Anton, ed. *Kino-Debatte: Texte zum Verhältnis von Literatur und Film 1909–1929.* Tubingen, 1978.

______. "Silent Cinema," *Monatshefte* 82, no. 3 (1990): 246–56.

______. *Weimarer Republik: Manifeste und Dokumente zur deutschen Literatur 1918–1933.* Stuttgart, 1983.

Kafka, Franz. "Letter to Max Brod, June 1921," *Briefe, 1902–1924,* ed. Max Brod, Vol. 8 (New York, 1958), 337.

Kater, Michael H. *Different Drummers: Jazz in the Culture of Nazi Germany.* New York, 1992.

Kaus, Gina. "Glück bei Männern." *Der Querschnitt* 9, no. 11 (November, 1932): 736–38.

Kessler, Harry. *Walter Rathenau: Sein Leben und sein Werk* . Berlin, 1928.

Kestner, Joseph A. *Mythology and Misogyny.* Madison, Wisc., 1989.

Keyserling, Count Hermann. " Introduction." In *The Book of Marriage,* ed. Count Hermann Keyserling. New York, 1926.

King, Lynda J. *Best-sellers by Design: Vicki Baum and the Ullstein Press.* Detroit, 1988.

______. "Probable or Possible? The Issue of Women's Emancipation in German Literature of the 1920s." *Rocky Mountain Review* 35, no. 2 (1981): 138–52.

______. "Vicki Baum and the "Making" of Popular Success: "Mass" Culture or "Popular" Culture?" *Women in German Yearbook,* 11 (1995): 151–69.

Kokula, Ilse. *Weibliche Homosexualität um 1900 in zeitgenössischen Dokumenten.* Munich, 1981.

Kosta, Barbara. "Employed Bodies: Female Servants in Works by Marieluise Fleisser." *German Studies Review* XI, no. 1 (February 1992): 47–63.

Kracauer, Siegfried. *From Caligari to Hitler: A Psychological History of the German Film.* Princeton, 1974.

______. *The Mass Ornament: Weimar Essays.* Translated and edited by Thomas Y. Levine. Cambridge, Mass., 1995.

Kuhn, Annette. "Sexual Disguise and Cinema." In *Popular Fiction: Technology, Ideology, Production, Reading,* ed. Tony Bennett, 169–88. London, 1990.

Lacey, Kate. *Feminine Frequencies: Gender, German Radio, and the Public Sphere, 1923–1945.* Ann Arbor, Mich., 1996.

Landau, Lola. "The Companionate Marriage." *The Weimar Republik Sourcebook,* eds. Anton Kaes, Martin Jay, and Edward Dimenberg, 702–703. Berkeley and Los Angeles, 1994.

Lethen, Helmut. *Verhaltenslehre der Kälte: Lebensversuche zwischen den Kriegen.* Frankfurt am Main, 1994.

Leipziger Illustrierte Zeitung, no. 4234 (May 6, 1926): 607.

Löwenthal, Leo. *Literature, Popular Culture, and Society.* Palo Alto, Calif., 1961.

Lucka, Emil. "Verwandlung der Frau." In *Die Frau von Morgen: Wie wir sie wünschen,* ed. Friedrich M. Huebner, 77–90. Leipzig, 1929.

Lungstrom, Janet. "*Metropolis* and the Technosexual Woman of German Modernity." In *Women in the Metropolis: Gender and Modernity in Weimar Culture,* ed. Katharina von Ankum, 128–44. Berkeley and Los Angeles, 1997.

Mamozai, Martha. *Komplizinnen* Hamburg, 1990.

Mandell, Richard D. *Sport: A Cultural History.* New York, 1984.

Mann, Thomas. "Marriage in Transition: An Open Letter to Count Hermann Keyserling." In *The Book of Marriage: A New Interpretation by Twentyfour Leaders of Contemporary Thought,* ed. Count Hermann Keyserling, 244–62. New York, 1926.

Marti, Madeleine. *Hinterlegte Botschaften. Die Darstellung lesbischer Frauen in der Deutschsprachigen Literatur seit 1945.* Stuttgart, 1992.

Mason, Tim. " Women in Germany 1925-1940: Family, Welfare and Work." Part 1. *History Workshop* 1, no. 1 (1976): 74–113.

McCormick, Richard. "From *Caligari* to Dietrich: Sexual, Social, and Cinematic Discourses in Weimar Film." *Signs* 18, no. 3 (Spring 1993): 640–68.

Meisl, Willy. "Der Sport am Scheidewege," in *Der Sport am Scheidewege*, ed. Willy Meisl. Heidelberg, 1928.
Melman, Billie. *Women and the Popular Imagination in the 20s: Flappers and Nymphs*. London, 1988.
Mizejewski, Linda. *Divine Decadence: Fascism, Female Spectacle, and the Makings of Sally Bowles*. Princeton, 1992.
Morgenrot (Advent 1922): 185–6.
Mosse, George. *The Culture of Western Europe*. Boulder, Colo., 1988.
______. *German Jews Beyond Judaism*. Cincinatti, Ohio, 1980.
______. *Masses and Man: Nationalist and Fascist Perceptions of Reality*. New York, 1980.
______. *Nationalism and Sexuality: Middle Class Morality and Sexual Norms in Modern Europe*. Madison, Wisc., 1985.
Murray, Bruce. *Film and the German Left in the Weimar Republic: From Caligari to Kuhle Wampe*. Austin, Texas, 1990.
Naremore, James and Patrick Brantlinger. "Introduction." In *Modernity and Mass Culture*, eds. James Naremore and Patrick Brantlinger, 1–23. Bloomington, Ind., 1991.
New German Critique 40 (Winter 1987). (Special issue on Weimar Film Theory).
New German Critique 51 (Fall 1990). (Special issue on Weimar Mass Culture).
Nicholson-Lord, David. "The Politics of Travel: Is Tourism Just Colonialism In Another Guise?" *The Nation* (October 6, 1997): 11–18.
Niewyk, Donald L. *The Jews in Weimar Germany*. Baton Rouge, 1980.
Nusser, Peter. *Trivialliteratur.* Sammlung Metzler, vol. 262. Stuttgart, 1991.
Nutz, Walter. *Der Trivialroman, seine Formen und seine Hersteller.* Cologne, 1966.
Opitz, May, Katharina Oguntoye & Dagmar Schultz, eds. *Showing Our Colors: Afro-German Women Speak Out.* Translated by Anne V. Adams. Amherst, Mass., 1992.
Parker, Andrew, Mary Russo, Doris Sommer, and Patricia Yaeger, eds. *Nationalisms and Sexualities*. New York, 1991.
Peiss, Kathy. "'Charity Girls' and City Pleasures: Historical Notes on Working Class Sexuality, 1880-1920." In *Powers of Desire: The Politics of Sexuality*, eds. Ann Snitow, Christine Stansel, and Sharon Thompson, 74–87. New York, 1983.
Petersen, Vibeke Rützou. "The Best of Both Worlds? Jewish Representations of Assimilation, Self, and Other in Weimar Popular Fiction." *The German Quarterly* 68, no. 2 (Spring 1995): 160–73.
Petro, Patrice. *Joyless Streets: Women and Melodramatic Representation in Weimar*.
______. "Perceptions of Difference: Woman as Spectator and Spectacle." In *Women in the Metropolis: Gender and Modernity in Weimar Culture*, Berkeley, 1997, ed. Katharina von Ankum, 41–66.
______. "Representation of Women in Weimar Germany." Paper presented at the Symposium on Hannah Höch, Walker Art Center, Minneapolis, Minn., October 20, 1996.

Peukert, Detlev, J.K. *The Weimar Republic: The Crisis of Classic Modernity*. New York, 1992.

Phelan, Anthony. *The Weimar Dilemma: Intellectuals in the Weimar Republic*. Manchester, UK, 1985.

Phillips, Anne. *Divided Loyalties: Dilemmas of Sex and Class*. London, 1987.

Pieterse, Jan Nederveen. *White on Black: Images of Africa and Blacks in Western Popular Culture*. New Haven, 1992.

Pinthus, Kurt. "Masculine Literature." In *The Weimar Republic Sourcebook.*, eds. Anton Kaes, Martin Jay, and Edward Dimendberg, 518–20. Berkeley and Los Angeles, 1994.

Prévost, Jean. "Boxkampftag." *Der Querschnitt* 9, no. 5 (March, 1929): 330–333.

Rabinach, Anson. *In the Shadow of Catastrophe: German Intellectuals Between Apocalypse and Enlightenment*. Berkeley and Los Angeles, 1997.

Radway, Janice. "Interpretive Communities and Variable Literacies: The Functions of Romance Reading." *Daedalus* 113, no, 3 (1984): 52.

______. "The Utopian Impulse in Popular Literature: Gothic Romances and "Feminist" Protest." *American Quarterly* 33, no. 2 (1981): 157–58.

Raiskin, Judith. "Inverts and Hybrids: Lesbian Rewritings of Sexual and Racial Identities." In *The Lesbian Postmodern*, ed. Laura Doan, 158–72. New York, 1994.

Reich, Wilhelm. *The Mass Psychology of Fascism*. 3rd ed. New York, 1988.

Remmling, Gunter W. "Prologue: Weimar Society in Retrospect." In *Towards the Holocaust: The Social and Economic Collapse of the Weimar Republic*, eds. Michael Dobkowski and Isidor Wallimann, 8–12. Westport, Conn., 1983.

Richards, Donald Ray. *The German Bestseller in the 20th Century: A Complete Bibliography and Analysis, 1940*. Bern, 1968.

Roberts, Mary Louise. *Civilization Without Sexes: Reconstructing Gender in Postwar France, 1917–1927*. Chicago, 1994.

Roof, Judith. *A Lure of Knowledge: Lesbian Sexuality and Theory*. New York, 1991.

Rosaldo, Michelle Zimbalist. "Woman, Culture, and Society: A Theoretical Overview." In *Woman Culture, & Society*, eds. Michelle Zimbalist Rosaldo and Louise Lamphere, 1–37. Stanford, 1982.

Rosenberg, Alfred. *Der Mythus des 20. Jahrhunderts: eine Wertung der seelisch-geistigen Gestaltenkämpfe unserer Zeit*. Munich, 1935.

Scarry, Elaine. *The Body in Pain: The Making and Unmaking of the World*. New York, 1985.

Schenk, Herrad. *Die feministische Herausforderung. 150 Jahre Frauenbewegung in Deutschland*. Munich, 1980.

Schoppman, Claudia. "Ein Lesbenroman aus der Weimarer Zeit: *Der Skorpion*." In *Eldorado: Homosexuelle Frauen und Männer in Berlin 1850–1950. Geschichte Alltag und Kultur*, ed. Michael Bollé, 197–99. Berlin, 1984.

Schrader, Bärbel and Jürgen Schebera. *The Golden Twenties: Art and Literature in the Weimar Republik*. New Haven, 1988.
Schröder, Fritz. "The Labor Market for White-Collar Workers." *Die Arbeit: Zeitschrift für Gewerkschaftspolitik und Wissenschaftskunde* I, 6 (1924):340–43. In *The Weimar Republic Sourcebook*, eds. Anton Kaes, Martin Jay, and Edward Dimenberg, 184–185. Berkeley and Los Angeles, 1994.
Schulte-Sasse, Jochen. "High/Low and Other Dichotomies." In *High and Low Cultures: German Attempts at Mediation*, eds. Reinhold Grimm and Jost Hermand, 3–18. Madison, Wisc., 1994.
Schütz, Erhard. *Romane der Weimarer Republik*. Munich, 1986.
Scott, Joan Wallach. *Gender and the Politics of History*. New York, 1988.
Sedgwick, Eve Kosofsky. *Between Men: English Literature and Male Homosocial Desire*. New York, 1985.
______. *Tendencies*. Durham, 1993.
Showalter, Elaine. *Sexual Anarchy: Gender and Culture at the Fin-de-Siècle*. New York, 1990.
Snitow, Ann Barr. "Mass Market Romance: Pornography for Women is Different." In *Powers of Desire: The Politics of Sexuality*, eds. Ann Snitow, Christine Stansel, and Sharon Thompson, 245–263. New York, 1983.
Sorkin, David. *The Transformation of German Jewry, 1789–1840*. New York, 1987.
Spencer, Daniel T. *Gay and Gaia: Ethics, Ecology, and the Erotic*. Cleveland, 1996.
Steakley, James D. *The Homosexual Emancipation Movement in Germany*. North Stratford, N.H., 1976.
Stephenson, Jill. *Women in Nazi Germany*. New York, 1975.
Stölzl, Christoph, ed. *Die Zwanziger Jahre In München: Katalog zur Ausstellung im Münchner Stadtmuseum Mai bis September 1979*. Munich, 1979.
Streese, Konstanze. *"Cric?"—"Crac!" Vier literarische Versuche mit dem Kolonialismus umzugehen*. Bern, 1991.
Suren, Hans. "Preface to the 61st Edition." In *The Weimar Republik Sourcebook* , eds. Anton Kaes, Martin Jay, and Edward Dimenberg, 678. Berkeley and Los Angeles, 1994.
Tatar, Maria. *Lustmord: Sexual Murder in Weimar Germany*. Princeton, 1995.
Theis, Wolfgang and Andreas Sternweiler. "Alltag im Kaiserreich und der Weimarer Republik." In *Eldorado: Homosexuelle Frauen und Männer in Berlin 1850–1950. Geschichte, Alltag und Kultur*, ed. Michael Bollé, 48–73. Berlin, 1984.
Theweleit, Klaus. *Male Fantasies. Women, Floods, Bodies, History*. Vol. 1. Minneapolis, 1987.
Trachtenberg, Joshua. *The Devil and the Jews: The Medieval Conception of the Jew and its Relation to Modern Antisemitism*. 1943. Cleveland, 1961.
Ungern-Sternberg, Leonie. "The Marriage of the Future." In *The Book of Marriage: A New Interpretation by Twentyfour Leaders of Contemporary Thought*, ed. Count Hermann Keyserling, 262–70. New York, 1926.

Usborne, Cornelie. *The Politics of the Body in Weimar Germany: Women's Reproductive Rights and Duties*. London, 1992.

Vaerting. M. *Die weibliche Eigenart im Männerstaat und die männliche Eigenart im Frauenstaat*. Karlsruhe, 1931.

Valentin, Veit. *Geschichte der Deutschen*. Cologne, 1979.

Vasold, Manfred. "Der Herr hat's gegeben; der Herr hat's genommen." *Die Zeit*. 10 (March 6, 1992): 13–14.

Völger, Gisela and Karin V. Welck, eds. *Männerbünde: Die Rolle des Mannes im Kulturvergleich*. 2 vols. Cologne, 1990.

von der Vring, George. "Offensive der Frau." In *Die Frau von Morgen: Wie wir sie wünschen*, ed. Friedrich M. Huebner, 49–56. Leipzig, 1929.

von See, Klaus. *Barbar—Germane—Arier: die Suche nach der Identität der Deutschen*. Heidelberg, 1994.

Weininger, Otto. *Sex and Character*. Authorized translation. New York, 1906.

Wertheimer, Jack. *Unwelcome Strangers*. New York, 1987.

Whalen, Robert Weldon. *Bitter Wounds: German Victims of the Great War, 1914–1939*. Ithaca, N.Y., 1984.

Widdig, Bernd. "Mann unter Männern: Männerbünde und die Angst vor der Masse in der Rede 'Von Deutscher Republik!'" *The German Quarterly* 66, no. 4 (Fall 1993): 524–36.

Willett, John. *Art and Politics in the Weimar Period: The New Sobriety 1917–1933*. New York, 1978.

Williams, John Alexander. "Steeling the Young Body: Official Attempts to Control Youth Hiking in Germany, 1913–1938." *Occasional Papers in German Studies* 12 (June 1997): 1–54.

Williams, Raymond. *The Politics of Modernism: Against the New Conformists*. London, 1989.

Wolff, Janet. *Feminine Sentences: Essays on Women and Culture*. Berkeley and Los Angeles, 1990.

______. "The Invisible Flaneuse: Women and the Literature of Modernity." In *The Problems of Modernity: Adorno and Benjamin*, ed. Andrew Benjamin. London: Routledge, 1989, 141–156.

Young, Robert. *White Mythologies: Writing History and the West*. New York, 1990.

Zimmermann, E. Michael. *Heidegger's Confrontation with Modernity: Technology, Politics, and Art*. Bloomington, Ind., 1990.

Index

N

O

P

R

S

T